WORDSWORTH CLASSICS
OF WORLD LITERATURE

General Editor: Tom Griffith

THUS SPAKE ZARATHUSTRA

Friedrich Nietzsche

Thus Spake Zarathustra

Translated by Thomas Common
Introduction by Nicholas Davey

WORDSWORTH CLASSICS
OF WORLD LITERATURE

For my husband

ANTHONY JOHN RANSON

with love from your wife, the publisher
Eternally grateful for your
unconditional love

Readers who are interested in other titles from
Wordsworth Editions are invited to visit our
website at www.wordsworth-editions.com

This edition published 1997 by Wordsworth Editions Limited
8B East Street, Ware, Hertfordshire SG12 9HJ

ISBN 978 1 85326 776 5

Wordsworth Editions is
the company founded in 1987 by

MICHAEL TRAYLER

Typeset in Great Britain by Antony Gray
Printed and bound by Clays Ltd, Elcograf S.p.A.

CONTENTS

SECOND PART

THIRD PART

FOURTH AND LAST PART

AN INTRODUCTION

> A testing and a questioning hath been all my travelling – and verily, one must also *learn* to answer such questioning! That, however, is my taste –
>
> ZARATHUSTRA III, *55 – The Spirit of Gravity*'

There is something truly uncanny about prophetic tidings. Their compelling force seems to have less to do with being bolts from the blue than with their ability to remind us – to make us more mindful – of what we already know, and might have wished for but have by circumstance or choice set aside. The Old Testament vision of a heavenly realm of milk and honey gains its (universal) power not from the paradisiacal ideality it projects but from the way it forces us to confront the violence, estrangement and disappointments of ordinary experience, and our only-too-human longing for something different or redemptive.[1] The compelling pull of the prophetic tiding resides in the fact that the vision and answer it communicates revitalises and returns us to the experiences and questions which inspire the quest for prophetic insight in the first place. The prophetic vision demands that we recognise and submit to the question which the prophetic tiding is an answer to. The truthfulness of the prophetic vision does not lie in the statemental or logical structure of its claim but in the extent to which it can be grasped as a legitimate and truthful, if not

1 Mary Grey argues that 'to redeem' can mean to 'recover from a state of submersion', to 'extricate from futility or meaninglessness, to reclaim, liberate, fulfil or realise'. See her book *Redeeming the Dream, Feminism, Redemption and Christian Tradition*, London, SPCK 1989

redemptive, response to the experiences and questions it addresses. The prophetic vision returns us to and relocates us within the fundamental questions it transfigures. *Thus Spake Zarathustra* gives voice to just such a prophetic response. It is prophetic in that it looks forward to and prophesies the imminent need for human beings to overcome their traditional values, and it is a response in that what it projects as needed constitutes Nietzsche's innermost response to the vital questions of human meaning and purpose.

More than any other philosopher, Nietzsche is linked to the phenomenon of the question in all its guises. His *critique* of the European tradition of epistemology and morality is so sustained and penetrating in its questioning as almost to deprive the notions of 'truth' and 'goodness' of credibility. In his philosophical interrogations Nietzsche's mistrust of universal claims is relentless. He is a practician of the hermeneutics of suspicion *par excellence*,[2] and explicitly raises doubts about 'the highest values' in an abrupt, rude and sometimes questionable manner. He revels in the frenzied excitement of both creating uncertainty and finding uncertainty creative, transforming Descartes's methodological scepticism into a stratagem for disrupting the alleged foundations of knowledge. The integrity of this philosophical questioning is, however, beyond reproach; he never spares himself from his own critical eye, once declaring that he was far too distrustful to accept his own (philosophical) system. And in his questioning, Nietzsche never fails to be the most questing of thinkers.

> But to stand in the midst of this *rerum concordia discors* and of this whole marvellous uncertainty and rich ambiguity of existence without questioning, without trembling with the craving and the rapture of such questioning . . . that is what I feel to be contemptible (*The Gay Science* 1, 2).

2 In the Preface of *Human All Too Human*, Nietzsche describes himself as being one of the most suspicious of thinkers: 'In fact I do not myself believe that anyone has looked into the world with an equally profound degree of suspicion . . . and any one who could divine something of the consequences that lie in that profound suspiciousness, something of the fears and frosts and isolations to which that unconditional disparity of view condemns him who is infected with it, will also understand'.

There is one question which all Nietzsche's works cautiously draw alongside: how much courage does one have for what one really knows? – 'How much truth can a spirit endure, how much truth does it dare?' (*Ecce Homo* Preface, Section 3). That which Nietzsche always knew and felt in the innermost core of his being was that human experience was a seething chaos of oppositions, contradictions, tensions and disruptions. The issue this question awakes is: how possible is it for us to live in a realm of perpetual and seemingly meaningless flux? It is as if this issue throws us off centre, reawakening an ancient anxiety. Was Silenus perhaps right after all? Is it indeed the case that 'what is best of all is utterly beyond . . . our reach: not to be born, not to be, to be nothing . . . (and that) the second best is to die soon' (*The Birth of Tragedy* 3)? Zarathustra remarks, with the tone of one who has wrestled with this question, 'Sombre is human life and as yet without meaning' (Prologue 7). As was suggested above, *Thus Spake Zarathustra* is a prophetic work, a disconcerting reminder that key questions 'from very far away and long ago' have not left us. Nietzsche openly acknowledges that the experiences surrounding the inception of *Thus Spake Zarathustra* transformed his understanding of these defining existential *aporias*.

Without doubt *Thus Spake Zarathustra* is one of Nietzsche's greatest, most questioning and question-provoking works. Like *The Birth of Tragedy*, the book can scarcely contain the explosive wealth of ideas it expresses. The doctrines of the will to power, the *Übermensch*,[3] *amor fati* (the love of fate) and the eternal recurrence all gain seminal expression, some for the first time. None of these doctrines is argued out philosophically in any traditional sense; they are made the subject of what are sometimes judged as tendentious poetic assertions. Their form has certainly contributed to the notoriety of the text. At one extreme, the book's celebration of

3 The word *Übermensch* has been left in German in order to avoid the misleading connotations of the customary English translation 'Superman'. For Nietzsche humanity is a transitional form, a life-form which although it has risen beyond inarticulate animality has not yet attained the power of full existential self-determination. In *Thus Spake Zarathustra* the notion of *Übermensch* refers to a life-form yet to come, a life-form free from anxiety and guilt, and reliant upon the values it has created for itself.

this-worldliness and the passions of creativity secured it almost biblical status amongst German Expressionists, whilst at the other, the text's announcement of God's death and the subsequent passing of Christian morality was utilised by British First World War propagandists to propagate the myth that Nietzsche's 'irreligious text' could be found in the field packs of every Prussian infantryman. Furthermore, because *Thus Spake Zarathustra* is *the* title by which Nietzsche is popularly known, the work's literary genre has placed considerable obstacles in the path of its author's reception as a serious philosopher. However, in Nietzsche's case, to question whether his writings are artistic or philosophical is profoundly misleading.

Though Nietzsche once lamented that he wrote rather than sang, for most of his creative life there was never any rigid distinction between the literary and philosophical dimensions of his thinking. His intellectual *corpus* reveals several bursts of seminal intellectual and creative expression, each of which establishes a provisional beachhead in a new mode of thought and sensibility which later works could reinforce in more conventional philosophical terms. *Beyond Good and Evil* was not written because *Thus Spake Zarathustra* failed but because what was revealed to Nietzsche in his creative reverie needed consolidation in other forms.[4] In *Thus Spake Zarathustra* Nietzsche allows his imagination full rein. To quibble about the philosophical or literary status of the text is foolish. What matters is the subject-matter of the endeavour rather than its formal idiom.[5] Furthermore, Nietzsche is a modern thinker whose *modus operandi* uniquely resides in the irresolvable tensions of his philosophical creativity – that is, within

4 Nietzsche is a thinker who believes, like his contemporary Wilhelm Dilthey, that the profoundest experiences are incomplete, that is, they are always forward-moving, showing ever more aspects of themselves, but never in fact becoming complete.

5 This is not to say that the question of idiom and style is not important in Nietzsche's case. On the contrary, it is a central issue. Nietzsche adopts a whole number of styles and perspectives in order to convey a philosophical point about the elusive nature of 'truth'. To adopt but one philosophical idiom is for Nietzsche to strait-jacket our understanding of the enigmatic character of being.

the productive confrontation of art and philosophy from which his creative daemon springs. Nietzsche's early text *The Birth of Tragedy* juxtaposes the quest for luminous philosophical intelligibility and the darker creative impetuses which agitate art. The Socratic enterprise is taken to be intimately connected with believing the world to be a knowable, articulable order. Philosophy's task is to reveal the truth of that order in as clear and distinct conceptual terms as possible: being is articulable. The same text's analysis of the Dionysian reveals that Nietzsche also knows that the creative spirit gains its freedom to re-interpret and re-mould the accepted and conventional at the high price of having to confront the terrors of chaos, the dissolution of rules and the destruction of intelligible forms on which it can rely. Whereas the philosophical mind strives to dispel the unintelligible in order to create new forms, the creative mind has in a certain sense to embrace it. The creative spirit has to confront 'a darkness on top of a void', to put itself at risk by entering the crucible wherein that which has not yet been has still to be forged. What is exceptional about Nietzsche's writings is that these two modes of 'knowing' fuse, charge and provoke each other.

The philosopher and historian of ideas in Nietzsche knows that his epoch's increasing recognition of the lived actuality of flux and becoming as the *only* world bespeaks the collapse of the greatest values hitherto – i.e. the death of western metaphysics. Nietzsche is haunted not so much by God's death but by the fact that the full consequences of that death have not dawned upon a civilisation as yet unaware of the incipient calamity surrounding it. For Nietzsche the combined forces of empirical science and Kant's critique of metaphysics expose the existence of an intelligible Being, the belief in fixed extra-mental truths, the efficacy of logical identity and the belief in a divinely legitimated moral good – indeed everything which philosophical intelligibility has relied on – as fictive constructs projected upon an inhospitable actuality in order to force some semblance of human meaningfulness upon it. *Thus Spake Zarathustra* expresses the nature of the latent crisis in the following terms.

> When the water hath planks, when gangways and railings o'erspan the stream, verily, he is not believed who then saith: 'All is in flux.'

But even the simpletons contradict him. 'What,' say the simpletons, 'all in flux? Planks and railings are still *over* the stream!'

'*Over* the stream all is stable, all the values of things, the bridges and bearings, all "good" and "evil': these are all *stable*!'

Cometh, however, the hard winter, the stream-tamer, then learn even the wittiest distrust, and verily, not only the simpletons then say: 'Should not everything – *stand still*?'

'Fundamentally standeth everything still' – that is an appropriate winter doctrine, good cheer for an unproductive period, a great comfort for winter-sleepers and fireside-loungers.

'Fundamentally standeth everything still' – but *contrary* thereto preacheth the thawing wind!

The thawing wind, a bullock which is no ploughing bullock – a furious bullock, a destroyer, which with angry horns breaketh the ice! The ice however – *breaketh gangways*!

O my brethren, is not everything *at present in flux*? Have not all railings and gangways fallen into the water? Who would still *hold on* to 'good' and 'evil'?

'Woe to us! Hail to us! The thawing wind bloweth!' Thus preach, my brethren, through all the streets.'

ZARATHUSTRA III, *56 – Old and New Tables*

Nietzsche's knowledge and becoming exclude one another. Everything humankind has clung to in order to assure itself of the universal status of its epistemological and moral preferences, is revealed as prejudice, fiction, untruth and deception. That which was received or projected as divine assurance is exposed as being no more than a subtle and clever creative inversion – a means of assuaging a terrifying sense of meaninglessness. *Incipit* nihilism.

As soon as man finds out that the (true) world is fabricated solely from psychological needs and (how) consequently he has no right to it, the last form of nihilism comes into being: it includes disbelief in any metaphysical world and forbids itself any belief in a true world. (*The Will to Power* 12A)

The most extreme form of nihilism would be the view that every belief, every considering something true, is necessarily false because there is no true world. (*The Will to Power* 13)

Nietzsche's theoretical analysis of European nihilism has both pessimistic and optimistic aspects. The pessimistic dimension concerns the realisation that continued belief in being, truth and intelligibility as the sole criteria of reality will only ever lead to disappointment. The formal incommensurability of becoming and knowing means that however we think of the world, our thinking and the nature of actuality will never coincide. What Nietzsche fears even more is the despair that might seize humanity when it realises that the enormous sacrifices undertaken in quest of the 'truth' have been in vain. The optimistic side of his analysis concerns the revaluation of humanity's ideals which an understanding of nihilism facilitates. That there is no true being, and no necessary equation between knowing and the good, does not empty these fictions of value. It is what the power of belief underwriting these fictions is capable of achieving that matters to Nietzsche, not the epistemological status of such fictions. Though the formal premises of western philosophy and science may turn out to be false, belief in the truth of those premises has harnessed enormous powers of disciplined observation which have enabled humanity to overcome its most immediate and instinctive reactions to the environment. Belief in such fictions has, in short, allowed humanity to transform itself, to articulate its circumstances, formulate its goals and ambitions. It has freed humanity from being a passive subject in the flux of actuality and has made its self-development (*Bildung*) possible. Without the creation of such fictions such a transformation would not have been possible. What concerns Nietzsche, therefore, is the life-enabling and life-enhancing value of the creativity which finds expression in these fictions, and not their veracity. *Beyond Good and Evil* suggests that we should not be ungrateful for such errors:

> The falseness of a judgement is for us not necessarily an objection to a judgement: in this respect our new language may sound strangest. The question is to what extent it is life-promoting, life-preserving, species-preserving, even species-cultivating. (*Beyond Good and Evil* 4)

However, the critical question which haunts Nietzsche concerns what might happen when humanity realises that the truths and values which have sustained its creative voyagings are exposed as fictions. In *On the Genealogy of Morals* Nietzsche remarks, 'All great things bring about their own destruction through an act of self-overcoming'. 'What then will happen when the will to truthfulness calls 'truth' into question? (*On the Genealogy of Morals* 3, 25, 27). To avoid the disaster of a culturally destructive nihilism, Nietzsche concludes that humanity's 'truths' need to be seen for what they are, namely, creative devices which have enabled it both to transform and discipline itself and to take an interest in the rich contradictions and struggles of its existence. If these fictions can no longer be sustained as 'truths', Nietzsche the theoretician sees the critical need for the creation of a new set of values which would enable humanity to confront actuality as it is, to take delight in actuality *per se* rather than to hanker after another true world of Being. *Incipit* Zarathustra and his prophetic appeal, not for the coming of a Christ figure capable of overcoming this world but for the coming of an *Übermensch* who by his or her creation of new values demonstrates that through its own creativity humanity is capable of yet a further overcoming of itself. The creativity of the *Übermensch* demonstrates that the worth of humanity does not derive from the fictions of Being and truth which it creates in order to believe in itself but from the creativity which produces such fictions in the first place. By revealing that its own creativity is the primary source of its value the *Übermensch* allows humanity to overcome its need to create the fiction of something other than itself in order to believe in and justify itself. Here is the crux of the matter.

Nietzsche the philosopher responds to the provocation of nihilism by articulating its character, but Nietzsche the artist knows equally well that an analytical description of nihilism is not enough. Nihilism's symptoms may be understood theoretically but its causes are not thereby eliminated. Nihilism is not so much to be solved as to be displaced by the creation of world-affirming values which neither lead to nor express an alienation from the flux of actuality. Nietzsche esteems Christ's ability to rise above the pain and suffering of existence as a mode of overcoming, but is perturbed by its negativity: the promise of another world of Being is the allure which makes the endurance of this world possible. What Nietzsche projects as the *Übermensch's* mode of overcoming is heralded as an affirmative mode of overcoming (*ja-sagen*). The pathos of existence is not denied but redeemed, in so far as the creativity it inspires is celebrated not as a means to escape or deny actuality but as a means to affirm, celebrate, enhance and transform this our worldly existence. No wonder then that *Thus Spake Zarathustra* was so beloved of German Expressionist artists, for Nietzsche understands that with regard to the problem of nihilism and cultural rejuvenation, the artist must take over from the philosopher.

> Artists: they at least fix an image of that which ought to be: they are productive to the extent that they actually alter and transform, unlike men of knowledge who leave everything as it is. (*The Will to Power* 585)

In conclusion, Nietzsche the philosopher may have a theoretical grasp of the need for awakening a profound and pervasive existential creativity, but as a theoretician he cannot strictly speaking bring it about. However, as a poet he can attempt to give voice to, invoke and celebrate an affirmative mode of existence purged of the despair of nihilism. As a text therefore, *Thus Spake Zarathustra* embodies Nietzsche's understanding that in order to respond to the world-historical crisis posed by nihilism he must turn from philosophy to artistic creativity. This turn does not constitute a denial of philosophy for as *Thus Spake Zarathustra* demonstrates, Nietzsche's poetic voice is underwritten by and gains its resonance from the philosophical vision which sustains it. Perhaps no other thinker-writer resides so effectively and yet so precariously in the tensions which constitute the philosophical imagination.

Nietzsche's juxtaposition of the theoretical and the creative shows how philosophy too stands upon imaginative forces of world-creating proportions. Like Heidegger, Nietzsche is acutely aware how both philosophical modes of thinking and works of art can fundamentally alter humanity's understanding of itself. Such works do not so much belong to history as enunciate and define new historical epochs. For Nietzsche the most profound philosophies are foundational in that they create *ex nihilo* the possibility of different worlds. The philosophical crisis to which *Thus Spake Zarathustra* responds concerns the realisation that if the value-worlds of post-Socratic and Christian philosophy are no longer credible, philosophy must once more stare into the 'darkness on top of a void', and create from within itself categories and values which do not deny or condemn the chaos and suffering of existence but celebrate and transform it. *Thus Spake Zarathustra* is Nietzsche's creative response to the philosophical and existential challenge of nihilism.

In *Beyond Good and Evil* Nietzsche comments that thoughts come when they want and not when we want them. There is no doubt that *Thus Spake Zarathustra* was written by Nietzsche as if he were possessed by a tormented and tormenting muse. *Ecce Homo* describes the inception of Zarathustra in passionate terms.

> Has anyone at the end of the nineteenth century a clear idea of what poets of strong ages have called *inspiration*? If not, I will describe it. If one had the slightest residue of superstition left in one's system, one could hardly reject altogether the idea that one is merely incarnation, merely mouthpiece, merely a medium of overpowering forces. The concept of revelation in the sense that suddenly and with indescribable certainty and subtlety, something becomes *visible*, audible, something that shakes one to the last depths and throws one down – that merely describes the facts. One hears, one does not seek; one accepts, one does not ask who gives; like lightning, a thought flashes up, with necessity, without hesitation regarding its form – I never had any choice . . .
>
> Everything happens involuntarily in the highest degree but as in a gale of a feeling of freedom, of absoluteness, of power, of divinity; – The involuntariness of image and metaphor is strangest of all; one no longer has any notion of what is image or metaphor: everything offers itself as the nearest, most obvious, simplest expression. It actually seems to allude to something Zarathustra says, as if the things themselves approached and offered themselves as metaphors. 'Here all things come caressingly to your discourse and flatter you: for they want to ride on your back. On every metaphor you ride to every truth . . . Here the words and word shrines of all being open up before you: here all being wishes to become word, all becoming wishes to learn from you how to speak.' (*Ecce Homo* 3)

It not surprising that Nietzsche speaks in such ecstatic terms of his literary child. In January 1883 he writes 'I have written my *best* book', and indeed within it he brings to articulation doctrines such as the will to power and the eternal return which have become synonymous with his later thought. Now although the moment of Nietzsche's revelation may have been arbitrary, the doctrines to which Zarathustra gives voice are not. *Thus Spake Zarathustra* is not a work that comes out of the blue. It represents Nietzsche's third response to questions concerning both the meaningfulness of existence and the relationship of art to existence. *Thus Spake Zarathustra* should be considered in the context of Nietzsche's thought as a whole and, as we shall see, the text brings to fruition a long-standing meditation on the existential and cultural significance of creative power.

Nietzsche's first response to the above questions – his tragical *Artisten-Metaphysik* – is characterised by a note of 1870/71.

> My philosophy (as) an inverted Platonism: indeed the further from actuality, the more pure, the more beautiful, the better it is. (*Die Unschuld des Werdens* I, 38)

In *The Birth of Tragedy* he claims:

> There is only one world, and this is false, cruel, contradictory, seductive, without meaning – A world thus constituted is the real world. We have need of lies in order to conquer this reality, this 'truth', that is in order to live.

The premise of this argument is that existence for both the Ancient Greek and for ourselves is 'cruel, contradictory, seductive and without meaning'. According to Nietzsche, the illusions of Christianity and metaphysics have blinded post-Greek civilisations to this 'truth', but now that Kantian scepticism and science have exposed the insecure foundations of such faiths, he senses that modern humanity is about to rediscover the 'eternal problem' in the guise of nihilism. Nietzsche's purpose in discussing the nature of Ancient Greek art is not to return to antiquity *per se* but to learn from it, to see *our* nihilistic situation through its eyes so that we may learn how the Ancient Greeks solved what is also our problem: the problem of existence.

Nietzsche detected in Greek culture three aesthetic responses to the existential problem: the Dionysian (ecstatic dance and revelry), the Apolline (the plastic arts where beauty, measure and the avoidance of excess provide the rule) and the Tragic (the dramatic form whereby we can distance ourselves from the cruelty and excess which afflict us daily, and see that within a wider whole such phenomena do perhaps have a certain necessity). Nietzsche entertains certain doubts about the value of Dionysian and Apolline aesthetics as existential palliatives. The Dionysian provides not an answer to, but a giving in to, the 'wound' of existence. A consciousness of the sorrowful end all beings must face (*The Birth of Tragedy* 17) may be obliterated by dance and revelry, but they succumb to precisely that flow of finitude which nurtures existential anxiety in the first place: the Dionysian can lead to self-annihilation through excess. Existential anxiety can also be stilled by the Apolline quest for self-forgetfulness in the contemplation of the beautiful image. Yet Nietzsche insists that the Apolline pursuit of the transfixing illusion is endless, and promotes an increasingly disillusioned wandering through cultural history. Art is used to escape the question of existence and not to resolve it. As the synthesis of Dionysus and Apollo, however, Greek tragedy neither submits to nor repudiates nihility. It celebrates the rise and fall of all beings, but by objectifying it within a dramatic art form, maintains a distance from it. It thereby avoids the damage of Dionysian excess. Because it provides images of Dionysian actuality, the Apolline allows actuality to be aesthetically graspable. Turning from a sensationalist quest to the task of beautifying existence, the Apolline desire for beauty is given limit by, and gains purpose from, the Dionysian. Apollo and Dionysus become intertwined within an art form which, because it confronts and transforms humanity's predicament, allows individuals to focus upon, reconcile themselves to, and even find their life desirable in, a Becoming without Being. As we shall see, this too is the aim of Zarathustra's teaching. Thus existence transformed by the tragic arts reverses the wisdom of Silenus: 'We might (now) say of the Greeks that to die soon is worst of all for them, the next worst is to die at all' (*The Birth of Tragedy* 3), for art alone knows how to turn the most nauseous thoughts about existence into something with which one can live (*The Birth of Tragedy* 7).

Yet Nietzsche regards the rebirth of tragic aesthetics as something he is looking towards and not at.

> Must we not suppose that the highest and indeed the truly serious task of art – to save the eye from gazing into the horrors of night and to deliver the subject by the healing balm of illusion from the spasms of the agitations of the will . . . (*The Birth of Tragedy* 19)

This is a curious passage, for it is *not* an advocacy of tragic aesthetics. It seems to indicate that until the rebirth of the tragic form, man's increasing Dionysian awareness must be countered with an Apolline aesthetic. Yet this exposes what is problematic in the *Artisten-Metaphysik*.

If the purpose of art is to transform an individual's existence by means of aesthetic illusion, the argument is deeply paradoxical. That which humanity is (a mode of Becoming) can only be enhanced by a forgetting of its proper being. In *Human All Too Human* Nietzsche suggests that Apolline aesthetics will 'soothe and heal only provisionally' (*Human All Too Human* 148), and that promises of beauty and Being will make the inevitable confrontation with the Dionysian more difficult. Nietzsche realises that the Apolline quest is based on the false premise that existence is meaningless in itself. If actuality fails to accord with *our* criterion of intelligible meaning, all that can be concluded is that our criterion fails to apply. To conclude that existence is intrinsically meaningless assumes humanity's principles of meaning to be universally valid. Pessimism becomes a 'laughing stock': the problem of Becoming lies not in the latter's nature but in our evaluation of it. Thus if a resolution of the existential predicament lies in a change of evaluations, it would be desirable to undermine precisely those values which because they present the spectre of a better, more desirable world serve only to alienate individuals from their actuality. The attempt to save this our lived world from being denigrated by other-worldly values is a primary feature of Zarathustra's appeal that we should remain true to the world. Such a concern becomes the basis of Nietzsche's attack on his former *Artisten-Metaphysik*.

Nietzsche's *Human All Too Human* initiates an attack on art and aesthetics which is Platonic in its ferocity. Rather than encouraging humanity to explore different modes of being-in-the-world to effect a change in their evaluation of actuality, Nietzsche sees in

Apolline art a positive hindrance to such attempts. 'Art', he comments wryly, 'can easily set the metaphysical strings which have long been silent, or indeed snapped apart, vibrating in sympathy' (*Human All Too Human* 148). By peddling the illusion of a stable realm of Being, artists 'even hinder men from working for a real improvement in their conditions by suspending and discharging in a palliative way the very passion which impels the discontented to action' (*Human All Too Human* 148). Thus between 1876 and 1882 Nietzsche insists upon 'historical philosophy', the study of different modes of life, value systems, diet and types of social organisation. All are attempts to break free from the world-alienating and alienated traditions of metaphysics. No longer is humanity's existential predicament to be solved by a flight into aesthetic illusion but by a seeking out of those values and modes of living which embrace and enhance the dynamism of the actual. There is, however, a serious flaw in Nietzsche's middle-period critique of art.

Thought-experiments, existential hypotheses and the values supporting them cannot be derived *ex vacuo*. With the passion of a Marxist demonstrating the historical alternatives to a prevalent metaphysical ideology, he advocates historical philosophy – social, psychological and anthropological enquiries into different value systems. The task is not to identify or relive past possibilities but to achieve a new mode of existential orientation. Experimentation clearly requires creative insight, projection and anticipation, yet the latter are intrinsic components of the Apolline aesthetics which his middle-period critique of art condemns. Considerations of what could be or might be more desirable (all essential elements in creative thinking) necessarily involve looking away from actuality towards as yet unrealised possibilities. Yet it is precisely this dissatisfaction with actuality that Nietzsche criticises in the Apolline. The latter is condemned as an obstacle to any reconciliation with the existent. Yet if experimentalism is to achieve a new reconciliation with actuality, it can do so only because it too possesses a creative capacity of imagined alternatives to the immediately given. Without a creative looking away from actuality, Nietzsche's middle-period experimentalism collapses. The stage is set for *Thus Spake Zarathustra*.

Thus Spake Zarathustra is a text which looks to creativity as a form of existential redemption. Like the wilful determination of a Beethoven *finale*, this text contains passages on art and aesthetics which swamp Nietzsche's previous arguments, yet lift them up and set them down in a new and final relation. Consider the following themes.

> Verily, men have given unto themselves all their good and bad. Verily, they took it not, they found it not, it came not unto them as a voice from heaven. (*The Thousand and One Goals*)

> But of time and of becoming shall the best similes speak; a praise shall they be, and a justification of all perishableness! (*In the Happy Isles*)

> Creating – that is the great salvation from suffering, and life's alleviation. But for the creator to appear, suffering itself is needed, and much transformation. (*Ibid*)

> Where is innocence? Where there is will to procreation . . . Where is beauty? Where I *must will* with my whole Will; where I will love and perish, that an image may not remain merely an image. (*Immaculate Perception*)

> Willing emancipateth; for willing is creating: so do I teach. And *only* for creating shall ye learn! (*Old and New Tables*)

Of paramount importance in these quotations is the conjunction of the terms willing, creating and suffering. It brings the question of art and its relation to humanity's existential predicament into a new and tight analytic alignment. In Nietzsche's works the term suffering denotes that alienation from actuality which emerges with the realisation that actuality can never correspond to the intelligible world of rational discourse. Suffering has, therefore, a double aspect: it is the tension between recognising what is and what might be, or between what was believed to be but is now known not to be the case. In *Thus Spake Zarathustra* the experience of this tension becomes the definitive expression of our existential predicament: such suffering is an inevitable fact of our being and not an objection to it! The concept of willing has the same double aspect. It entails a conflict between what is recognised to be the case and a projection of what is wished for. In *Beyond Good and Evil* Nietzsche states that all willing entails a simultaneous 'towards which' and 'away from which' (*Beyond Good and Evil* 19), whilst in the *Nachlass* he declares:

> Every drive that desires to be satisfied expresses its dissatisfaction with the present state of things: what, is the whole perhaps composed of dissatisfied parts, which all have desiderata in their heads? Is the 'course of things' perhaps precisely this 'away from here, away from actuality!' – eternal dissatisfaction itself? (*The Will to Power* 331)

What can be said for willing holds also for the concept of Becoming, for as will to power it also has two moments, one of coming to be and one of passing away. Creativity equally embraces the imminent simultaneity of two aspects: it is both an 'away from here' and a 'towards which', 'a desire to create a world as it ought to be' (*The Will to Power* 585) to make that which is image not remain merely an image (*Thus Spake Zarathustra, Immaculate Perception*).

What this quartet of double-aspect terms points to is a monistic ontology in which artistic creativity is a transforming vehicle of humanity's being as a mode of Becoming. Whereas the *Artisten-Metaphysik* suggests that individuals are alienated from actuality, the synchronicity of the terms suffering, willing and becoming implies that the experience of alienation speaks not so much of humanity's isolation from actuality but of the point of its most intimate union with it: 'This world is the will to power – and nothing besides! And you yourselves are also this will to power – and nothing besides!' (*The Will to Power* 1067). Pain, suffering and contradiction are no longer objections to existence but an expression of the tensions of existence itself. The linking of willing and creating has self-evident implications.

The creative act is a moment of Becoming itself and thus entails the most intimate unity of an individual and actuality. In such a moment, the creative act is an instant of fatality, a determination of what will be. As such, artists as value creators are the engine of Becoming. The values which inspire and structure art works are not subjective appendages to a supposed world of objective fact but the ground and substance of those perspectives and interpretations through which possible experiential worlds become apparent. Artistic creativity is therefore the principal determinant of existential possibility. As Nietzsche declares in *Thus Spake Zarathustra*, 'valuing is creating' (*The Thousand and One Goals*). Not only does this conception of creativity complete the former hollowness of Nietzsche's existential experimentalism, but it also asserts that the creative individual is the embodiment of the life processes which are actuality. This does not rid the individual of suffering, but transforms his or her evaluation of it. It becomes a criterion of oneness with the flow of all beings.

Whereas the pessimist is mentally spread-eagled between rejecting the world as it is and longing for it to be something that it is not, the artist achieves through a creation of possible experiential worlds not only a mediation of actuality but a oneness with the process of actuality itself. The torment of the existential predicament – the 'away from which' and the 'towards which' – is no longer an objection to being-in-the-world but becomes the experience of existence *par excellence*. The question of the intrinsic meaning or meaninglessness of Becoming is set aside as the meaning of existence is re-determined by each creative assertion of 'thus, now, shall it be'. This is the basis of Nietzsche's declaration that the world is an art work that continually gives birth to itself. The creative moment permits actuality to achieve a new determination of its being or, as Heidegger might put it, allows the world to 'world'. Thus the fusion of 'willing, suffering and Becoming' does not strictly solve the question of art's relation to existence. It dissolves it. It is no longer an issue of art relating to existence but of art articulating it. As the redemption of suffering, the creative will is the apotheosis of existential tension. It is the yearning to be, to become, to become more.

Apart from its existential import, Nietzsche's final aesthetic achieves a new alignment of the Dionysian and Apolline. The Apolline quest to fix and perfect stable images is no longer seen as antithetical to change, but as a means to its enhancement. The expression and projection of new values and perspectives give rise to new experiential possibilities. Apollo becomes an agent of Dionysus. Yet the will to form new possibilities inevitably entails the destruction of established perspectives: 'always doth he destroy who hath to be a creator' (*The Thousand and One Goals*). Furthermore, each new possibility must itself be overcome or surpassed: 'Ready must thou be to burn thyself in thine own flame; how couldst thou become new if thou have not first become ashes?' (*The Way of the Creating One*). Dionysus cut to pieces finally appears as a promise of life's continual renewal: 'it will be eternally reborn and return again from destruction' (*The Will to Power* 1052). The creative act emerges as the apotheosis of the tragic. In order to be re-born, the artist must 'create beyond himself and perish'. In his wish to be 'away from here' and 'towards which' the artist, in the words of *The Birth of Tragedy,* becomes 'primordial being itself, feeling its raging desire for existence and joy in existence' (*The Birth of Tragedy* 17). This emphasises what Nietzsche's final aesthetic celebrates above all: not the creator nor the created but the *creating*. The creative moment is the eternal being of all Becoming.

The tight analytic relationship between the concepts of suffering, becoming, willing and creating which *Thus Spake Zarathustra* achieves is enormously impressive. Not only does it constitute Nietzsche's third response to the question of art and its relationship to humanity's existential predicament; it also combines creativity with the doctrines of the *amor fati* and the eternal recurrence. The combination is poignant, for despite its undeniable bombast there can be little doubt that *Thus Spake Zarathustra* is also a work of piety and faith. Given Nietzsche's vigorous attack on Christianity both in *Thus Spake Zarathustra* and in *The Anti-Christ*, such a claim might seem somewhat surprising. Yet Nietzsche's text speaks for itself. *Thus Spake Zarathustra* makes repeated references to the *redemptive* (*Erlösung*) nature of creativity and to the importance of remaining true to the 'earth'. *Thus Spake Zarathustra* does not formulate a new religion, but it clearly strives for a grace-like acceptance of the world as it is in *all* its aspects. This is made apparent by the relationship between creativity and the *amor fati*.

Insofar as suffering goads the individual to the creation of new perspectives whereby his or her existence can become meaningful, an individual's creativity, for Nietzsche, redeems all human suffering. Rather than being unimportant within the 'ocean of Becoming', the individual, as the site of numerous form-giving forces, gains an enormous importance. Although the evaluative and cultural forces which shape an individual are effective well before that individual comes into existence, they can nevertheless achieve a decisive formation within an individual's creative activity. Zarathustra asserts that all things are 'enlinked, enlaced and enamoured' (*The Drunken Song*), so that in any moment within the 'hour-glass of existence', all previous moments effectively pour into it. The joy of the creative moment can be an ecstatic affirmation of all the pre-conditions which have brought it into being. Zarathustra comments,

> Pain is also a joy, curse is also a blessing, night is also a sun . . . Said ye ever Yea to one joy? O my friends, then said ye Yea also unto all woe . . . Wanted ye ever once to come twice; said ye ever: 'Thou pleasest me, happiness! Instant! Moment!' then wanted ye *all* to come back again! (*The DrunkenSong*).

Not only is everything that has gone before a necessary prelude to the moment of an individual's creative act, but also the meaningfulness of everything that has gone before hangs in the balance, awaiting affirmation or denial. Thus the destiny of the future depends upon what is decided in the world-historical vortex of creative moment: 'Every moment beginneth existence, around every "Here" rolleth the ball "There". The middle is everywhere.' (*The Convalescent*). Far from being extraneous to existence, the creative individual is thus a pivot around which that which is at play within Becoming unfolds. In this context, Nietzsche's quizzical remark in *Ecce Homo*, 'Why I Am A Destiny', is neither peculiar nor particular. Nietzsche sees the creative affirmation of existential suffering as unavoidable – as the first act which can turn the apparent meaninglessness and uncertainty of the existential predicament into something meaningful. The statement 'All "it was" is fragment, a riddle, a dreadful chance – until the creative will says "But I willed it thus" ' does not imply a fatalistic acceptance of the past, but a joyous acceptance of the 'all it was' as a necessary prelude to the creative moment. By allowing us to see meaning and significance where we had previously seen none, the creative act actualises previously hidden and unrealised potentials of meaningfulness. The 'it was' no longer appears as riddle but as a necessary aspect of an unfolding meaningfulness. In other words, the 'Thus shall I will it' of the creative will redeems the past by giving it a future. Zarathustra comments on the moment of creative intervention,

> Observe this Moment! From the gateway, This Moment, there runneth a long eternal lane *backwards*; behind us lieth an eternity. (*The Vision and the Enigma*)

Yet he also knows that through this gateway an eternity runs before us. He remarks, '[I did] teach them to create the future, and all that *hath been* – to redeem by creating.' (*Old and New Tables*) Zarathustra asks whether we can address that moment and say 'I will it thus', because we are provoked by it into creative action, because we are able to form or move towards forming a meaning for our predicament and thereby affirm the necessity of our suffering. And so Zarathustra remarks, 'Wanted ye ever once to come twice . . . then wanted ye *all* to come back again.' (*The Drunken Song*). Because in the creative moment the agonies of being are grasped as worthwhile, existence with all its pain and suffering is eternally redeemed. Zarathustra's philosophy of creativity articulates a redemptive grace: a grateful, loving, accepting celebration of the world as it is. Whereas Christ overcame the world by denying it, Zarathustra 'so loves the world' that he is prepared to give himself completely to it, to sacrifice himself, (*untergehen*) to that which is larger than himself, i.e. to the quest for what is yet to come – world-affirming and world-redeeming values.

Thus Spake Zarathustra reveals the darker side of Nietzsche's doctrine of the eternal recurrence. To fail to shape the suffering within us into a tolerable meaningfulness condemns us to the terrifying prospect of the endless return of our suffering. Failure to redeem everything that belongs to the 'it was', and therefore failure to secure the meaningfulness of what has yet to come, guarantees what Nietzsche describes as the eternal recurrence of the same. Without the redemption of the creative moment we are condemned to the eternal return of the same suffering. This further emphasises the motif of questioning in *Thus Spake Zarathustra*. What the moment of suffering questions in each and every one of us is whether we have the creative capacity to attribute a meaningfulness to our pain and thereby redeem all that has flowed into it and all that will flow from it. The truly searching test set by the doctrine of the eternal recurrence is a stark one: confront the suffering of the moment and in creating a meaning for your being redeem both yourself and all that sustains you. Fail to do so, and be condemned by your weakness to remain within the same cycle of eternal meaninglessness. That the doctrine of eternal recurrence effectively provokes and questions the extent of our creative-philosophical powers brings our introduction full circle.

We suggested that part of the nature of a prophetic vision is to return us to and relocate us within the fundamental questions it seeks to transfigure. *Thus Spake Zarathustra* is an enormously rich and varied text which discusses the virtues of suicide and criticises the modern state and the bourgeois values it sustains. Yet underlying its complexity remains Nietzsche's concern with the 'eternal question': the question of the meaningfulness of human existence within endless flux. Zarathustra's role is in part provocative, for in addressing this question he brings us back to it. Yet Nietzsche's motive for reminding us of it is clear. Christianity and western metaphysics have veiled this question, but now that their intellectual credibility has come into question, Nietzsche fears the destructive nihilistic despair which will seize humanity when it realises that its quest for philosophical and scientific truth has been in vain. Nietzsche's sense of an urgent cultural mission (Zarathustra's occasional anxiety about being heard) explains some of the violent and shrill rhetoric of his work. Nevertheless, despite Nietzsche's many styles and masks, there is a consistency of purpose: to bring us back to, and precipitate the possibility of, a creative confrontation with 'the eternal question'. If we understand Zarathustra's teaching as a response to the existential and philosophical dilemmas it confronts, we will also understand that these questions are necessarily larger than Zarathustra's interpretation of them. In other words, if we think with Nietzsche, we know we will have to face and be questioned by such questions ourselves. Zarathustra does not really seek followers: 'one requiteth a teacher badly if one remain merely a scholar' (*The Bestowing Virtue*). He asserts, 'I make for my goal, I follow my course' (*Prologue 9*), for 'thus did I answer those who asked me "the way". For *the* way – it doth not exist!' (*The Spirit of Gravity*). This is perhaps Zarathustra's hidden gift, his unwritten doctrine, for in the midst of the uncertainty and ambiguity of existence, each has to make his or her own way. If, in conclusion, we come to understand the nature and implications of the questions Zarathustra returns us to, we might also appreciate that the fulfilment of Zarathustra's prophetic quest lies in the individual creation of world-affirming perspectives of meaningfulness which might overcome and thereby redeem the need for his teaching. Zarathustra's 'truth' is realised in the moment of its 'down-going'.

NICHOLAS DAVEY
University of Dundee

SUGGESTIONS FOR FURTHER READING

For those readers who are new to Nietzsche and enjoy his style, the following might be of interest. Nietzsche was very much influenced by the style and content of Montaigne, La Rochefoucauld and Ralph Waldo Emerson.

Michel de Montaigne, *The Complete Essays*, Penguin Classics, London 1993

La Rochefoucauld, *Maxims*, Wordsworth 1997

Ralph Waldo Emerson, *A Modern Anthology*, Dell Publishing Co., New York 1958

The figure of Nietzsche and Nietzschean motifs appear in the novels of Herman Hesse (see *Steppenwolf* and *The Glass Bead Game*) and more especially in the works of Thomas Mann. Mann's treatment of the victory of life over death in the closing sections of *The Magic Mountain* has a sharp Nietzschean ring to it. The figure of Dr Leverkuhn in *Dr Faustus* is an unmistakeable portrait of Nietzschean pride (See R. A. Nicholls, *Nietzsche in the Early Work of Thomas Mann*, Russel and Russel, New York 1955). Nietzsche's impact upon German society is fully discussed in R. Hinton Thomas, *Nietzsche in German Politics and Society 1890–1918*, Manchester University Press. Nietzsche's influence on Jack London, D. H. Lawrence, W. B. Yeats and Eugene O'Neill is widely discussed in P. Broadwater, *Nietzsche in Anglo-Saxony*, Leicester University Press 1972. For Nietzsche's influence on André Gide and other French thinkers, see Ernst Behler, 'Nietzsche's Influence in the Twentieth Century' and Alan Shrift's 'Nietzsche's French Legacy' in *The Cambridge Companion to Nietzsche*, ed. B. Magnus and K. M. Higgens, Cambridge University Press 1996.

Richard Strauss's tone poem *Also Sprach Zarathustra* is the best-known musical interpretation of Nietzsche's text; less well known are both Gustav Mahler's setting to music of extracts from Zarathustra in his Third Symphony and Frederick Delius's quotations from Zarathustra in his Mass of Life.

ENDNOTES

The versions of Nietzsche's texts cited in this essay are:

The Birth of Tragedy, trans. W. Kaufmann, Vintage, New York 1967

Human All Too Human, trans. R. Hollingdale, Cambridge University Press 1986

The Gay Science, trans. W. Kaufmann, Vintage, New York 1974

Beyond Good and Evil, trans. W. Kaufmann, Vintage, New York 1966

On the Genealogy of Morals, trans. W. Kaufmann, Vintage, New York 1965

Ecce Homo, trans. W. Kaufmann, Vintage, New York 1969

The Will to Power, trans. W. Kaufmann and R. Hollingdale, Weidenfeld and Nicolson, London 1968

Die Unschuld des Werdens, Kromer, Stuttgart 1968.

THUS SPAKE ZARATHUSTRA

FIRST PART

ZARATHUSTRA'S PROLOGUE

1

When Zarathustra was thirty years old, he left his home and the lake of his home, and went into the mountains. There he enjoyed his spirit and his solitude, and for ten years did not weary of it. But at last his heart changed, and rising one morning with the rosy dawn, he went before the sun, and spake thus unto it:

Thou great star! What would be thy happiness if thou hadst not those for whom thou shinest!

For ten years hast thou climbed hither unto my cave: thou wouldst have wearied of thy light and of the journey, had it not been for me, mine eagle and my serpent.

But we awaited thee every morning, took from thee thine overflow, and blessed thee for it.

Lo! I am weary of my wisdom, like the bee that hath gathered too much honey; I need hands outstretched to take it.

I would fain bestow and distribute, until the wise have once more become joyous in their folly, and the poor happy in their riches.

Therefore must I descend into the deep: as thou doest in the evening, when thou goest behind the sea, and givest light also to the nether-world, thou exuberant star!

Like thee must I go *down*, as men say, to whom I shall descend.

Bless me, then, thou tranquil eyes that canst behold even the greatest happiness without envy!

Bless the cup that is about to overflow, that the water may flow golden out of it, and carry everywhere the reflection of thy bliss.

Lo! This cup is again going to empty itself, and Zarathustra is again going to be a man.

Thus began Zarathustra's down-going.

2

Zarathustra went down the mountain alone, no one meeting him. When he entered the forest, however, there suddenly stood before him an old man, who had left his holy cot to seek roots. And thus spake the old man to Zarathustra:

No stranger to me is this wanderer: many years ago passed he by. Zarathustra he was called, but he hath altered.

Then thou carriedst thine ashes into the mountains: wilt thou now carry thy fire into the valleys? Fearest thou not the incendiary's doom?

Yea, I recognise Zarathustra. Pure is his eye, and no loathing lurketh about his mouth. Goeth he not along like a dancer?

Altered is Zarathustra; a child hath Zarathustra become; an awakened one is Zarathustra: what wilt thou do in the land of the sleepers?

As in the sea hast thou lived in solitude, and it hath borne thee up. Alas, wilt thou now go ashore? Alas, wilt thou again drag thy body thyself?

Zarathustra answered: I love mankind.

Why, said the saint, did I go into the forest and the desert? Was it not because I loved men far too well?

Now I love God: men I do not love. Man is a thing too imperfect for me. Love to man would be fatal to me.

Zarathustra answered: What spake I of love! I am bringing gifts unto men.

Give them nothing, said the saint. Take rather part of their load, and carry it along with them – that will be most agreeable unto them: if only it be agreeable unto thee!

If, however, thou wilt give unto them, give them no more than an alms, and let them also beg for it!

No, replied Zarathustra, I give no alms. I am not poor enough for that.

The saint laughed at Zarathustra, and spake thus: Then see to it that they accept thy treasures! They are distrustful of anchorites, and do not believe that we come with gifts.

The fall of our footsteps ringeth too hollow through their streets. And just as at night, when they are in bed and hear a man abroad long before sunrise, so they ask themselves concerning us: Where goeth the thief?

Go not to men, but stay in the forest! Go rather to the animals! Why not be like me – a bear amongst bears, a bird amongst birds?

And what doth the saint in the forest? asked Zarathustra.

The saint answered: I make hymns and sing them; and in making hymns I laugh and weep and mumble: thus do I praise God.

With singing, weeping, laughing and mumbling do I praise the God who is my God. But what dost thou bring us as a gift?

When Zarathustra had heard these words, he bowed to the saint and said: What should I have to give thee! Let me rather hurry hence lest I take aught away from thee! And thus they parted from one another, the old man and Zarathustra, laughing like schoolboys.

When Zarathustra was alone, however, he said to his heart: Could it be possible! This old saint in the forest hath not yet heard of it, that *God is dead*!

3

When Zarathustra arrived at the nearest town which adjoineth the forest, he found many people assembled in the market-place, for it had been announced that a rope-dancer would give a performance. And Zarathustra spake thus unto the people:

I teach you the Superman. Man is something that is to be surpassed. What have ye done to surpass man?

All beings hitherto have created something beyond themselves: and ye want to be the ebb of that great tide, and would rather go back to the beast than surpass man?

What is the ape to man? A laughing-stock, a thing of shame. And just the same shall man be to the Superman: a laughing-stock, a thing of shame.

Ye have made your way from the worm to man, and much within you is still worm. Once were ye apes, and even yet man is more of an ape than any of the apes.

Even the wisest among you is only a disharmony and hybrid of plant and phantom. But do I bid you become phantoms or plants?

Lo, I teach you the Superman!

The Superman is the meaning of the earth. Let your will say: The Superman *shall be* the meaning of the earth!

I conjure you, my brethren, *remain true to the earth*, and believe not those who speak unto you of super-earthly hopes! Poisoners are they, whether they know it or not.

Despisers of life are they, decaying ones and poisoned ones themselves, of whom the earth is weary: so away with them!

Once blasphemy against God was the greatest blasphemy; but God died, and therewith also those blasphemers. To blaspheme the earth is now the dreadfulest sin, and to rate the heart of the unknowable higher than the meaning of the earth!

Once the soul looked contemptuously on the body, and then that contempt was the supreme thing: the soul wished the body meagre, ghastly and famished. Thus it thought to escape from the body and the earth.

Oh, that soul was itself meagre, ghastly and famished; and cruelty was the delight of that soul!

But ye, also, my brethren, tell me: what doth your body say

about your soul? Is your soul not poverty and pollution and wretched self-complacency?

Verily, a polluted stream is man. One must be a sea, to receive a polluted stream without becoming impure.

Lo, I teach you the Superman: he is that sea: in him can your great contempt be submerged.

What is the greatest thing ye can experience? It is the hour of great contempt. The hour in which even your happiness becometh loathsome unto you, and so also your reason and virtue.

The hour when ye say: 'What good is my happiness! It is poverty and pollution and wretched self-complacency. But my happiness should justify existence itself!'

The hour when ye say: 'What good is my reason! Doth it long for knowledge as the lion for his food? It is poverty and pollution and wretched self-complacency!'

The hour when ye say: 'What good is my virtue! As yet it hath not made me passionate. How weary I am of my good and my bad! It is all poverty and pollution and wretched self-complacency!'

The hour when ye say: 'What good is my justice! I do not see that I am fervour and fuel. The just, however, are fervour and fuel!'

The hour when we say: 'What good is my pity! Is not pity the cross on which he is nailed who loveth man? But my pity is not a crucifixion.'

Have ye ever spoken thus? Have ye ever cried thus? Ah! would that I had heard you crying thus!

It is not your sin – it is your self-satisfaction that crieth unto heaven; your very sparingness in sin crieth unto heaven!

Where is the lightning to lick you with its tongue? Where is the frenzy with which ye should be inoculated?

Lo, I teach you the Superman: he is that lightning, he is that frenzy!

When Zarathustra had thus spoken, one of the people called out: We have now heard enough of the rope-dancer; it is time now for us to see him! And all the people laughed at Zarathustra. But the rope-dancer, who thought the words applied to him, began his performance.

4

Zarathustra, however, looked at the people and wondered. Then he spake thus:

Man is a rope stretched between the animal and the Superman – a rope over an abyss.

A dangerous crossing, a dangerous wayfaring, a dangerous looking-back, a dangerous trembling and halting.

What is great in man is that he is a bridge and not a goal: what is lovable in man is that he is an *over-going* and a *down-going*.

I love those that know not how to live except as down-goers, for they are the over-goers.

I love the great despisers, because they are the great adorers, and arrows of longing for the other shore.

I love those who do not first seek a reason beyond the stars for going down and being sacrifices, but sacrifice themselves to the earth, that the earth of the Superman may hereafter arrive.

I love him who liveth in order to know, and seeketh to know in order that the Superman may hereafter live. Thus seeketh he his own down-going.

I love him who laboureth and inventeth, that he may build the house for the Superman, and prepare for him earth, animal and plant – for thus seeketh he his own down-going.

I love him who loveth his virtue: for virtue is the will to down-going, and an arrow of longing.

I love him who reserveth no share of spirit for himself, but wanteth to be wholly the spirit of his virtue: thus walketh he as spirit over the bridge.

I love him who maketh his virtue his inclination and destiny: thus, for the sake of his virtue, he is willing to live on, or live no more.

I love him who desireth not too many virtues. One virtue is more of a virtue than two, because it is more of a knot for one's destiny to cling to.

I love him whose soul is lavish, who wanteth no thanks and doth not give back: for he always bestoweth, and desireth not to keep for himself.

I love him who is ashamed when the dice fall in his favour, and who then asketh: 'Am I a dishonest player?' – for he is willing to succumb.

I love him who scattereth golden words in advance of his deeds, and always doeth more than he promiseth: for he seeketh his own down-going.

I love him who justifieth the future ones, and redeemeth the past ones: for he is willing to succumb through the present ones.

I love him who chasteneth his God, because he loveth his God: for he must succumb through the wrath of his God.

I love him whose soul is deep even in the wounding, and may succumb through a small matter: thus goeth he willingly over the bridge.

I love him whose soul is so over-full that he forgetteth himself, and all things are in him: thus all things become his down-going.

I love him who is of a free spirit and a free heart: thus is his head only the bowels of his heart; his heart, however, causeth his down-going.

I love all who are like heavy drops falling one by one out of the dark cloud that lowereth over man: they herald the coming of the lightning, and succumb as heralds.

Lo, I am a herald of the lightning, and a heavy drop out of the cloud: the lightning, however, is the *Superman*.

5

When Zarathustra had spoken these words, he again looked at the people, and was silent. There they stand, said he to his heart. There they laugh: they understand me not; I am not the mouth for these ears.

Must one first batter their ears, that they may learn to hear with their eyes? Must one clatter like kettledrums and penitential preachers? Or do they only believe the stammerer?

They have something whereof they are proud. What do they call it, that which maketh them proud? Culture, they call it; it distinguisheth them from the goat-herds.

They dislike, therefore, to hear of 'contempt' of themselves. So I will appeal to their pride.

I will speak unto them of the most contemptible thing; that, however, is *the last man*!

And thus spake Zarathustra unto the people:

It is time for man to fix his goal. It is time for man to plant the germ of his highest hope.

Still is his soil rich enough for it. But that soil will one day be poor and exhausted, and no lofty tree will any longer be able to grow thereon.

Alas! there cometh the time when man will no longer launch the arrow of his longing beyond man – and the string of his bow will have unlearned to whizz!

I tell you: one must still have chaos in one, to give birth to a dancing star. I tell you: ye have still chaos in you.

Alas! There cometh the time when man will no longer give birth to any star. Alas! There cometh the time of the most despicable man, who can no longer despise himself.

Lo! I show you *the last man*.

'What is love? What is creation? What is longing? What is a star?' So asketh the last man and blinketh.

The earth hath then become small, and on it there hoppeth the last man who maketh everything small. His species is ineradicable like that of the ground-flea; the last man liveth longest.

'We have discovered happiness,' say the last men, and blink thereby.

They have left the regions where it is hard to live; for they need warmth. One still loveth one's neighbour and rubbeth against him; for one needeth warmth.

Turning ill and being distrustful they consider sinful: they walk warily. He is a fool who still stumbleth over stones or men!

A little poison now and then: that maketh pleasant dreams. And much poison at last for a pleasant death.

One still worketh, for work is a pastime. But one is careful lest the pastime should hurt one.

One no longer becometh poor or rich; both are too burdensome. Who still wanteth to rule? Who still wanteth to obey? Both are too burdensome.

No shepherd, and one herd! Every one wanteth the same; every one is equal: he who hath other sentiments goeth voluntarily into the madhouse.

'Formerly all the world was insáne,' say the subtlest of them, and blink thereby.

They are clever and know all that hath happened: so there is no end to their raillery. People still fall out, but are soon reconciled – otherwise it spoileth their stomachs.

They have their little pleasures for the day, and their little pleasures for the night: but they have a regard for health.

'We have discovered happiness,' say the last men, and blink thereby.

And here ended the first discourse of Zarathustra, which is also called 'The Prologue': for at this point the shouting and mirth of the multitude interrupted him. Give us this last man, O Zarathustra, they called out. Make us into these last men! Then will we make thee a present of the Superman! And all the people exulted and smacked their lips. Zarathustra, however, turned sad, and said to his heart:

They understand me not: I am not the mouth for these ears.

Too long, perhaps, have I lived in the mountains; too much have I hearkened unto the brooks and trees: now do I speak unto them as unto the goat-herds.

Calm is my soul, and clear, like the mountains in the morning. But they think me cold, and a mocker with terrible jests.

And now do they look at me and laugh: and while they laugh they hate me too. There is ice in their laughter.

6

Then, however, something happened which made every mouth mute and every eye fixed. In the meantime, of course, the rope-dancer had commenced his performance: he had come out at a little door, and was going along the rope which was stretched between two towers, so that it hung above the market-place and the people. When he was just midway across, the little door opened once more, and a gaudily-dressed fellow like a buffoon sprang out, and went rapidly after the first one. Go on, halt-foot, cried his frightful voice. Go on, lazy-bones, interloper, sallow-face – lest I tickle thee with my heel! What dost thou here between the towers? In the tower is the place for thee, thou shouldst be locked up; to one better than thyself thou blockest the way! And with every word he came nearer and nearer the first one. When, however, he was but a step behind, there happened the frightful thing which made every mouth mute and every eye fixed: he uttered a yell like a devil, and jumped over the other who was in his way. The latter, however, when he thus saw his rival triumph, lost at the same time his head and his footing on the rope; he threw his pole away, and shot downwards faster than it, like an eddy of arms and legs, into the depth. The market-place and the people were like the sea when the storm cometh on: they all flew apart and in disorder, especially where the body was about to fall.

Zarathustra, however, remained standing, and just beside him fell the body, badly injured and disfigured, but not yet dead. After a while consciousness returned to the shattered man, and he saw Zarathustra kneeling beside him. What art thou doing there? said he at last. I knew long ago that the devil would trip me up. Now he draggeth me to hell: wilt thou prevent him?

On mine honour, my friend, answered Zarathustra, there is nothing of all that whereof thou speakest: there is no devil and no hell. Thy soul will be dead even sooner than thy body: fear, therefore, nothing any more!

The man looked up distrustfully. If thou speakest the truth, said he, I lose nothing when I lose my life. I am not much more than an animal which hath been taught to dance by blows and scanty fare.

Not at all, said Zarathustra. Thou hast made danger thy calling;

therein there is nothing contemptible. Now thou perishest by thy calling: therefore will I bury thee with mine own hands.

When Zarathustra had said this, the dying one did not reply further; but he moved his hand as if he sought the hand of Zarathustra in gratitude.

7

Meanwhile the evening came on, and the market-place veiled itself in gloom. Then the people dispersed, for even curiosity and terror become fatigued. Zarathustra, however, still sat beside the dead man on the ground, absorbed in thought: so he forgot the time. But at last it became night, and a cold wind blew upon the lonely one. Then arose Zarathustra and said to his heart:

Verily, a fine catch of fish hath Zarathustra made today! It is not a man he hath caught, but a corpse.

Sombre is human life, and as yet without meaning: a buffoon may be fateful to it.

I want to teach men the sense of their existence, which is the Superman, the lightning out of the dark cloud – man.

But still am I far from them, and my sense speaketh not unto their sense. To men I am still something between a fool and a corpse.

Gloomy is the night, gloomy are the ways of Zarathustra. Come, thou cold and stiff companion! I carry thee to the place where I shall bury thee with mine own hands.

8

When Zarathustra had said this to his heart, he put the corpse upon his shoulders and set out on his way. Yet had he not gone a hundred steps, when there stole a man up to him and whispered in his ear – and lo! he that spake was the buffoon from the tower. Leave this town, O Zarathustra, said he. There are too many here who hate thee. The good and just hate thee, and call thee their enemy and despiser; the believers in the orthodox belief hate thee, and call thee a danger to the multitude. It was thy good fortune to be laughed at: and verily thou spakest like a buffoon. It was thy good fortune to associate with the dead dog; by so humiliating thyself thou hast saved thy life today. Depart, however, from this town, or tomorrow I shall jump over thee, a living man over a dead one. And when he had said this, the buffoon vanished; Zarathustra, however, went on through the dark streets.

At the gate of the town the grave-diggers met him: they shone their torch on his face, and recognising Zarathustra, they sorely derided him. Zarathustra is carrying away the dead dog: a fine thing that Zarathustra hath turned a grave-digger! For our hands are too cleanly for that roast. Will Zarathustra steal the bite from the devil? Well then, good luck to the repast! If only the devil is not a better thief than Zarathustra – he will steal them both, he will eat them both! And they laughed among themselves, and put their heads together.

Zarathustra made no answer thereto, but went on his way. When he had gone on for two hours, past forests and swamps, he had heard too much of the hungry howling of the wolves, and he himself became a-hungry. So he halted at a lonely house in which a light was burning.

Hunger attacketh me, said Zarathustra, like a robber. Among forests and swamps my hunger attacketh me, and late in the night.

Strange humours hath my hunger. Often it cometh to me only after a repast, and all day it hath failed to come: where hath it been?

And thereupon Zarathustra knocked at the door of the house. An old man appeared who carried a light, and asked: Who cometh unto me and my bad sleep?

A living man and a dead one, said Zarathustra. Give me something to eat and drink, I forgot it during the day. He that feedeth the hungry refresheth his own soul, saith wisdom.

The old man withdrew, but came back immediately and offered Zarathustra bread and wine. A bad country for the hungry, said he; that is why I live here. Animal and man come unto me, the anchorite. But bid thy companion eat and drink also, he is wearier than thou. Zarathustra answered: My companion is dead; I shall hardly be able to persuade him to eat. That doth not concern me, said the old man sullenly; he that knocketh at my door must take what I offer him. Eat, and fare ye well!

Thereafter Zarathustra again went on for two hours, trusting to the path and the light of the stars: for he was an experienced night-walker, and liked to look into the face of all that slept. When the morning dawned, however, Zarathustra found himself in a thick forest, and no path was any longer visible. He then put the dead man in a hollow tree at his head – for he wanted to protect him from the wolves – and laid himself down on the ground and moss. And immediately he fell asleep, tired in body, but with a tranquil soul.

9

Long slept Zarathustra; and not only the rosy dawn passed over his head, but also the morning. At last, however, his eyes opened, and amazedly he gazed into the forest and the stillness, amazedly he gazed into himself. Then he arose quickly, like a seafarer who all at once seeth the land; and he shouted for joy, for he saw a new truth. And he spake thus to his heart:

A light hath dawned upon me: I need companions – living ones, not dead companions and corpses, which I carry with me where I will.

But I need living companions who will follow me because they want to follow themselves – and to the place where I will.

A light hath dawned upon me. Not to the people is Zarathustra to speak, but to companions! Zarathustra shall not be the herd's herdsman and hound!

To allure many from the herd – for that purpose have I come. The people and the herd must be angry with me: a robber shall Zarathustra be called by the herdsmen.

Herdsmen, I say, but they call themselves the good and just. Herdsmen, I say, but they call themselves the believers in the orthodox belief.

Behold the good and just! Whom do they hate most? Him who breaketh up their tables of values, the breaker, the law-breaker: he, however, is the creator.

Behold the believers of all beliefs! Whom do they hate most? Him who breaketh up their tables of values, the breaker, the law-breaker: he, however, is the creator.

Companions the creator seeketh, not corpses – and not herds or believers either. Fellow-creators the creator seeketh – those who grave new values on new tables.

Companions the creator seeketh, and fellow-reapers: for everything is ripe for the harvest with him. But he lacketh the hundred sickles, so he plucketh the ears of corn and is vexed.

Companions the creator seeketh, and such as know how to whet their sickles. Destroyers will they be called, and despisers of good and evil. But they are the reapers and rejoicers.

Fellow-creators Zarathustra seeketh; fellow-reapers and fellow-rejoicers Zarathustra seeketh: what hath he to do with herds and herdsmen and corpses!

And thou, my first companion, rest in peace! Well have I buried thee in thy hollow tree; well have I hid thee from the wolves.

But I part from thee; the time hath arrived. 'Twixt rosy dawn and rosy dawn there came unto me a new truth.

I am not to be a herdsman; I am not to be a grave-digger. Not any more will I discourse unto the people; for the last time have I spoken unto the dead.

With the creators, the reapers and the rejoicers will I associate: the rainbow will I show them, and all the stairs to the Superman.

To the lone-dwellers will I sing my song, and to the twain-dwellers; and unto him who hath still ears for the unheard will I make the heart heavy with my happiness.

I make for my goal, I follow my course; over the loitering and tardy will I leap. Thus let my on-going be their down-going!

10

This had Zarathustra said to his heart when the sun stood at noontide. Then he looked inquiringly aloft, for he heard above him the sharp call of a bird. And behold! An eagle swept through the air in wide circles, and on it hung a serpent, not like a prey, but like a friend: for it kept itself coiled round the eagle's neck.

They are mine animals, said Zarathustra, and rejoiced in his heart.

The proudest animal under the sun, and the wisest animal under the sun – they have come out to reconnoitre.

They want to know whether Zarathustra still liveth. Verily, do I still live?

More dangerous have I found it among men than among animals; in dangerous paths goeth Zarathustra. Let mine animals lead me!

When Zarathustra had said this, he remembered the words of the saint in the forest. Then he sighed and spake thus to his heart:

Would that I were wiser! Would that I were wise from the very heart, like my serpent!

But I am asking the impossible. Therefore do I ask my pride to go always with my wisdom!

And if my wisdom should some day forsake me: alas! it loveth to fly away! May my pride then fly with my folly!

Thus began Zarathustra's down-going.

ZARATHUSTRA'S DISCOURSES

1 *The Three Metamorphoses*

Three metamorphoses of the spirit do I designate to you: how the spirit becometh a camel, the camel a lion, and the lion at last a child.

Many heavy things are there for the spirit, the strong load-bearing spirit in which reverence dwelleth: for the heavy and the heaviest longeth its strength.

What is heavy? So asketh the load-bearing spirit; then kneeleth it down like the camel, and wanteth to be well laden.

What is the heaviest thing, ye heroes, asketh the load-bearing spirit, that I may take it upon me and rejoice in my strength?

Is it not this: to humiliate oneself in order to mortify one's pride? To exhibit one's folly in order to mock at one's wisdom?

Or is it this: to desert our cause when it celebrateth its triumph? To ascend high mountains to tempt the tempter?

Or is it this: to feed on the acorns and grass of knowledge, and for the sake of truth to suffer hunger of soul?

Or is it this: to be sick and dismiss comforters, and make friends of the deaf, who never hear thy requests?

Or is it this: to go into foul water when it is the water of truth, and not disclaim cold frogs and hot toads?

Or is it this: to love those who despise us, and give one's hand to the phantom when it is going to frighten us?

All these heaviest things the load-bearing spirit taketh upon itself; and like the camel, which when laden hasteneth into the wilderness, so hasteneth the spirit into its wilderness.

But in the loneliest wilderness happeneth the second metamorphosis: here the spirit becometh a lion; freedom will it capture, and lordship in its own wilderness.

Its last Lord it here seeketh: hostile will it be to him, and to its last God; for victory will it struggle with the great dragon.

What is the great dragon which the spirit is no longer inclined to call Lord and God? 'Thou-shalt' is the great dragon called. But the spirit of the lion saith, 'I will.'

'Thou-shalt' lieth in its path, sparkling with gold – a scale-covered beast; and on every scale glittereth golden, 'Thou shalt!'

The values of a thousand years glitter on these scales, and thus speaketh the mightiest of all dragons: 'All the values of things – glitter on me.

All values have already been created, and all created values – do I represent. Verily, there shall be no "I will" any more.' Thus speaketh the dragon.

My brethren, wherefore is there need of the lion in the spirit? Why sufficeth not the beast of burden, which renounceth and is reverent?

To create new values – that even the lion cannot yet accomplish: but to create itself freedom for new creating – that can the might of the lion do.

To create itself freedom, and give a holy Nay even unto duty: for that, my brethren, there is need of the lion.

To assume the right to new values – that is the most formidable assumption for a load-bearing and reverent spirit. Verily, unto such a spirit it is preying, and the work of a beast of prey.

As its holiest, it once loved 'Thou-shalt': now is it forced to find illusion and arbitrariness even in the holiest things, that it may capture freedom from its love: the lion is needed for this capture.

But tell me, my brethren, what the child can do, which even the lion could not do? Why hath the preying lion still to become a child?

Innocence is the child, and forgetfulness, a new beginning, a game, a self-rolling wheel, a first movement, a holy Yea.

Aye, for the game of creating, my brethren, there is needed a holy Yea unto life: *its own* will willeth now the spirit; *his own* world winneth the world's outcast.

Three metamorphoses of the spirit have I designated to you: how the spirit became a camel, the camel a lion, and the lion at last a child.

Thus spake Zarathustra. And at that time he abode in the town which is called The Pied Cow.

2 *The Academic Chairs of Virtue*

People commended unto Zarathustra a wise man, as one who could discourse well about sleep and virtue; greatly was he honoured and rewarded for it, and all the youths sat before his chair. To him went Zarathustra, and sat among the youths before his chair. And thus spake the wise man:

Respect and modesty in presence of sleep! That is the first thing! And to go out of the way of all who sleep badly and keep awake at night!

Modest is even the thief in presence of sleep; he always stealeth softly through the night. Immodest, however, is the nightwatchman; immodestly he carrieth his horn.

No small art is it to sleep; it is necessary for that purpose to keep awake all day.

Ten times a day must thou overcome thyself; that causeth wholesome weariness, and is poppy to the soul.

Ten times must thou reconcile again with thyself; for overcoming is bitterness, and badly sleep the unreconciled.

Ten truths must thou find during the day; otherwise wilt thou seek truth during the night, and thy soul will have been hungry.

Ten times must thou laugh during the day, and be cheerful; otherwise thy stomach, the father of affliction, will disturb thee in the night.

Few people know it, but one must have all the virtues in order to sleep well. Shall I bear false witness? Shall I commit adultery?

Shall I covet my neighbour's maidservant? All that would ill accord with good sleep.

And even if one have all the virtues, there is still one thing needful: to send the virtues themselves to sleep at the right time.

That they may not quarrel with one another, the good females! And about thee, thou unhappy one!

Peace with God and thy neighbour: so desireth good sleep. And peace also with thy neighbour's devil! Otherwise it will haunt thee in the night.

Honour to the government, and obedience, and also to the

crooked government! So desireth good sleep. How can I help it, if power like to walk on crooked legs?

He who leadeth his sheep to the greenest pasture, shall always be for me the best shepherd; so doth it accord with good sleep.

Many honours I want not, nor great treasures; they excite the spleen. But it is bad sleeping without a good name and a little treasure.

A small company is more welcome to me than a bad one; but they must come and go at the right time. So doth it accord with good sleep.

Well also do the poor in spirit please me; they promote sleep. Blessed are they, especially if one always give in to them.

Thus passeth the day unto the virtuous. When night cometh, then take I good care not to summon sleep. It disliketh to be summoned – sleep, the lord of the virtues!

But I think of what I have done and thought during the day. Thus ruminating, patient as a cow, I ask myself, What were thy ten overcomings?

And what were the ten reconciliations, and the ten truths, and the ten laughters with which my heart enjoyed itself?

Thus pondering, and cradled by forty thoughts, it overtaketh me all at once – sleep, the unsummoned, the lord of the virtues.

Sleep tappeth on mine eye, and it turneth heavy. Sleep toucheth my mouth, and it remaineth open.

Verily, on soft soles doth it come to me, the dearest of thieves, and stealeth from me my thoughts; stupid do I then stand. Like this academic chair.

But not much longer do I then stand; I already lie.

When Zarathustra heard the wise man thus speak, he laughed in his heart, for thereby had a light dawned upon him. And thus spake he to his heart:

A fool seemeth this wise man with his forty thoughts; but I believe he knoweth well how to sleep.

Happy even is he who liveth near this wise man! Such sleep is contagious – even through a thick wall it is contagious.

A magic resideth even in his academic chair. And not in vain did the youths sit before the preacher of virtue.

His wisdom is to keep awake in order to sleep well. And verily, if life had no sense, and had I to choose nonsense, this would be the most desirable nonsense for me also.

Now know I well what people sought formerly above all else when they sought teachers of virtue. Good sleep they sought for themselves, and poppy-head virtues to promote it!

To all those belauded sages of the academic chairs, wisdom was sleep without dreams; they knew no higher significance of life.

Even at present, to be sure, there are some like this preacher of virtue, and not always so honourable; but their time is past. And not much longer do they stand; there they already lie.

Blessed are those drowsy ones, for they shall soon nod to sleep.

Thus spake Zarathustra.

3 *Backworldsmen*

Once on a time, Zarathustra also cast his fancy beyond man, like all backworldsmen. The work of a suffering and tortured God did the world then seem to me.

The dream – and diction – of a God did the world then seem to me; coloured vapours before the eyes of a divinely dissatisfied one.

Good and evil, and joy and woe, and I and thou – coloured vapours did they seem to me before creative eyes. The creator wished to look away from himself – thereupon he created the world.

Intoxicating joy is it for the sufferer to look away from his suffering and forget himself. Intoxicating joy and self-forgetting did the world once seem to me.

This world, the eternally imperfect, an eternal contradiction's image and imperfect image – an intoxicating joy to its imperfect creator: thus did the world once seem to me.

Thus, once on a time, did I also cast my fancy beyond man, like all backworldsmen. Beyond man, forsooth?

Ah, ye brethren, that God whom I created was human work and human madness, like all the Gods!

A man was he, and only a poor fragment of a man and ego. Out of mine own ashes and glow it came unto me, that phantom. And verily, it came not unto me from the beyond!

What happened, my brethren? I surpassed myself, the suffering one; I carried mine own ashes to the mountain; a brighter flame I contrived for myself. And lo, thereupon the phantom *withdrew* from me!

To me the convalescent would it now be suffering and torment to believe in such phantoms; suffering would it now be to me, and humiliation. Thus speak I to backworldsmen.

Suffering was it, and impotence, that created all backworlds; and the short madness of happiness, which only the greatest sufferer experienceth.

Weariness, which seeketh to get to the ultimate with one leap, with a death-leap; a poor ignorant weariness, unwilling even to will any longer, that created all Gods and backworlds.

Believe me, my brethren! It was the body which despaired of the body – it groped with the fingers of the infatuated spirit at the ultimate walls.

Believe me, my brethren! It was the body which despaired of the earth – it heard the bowels of existence speaking unto it.

And then it sought to get through the ultimate walls with its head – and not with its head only – into 'the other world'.

But that 'other world' is well concealed from man, that dehumanised, inhuman world which is a celestial naught, and the bowels of existence do not speak unto man, except as man.

Verily, it is difficult to prove all being, and hard to make it speak. Tell me, ye brethren, is not the strangest of all things best proved?

Yea, this ego, with its contradiction and perplexity, speaketh most uprightly of its being – this creating, willing, evaluing ego, which is the measure and value of things.

And this most upright existence, the ego – it speaketh of the body, and still implieth the body, even when it museth and raveth and fluttereth with broken wings.

Always more uprightly learneth it to speak, the ego; and the more it learneth, the more doth it find titles and honours for the body and the earth.

A new pride taught me mine ego, and that teach I unto men: no longer to thrust one's head into the sand of celestial things, but to carry it freely, a terrestrial head, which giveth meaning to the earth!

A new will teach I unto men: to choose that path which man hath followed blindly, and to approve of it – and no longer to slink aside from it, like the sick and perishing!

The sick and perishing – it was they who despised the body and the earth, and invented the heavenly world, and the redeeming blood-drops; but even those sweet and sad poisons they borrowed from the body and the earth!

From their misery they sought escape, and the stars were too remote for them. Then they sighed: 'O that there were heavenly paths by which to steal into another existence and into happiness!' Then they contrived for themselves their by-paths and bloody draughts!

Beyond the sphere of their body and this earth they now fancied themselves transported, these ungrateful ones. But to what did they owe the convulsion and rapture of their transport? To their body and this earth.

Gentle is Zarathustra to the sickly. Verily, he is not indignant at their modes of consolation and ingratitude. May they become convalescents and overcomers, and create higher bodies for themselves!

Neither is Zarathustra indignant at a convalescent who looketh tenderly on his delusions, and at midnight stealeth round the grave of his God; but sickness and a sick frame remain even in his tears.

Many sickly ones have there always been among those who muse, and languish for God; violently they hate the discerning ones, and the latest of virtues, which is uprightness.

Backward they always gaze toward dark ages: then indeed were delusion and faith something different. Raving of the reason was likeness to God, and doubt was sin.

Too well do I know those godlike ones; they insist on being believed in, and that doubt is sin. Too well, also, do I know what they themselves most believe in.

Verily, not in backworlds and redeeming blood-drops, but in the body do they also believe most; and their own body is for them the thing-in-itself.

But it is a sickly thing to them, and gladly would they get out of their skin. Therefore hearken they to the preachers of death, and themselves preach backworlds.

Hearken rather, my brethren, to the voice of the healthy body; it is a more upright and pure voice.

More uprightly and purely speaketh the healthy body, perfect and square-built; and it speaketh of the meaning of the earth.

Thus spake Zarathustra.

4 *The Despisers of the Body*

To the despisers of the body will I speak my word. I wish them neither to learn afresh, nor teach anew, but only to bid farewell to their own bodies – and thus be dumb.

'Body am I, and soul' – so saith the child. And why should one not speak like children?

But the awakened one, the knowing one, saith: 'Body am I entirely, and nothing more; and soul is only the name of something in the body.'

The body is a big sagacity, a plurality with one sense, a war and a peace, a flock and a shepherd.

An instrument of thy body is also thy little sagacity, my brother, which thou callest 'spirit' – a little instrument and plaything of thy big sagacity.

'Ego,' sayest thou, and art proud of that word. But the greater thing – in which thou art unwilling to believe – is thy body with its big sagacity; it saith not 'ego', but doeth it.

What the sense feeleth, what the spirit discerneth, hath never its end in itself. But sense and spirit would fain persuade thee that they are the end of all things, so vain are they.

Instruments and playthings are sense and spirit; behind them there is still the Self. The Self seeketh with the eyes of the senses, it hearkeneth also with the ears of the spirit.

Ever hearkeneth the Self, and seeketh; it compareth, mastereth, conquereth, and destroyeth. It ruleth, and is also the ego's ruler.

Behind thy thoughts and feelings, my brother, there is a mighty lord, an unknown sage – it is called Self; it dwelleth in thy body, it is thy body.

There is more sagacity in thy body than in thy best wisdom. And who then knoweth why thy body requireth just thy best wisdom?

Thy Self laugheth at thine ego and its proud prancings. 'What are these prancings and flights of thought unto me?' it saith to itself. 'A by-way to my purpose. I am the leading-string of the ego, and the prompter of its notions.'

The Self saith unto the ego: 'Feel pain!' And thereupon it

suffereth and thinketh how it may put an end thereto – and for that very purpose it *is meant* to think.

The Self saith unto the ego: 'Feel pleasure!' Thereupon it rejoiceth, and thinketh how it may ofttimes rejoice – and for that very purpose it *is meant* to think.

To the despisers of the body will I speak a word. That they despise is caused by their esteem. What is it that created esteeming and despising and worth and will?

The creating Self created for itself esteeming and despising, it created for itself joy and woe. The creating body created for itself spirit, as a hand to its will.

Even in your folly and despising ye each serve your Self, ye despisers of the body. I tell you, your very Self wanteth to die, and turneth away from life.

No longer can your Self do that which it desireth most – create beyond itself. That is what it desireth most; that is all its fervour.

But it is now too late to do so; so your Self wisheth to succumb, ye despisers of the body.

To succumb – so wisheth your Self; and therefore have ye become despisers of the body. For ye can no longer create beyond yourselves.

And therefore are ye now angry with life and with the earth. And unconscious envy is in the sidelong look of your contempt.

I go not your way, ye despisers of the body! Ye are no bridges for me to the Superman!

Thus spake Zarathustra.

5 *Joys and Passions*

My brother, when thou hast a virtue, and it is thine own virtue, thou hast it in common with no one.

To be sure, thou wouldst call it by name and caress it; thou wouldst pull its ears and amuse thyself with it.

And lo, then hast thou its name in common with the people, and hast become one of the people and the herd with thy virtue!

Better for thee to say: 'Ineffable is it, and nameless, that which is pain and sweetness to my soul, and also the hunger of my bowels.'

Let thy virtue be too high for the familiarity of names; and if thou must speak of it, be not ashamed to stammer about it.

Thus speak and stammer: 'That is *my* good! That do I love, thus doth it please me entirely, thus only do I desire the good.

Not as the law of a God do I desire it, not as a human law or a human need do I desire it; it is not to be a guidepost for me to superearths and paradises.

An earthly virtue is it which I love; little prudence is therein, and the least everyday wisdom.

But that bird built its nest beside me; therefore I love and cherish it – now sitteth it beside me on its golden eggs.'

Thus shouldst thou stammer, and praise thy virtue.

Once hadst thou passions and calledst them evil. But now hast thou only thy virtues; they grew out of thy passions.

Thou implantedst thy highest aim into the heart of those passions; then became they thy virtues and joys.

And though thou wert of the race of the hot-tempered, or of the voluptuous, or of the fanatical, or the vindictive, all thy passions in the end became virtues, and all thy devils angels.

Once hadst thou wild dogs in thy cellar; but they changed at last into birds and charming songstresses.

Out of thy poisons brewedst thou balsam for thyself; thy cow, affliction, milkedst thou – now drinketh thou the sweet milk of her udder.

And nothing evil groweth in thee any longer, unless it be the evil that groweth out of the conflict of thy virtues.

My brother, if thou be fortunate, then wilt thou have one virtue and no more: thus goest thou easier over the bridge.

Illustrious is it to have many virtues, but a hard lot; and many a one hath gone into the wilderness and killed himself, because he was weary of being the battle and battlefield of virtues.

My brother, are war and battle evil? Necessary, however, is the evil; necessary are the envy and the distrust and the backbiting among the virtues.

Lo, how each of thy virtues is covetous of the highest place! It wanteth thy whole spirit to be its herald; it wanteth thy whole power, in wrath, hatred and love.

Jealous is every virtue of the others, and a dreadful thing is jealousy. Even virtues may succumb by jealousy.

He whom the flame of jealousy encompasseth, turneth at last, like the scorpion, the poisoned sting against himself.

Ah, my brother, hast thou never seen a virtue backbite and stab itself?

Man is something that hath to be surpassed; and therefore shalt thou love thy virtues – for thou wilt succumb by them.

Thus spake Zarathustra.

6 *The Pale Criminal*

Ye do not mean to slay, ye judges and sacrificers, until the animal hath bowed its head? Lo, the pale criminal hath bowed his head! Out of his eye speaketh the great contempt.

'Mine ego is something which is to be surpassed; mine ego is to me the great contempt of man': so speaketh it out of that eye.

When he judged himself – that was his supreme moment; let not the exalted one relapse again into his low estate!

There is no salvation for him who thus suffereth from himself, unless it be speedy death.

Your slaying, ye judges, shall be pity and not revenge; and in that ye slay, see to it that ye yourselves justify life!

It is not enough that ye should reconcile with him whom ye slay. Let your sorrow be love to the Superman: thus will ye justify your own survival!

'Enemy' shall ye say, but not 'villain'; 'invalid' shall ye say, but not 'wretch'; 'fool' shall ye say, but not 'sinner'.

And thou, red judge, if thou would say audibly all thou hast done in thought, then would every one cry: 'Away with the nastiness and the virulent reptile!'

But one thing is the thought, another thing is the deed, and another thing is the idea of the deed. The wheel of causality doth not roll between them.

An idea made this pale man pale. Adequate was he for his deed when he did it, but the idea of it he could not endure when it was done.

Evermore did he now see himself as the doer of one deed. Madness, I call this: the exception reversed itself to the rule in him.

The streak of chalk bewitcheth the hen; the stroke he struck bewitched his weak reason. Madness *after* the deed, I call this.

Hearken, ye judges! There is another madness besides, and it is *before* the deed. Ah, ye have not gone deep enough into this soul!

Thus speaketh the red judge: 'Why did this criminal commit murder? He meant to rob.' I tell you, however, that his soul wanted blood, not booty: he thirsted for the happiness of the knife!

But his weak reason understood not this madness, and it persuaded him. 'What matter about blood!' it said; 'wishest thou not, at least, to make booty thereby? Or take revenge?'

And he hearkened unto his weak reason; like lead lay its words upon him – thereupon he robbed when he murdered. He did not mean to be ashamed of his madness.

And now once more lieth the lead of his guilt upon him, and once more is his weak reason so benumbed, so paralysed and so dull.

Could he only shake his head, then would his burden roll off, but who shaketh that head?

What is this man? A mass of diseases that reach out into the world through the spirit; there they want to get their prey.

What is this man? A coil of wild serpents that are seldom at peace among themselves – so they go forth apart and seek prey in the world.

Look at that poor body! What it suffered and craved, the poor soul interpreted to itself – it interpreted it as murderous desire, and eagerness for the happiness of the knife.

Him who now turneth sick, the evil overtaketh which is now the evil: he seeketh to cause pain with that which causeth him pain. But there have been other ages, and another evil and good.

Once was doubt evil, and the will to Self. Then the invalid became a heretic or sorcerer; as heretic or sorcerer he suffered, and sought to cause suffering.

But this will not enter your ears; it hurteth your good people, ye tell me. But what doth it matter to me about your good people!

Many things in your good people cause me disgust; and verily, not their evil. I would that they had a madness by which they succumbed, like this pale criminal!

Verily, I would that their madness were called truth, or fidelity, or justice: but they have their virtue in order to live long, and in wretched self-complacency.

I am a railing alongside the torrent; whoever is able to grasp me may grasp me! Your crutch, however, I am not.

Thus spake Zarathustra.

7 *Reading and Writing*

Of all that is written, I love only what a person hath written with his blood. Write with blood, and thou wilt find that blood is spirit.

It is no easy task to understand unfamiliar blood; I hate the reading idlers.

He who knoweth the reader, doth nothing more for the reader. Another century of readers – and spirit itself will stink.

Every one being allowed to learn to read, ruineth in the long run not only writing but also thinking.

Once spirit was God, then it became man, and now it even becometh populace.

He that writeth in blood and proverbs doth not want to be read, but learnt by heart.

In the mountains the shortest way is from peak to peak, but for that route thou must have long legs. Proverbs should be peaks, and those spoken to should be big and tall.

The atmosphere rare and pure, danger near and the spirit full of a joyful wickedness: thus are things well matched.

I want to have goblins about me, for I am courageous. The courage which scareth away ghosts, createth for itself goblins – it wanteth to laugh.

I no longer feel in common with you; the very cloud which I see beneath me, the blackness and heaviness at which I laugh – that is your thunder-cloud.

Ye look aloft when ye long for exaltation; and I look downward because I am exalted.

Who among you can at the same time laugh and be exalted?

He who climbeth on the highest mountains, laugheth at all tragic plays and tragic realities.

Courageous, unconcerned, scornful, coercive – so wisdom wisheth us; she is a woman, and ever loveth only a warrior.

Ye tell me, 'Life is hard to bear.' But for what purpose should ye have your pride in the morning and your resignation in the evening?

Life is hard to bear; but do not affect to be so delicate! We are all of us fine sumpter asses and she-asses.

What have we in common with the rose-bud, which trembleth because a drop of dew hath formed upon it?

It is true we love life; not because we are wont to live, but because we are wont to love.

There is always some madness in love. But there is always, also, some method in madness.

And to me also, who appreciate life, the butterflies and soap-bubbles and whatever is like them amongst us seem most to enjoy happiness.

To see these light, foolish, pretty, lively little sprites flit about – that moveth Zarathustra to tears and songs.

I should only believe in a God that would know how to dance.

And when I saw my devil, I found him serious, thorough, profound, solemn: he was the spirit of gravity – through him all things fall.

Not by wrath, but by laughter do we slay. Come, let us slay the spirit of gravity!

I learned to walk; since then have I let myself run. I learned to fly; since then I do not need pushing in order to move from a spot.

Now am I light, now do I fly; now do I see myself under myself. Now there danceth a God in me.

Thus spake Zarathustra.

8 *The Tree on the Hill*

Zarathustra's eye had perceived that a certain youth avoided him. And as he walked alone one evening over the hills surrounding the town called 'The Pied Cow', behold, there found he the youth sitting leaning against a tree, and gazing with wearied look into the valley. Zarathustra thereupon laid hold of the tree beside which the youth sat, and spake thus:

If I wished to shake this tree with my hands, I should not be able to do so.

But the wind, which we see not, troubleth and bendeth it as it listeth. We are sorest bent and troubled by invisible hands.

Thereupon the youth arose disconcerted, and said: I hear Zarathustra, and just now was I thinking of him! Zarathustra answered:

Why art thou frightened on that account? But it is the same with man as with the tree.

The more he seeketh to rise into the height and light, the more vigorously do his roots struggle earthward, downward, into the dark and deep – into the evil.

Yea, into the evil! cried the youth. How is it possible that thou hast discovered my soul?

Zarathustra smiled, and said: Many a soul one will never discover, unless one first invent it.

Yea, into the evil! cried the youth once more.

Thou saidst the truth, Zarathustra. I trust myself no longer since I sought to rise into the height, and nobody trusteth me any longer; how doth that happen?

I change too quickly: my today refuteth my yesterday. I often overleap the steps when I clamber; for so doing, none of the steps pardon me.

When aloft, I find myself always alone. No one speaketh unto me; the frost of solitude maketh me tremble. What do I seek on the height?

My contempt and my longing increase together; the higher I clamber, the more do I despise him who clambereth. What doth he seek on the height?

How ashamed I am of my clambering and stumbling! How I mock at my violent panting! How I hate him who flieth! How tired I am on the height!

Here the youth was silent. And Zarathustra contemplated the tree beside which they stood, and spake thus:

This tree standeth lonely here on the hills; it hath grown up high above man and beast.

And if it wanted to speak, it would have none who could understand it; so high hath it grown.

Now it waiteth and waiteth – for what doth it wait? It dwelleth too close to the seat of the clouds; it waiteth perhaps for the first lightning?

When Zarathustra had said this, the youth called out with violent gestures: Yea, Zarathustra, thou speakest the truth. My destruction I longed for, when I desired to be on the height, and thou art the lightning for which I waited! Lo, what have I been since thou hast appeared amongst us? It is mine envy of thee that hath destroyed me! Thus spake the youth, and wept bitterly. Zarathustra, however, put his arm about him, and led the youth away with him.

And when they had walked a while together, Zarathustra began to speak thus:

It rendeth my heart. Better than thy words express it, thine eyes tell me all thy danger.

As yet thou art not free; thou still *seekest* freedom. Too unslept hath thy seeking made thee, and too wakeful.

On the open height wouldst thou be; for the stars thirsteth thy soul. But thy bad impulses also thirst for freedom.

Thy wild dogs want liberty; they bark for joy in their cellar when thy spirit endeavoureth to open all prison doors.

Still art thou a prisoner – it seemeth to me – who deviseth liberty for himself; ah, sharp becometh the soul of such prisoners, but also deceitful and wicked.

To purify himself is still necessary for the freedman of the spirit. Much of the prison and the mould still remaineth in him; pure hath his eye still to become.

Yea, I know thy danger. But by my love and hope I conjure thee: cast not thy love and hope away!

Noble thou feelest thyself still, and noble others also feel thee still, though they bear thee a grudge and cast evil looks. Know this, that to everybody a noble one standeth in the way.

Also to the good, a noble one standeth in the way; and even when they call him a good man, they want thereby to put him aside.

The new would the noble man create, and a new virtue. The old wanteth the good man, and that the old should be conserved.

But it is not the danger of the noble man to turn a good man, but lest he should become a blusterer, a scoffer or a destroyer.

Ah, I have known noble ones who lost their highest hope. And then they disparaged all high hopes.

Then lived they shamelessly in temporary pleasures, and beyond the day had hardly an aim.

'Spirit is also voluptuousness,' said they. Then broke the wings of their spirit; and now it creepeth about, and defileth where it gnaweth.

Once they thought of becoming heroes; but sensualists are they now. A trouble and a terror is the hero to them.

But by my love and hope I conjure thee: cast not away the hero in thy soul! Maintain holy thy highest hope!

Thus spake Zarathustra.

9 *The Preacher of Death*

There are preachers of death; and the earth is full of those to whom desistance from life must be preached.

Full is the earth of the superfluous; marred is life by the many-too-many. May they be decoyed out of this life by the 'life eternal'!

'The yellow ones': so are called the preachers of death; or 'the black ones'. But I will show them unto you in other colours besides.

There are the terrible ones who carry about in themselves the beast of prey, and have no choice except lusts or self-laceration. And even their lusts are self-laceration.

They have not yet become men, those terrible ones; may they preach desistance from life and pass away themselves!

There are the spiritually consumptive ones; hardly are they born when they begin to die, and long for doctrines of lassitude and renunciation.

They would fain be dead, and we should approve of their wish! Let us beware of awakening those dead ones, and of damaging those living coffins!

They meet an invalid, or an old man, or a corpse – and immediately they say: 'Life is refuted!'

But only they are refuted, and their eye, which seeth only one aspect of existence.

Shrouded in thick melancholy, and eager for the little casualties that bring death: thus do they wait, and clench their teeth.

Or else, they grasp at sweetmeats, and mock at their childishness thereby; they cling to their straw of life, and mock at their still clinging to it.

Their wisdom speaketh thus: 'A fool, he who remaineth alive; but so far are we fools! And that is the foolishest thing in life!'

'Life is only suffering?' So say others, and lie not. Then see to it that ye cease! See to it that the life ceaseth which is only suffering!

And let this be the teaching of your virtue: 'Thou shalt slay thyself! Thou shalt steal away from thyself!'

'Lust is sin.' So say some who preach death. 'Let us go apart and beget no children!'

'Giving birth is troublesome,' say others. 'Why still give birth? One beareth only the unfortunate!' And they also are preachers of death.

'Pity is necessary,' So saith a third party. 'Take what I have! Take what I am! So much less doth life bind me!'

Were they consistently pitiful, then would they make their neighbours sick of life. To be wicked – that would be their true goodness.

But they want to be rid of life; what care they if they bind others still faster with their chains and gifts!

And ye also, to whom life is rough labour and disquiet, are ye not very tired of life? Are ye not very ripe for the sermon of death?

All ye to whom rough labour is dear, and the rapid, new and strange – ye put up with yourselves badly; your diligence is flight, and the will to self-forgetfulness.

If ye believed more in life, then would ye devote yourselves less to the momentary. But for waiting, ye have not enough of capacity in you – nor even for idling!

Everywhere resoundeth the voice of those who preach death; and the earth is full of those to whom death hath to be preached.

Or 'life eternal'; it is all the same to me – if only they pass away quickly!

Thus spake Zarathustra.

10 *War and Warriors*

By our best enemies we do not want to be spared, nor by those either whom we love from the very heart. So let me tell you the truth!

My brethren in war! I love you from the very heart. I am, and was ever, your counterpart. And I am also your best enemy. So let me tell you the truth!

I know the hatred and envy of your hearts. Ye are not great enough not to know of hatred and envy. Then be great enough not to be ashamed of them!

And if ye cannot be saints of knowledge, then I pray you, be at least its warriors. They are the companions and forerunners of such saintship.

I see many soldiers; could I but see many warriors! 'Uniform' one calleth what they wear; may it not be uniform what they therewith hide!

Ye shall be those whose eyes ever seek for an enemy – for your enemy. And with some of you there is hatred at first sight.

Your enemy shall ye seek; your war shall ye wage, and for the sake of your thoughts! And if your thoughts succumb, your uprightness shall still shout triumph thereby!

Ye shall love peace as a means to new wars – and the short peace more than the long.

You I advise not to work, but to fight. You I advise not to peace, but to victory. Let your work be a fight, let your peace be a victory!

One can only be silent and sit peacefully when one hath arrow and bow; otherwise one prateth and quarrelleth. Let your peace be a victory!

Ye say it is the good cause which halloweth even war? I say unto you: it is the good war which halloweth every cause.

War and courage have done more great things than charity. Not your sympathy, but your bravery hath hitherto saved the victims.

'What is good?' ye ask. To be brave is good. Let the little girls say: 'To be good is what is pretty, and at the same time touching.'

They call you heartless; but your heart is true, and I love the bashfulness of your goodwill. Ye are ashamed of your flow, and others are ashamed of their ebb.

Ye are ugly? Well then, my brethren, take the sublime about you, the mantle of the ugly!

And when your soul becometh great, then doth it become haughty, and in your sublimity there is wickedness. I know you.

In wickedness the haughty man and the weakling meet. But they misunderstand one another. I know you.

Ye shall only have enemies to be hated, but not enemies to be despised. Ye must be proud of your enemies; then the successes of your enemies are also your successes.

Resistance – that is the distinction of the slave. Let your distinction be obedience. Let your commanding itself be obeying!

To the good warrior soundeth 'thou shalt' pleasanter than 'I will.' And all that is dear unto you, ye shall first have it commanded unto you.

Let your love to life be love to your highest hope; and let your highest hope be the highest thought of life!

Your highest thought, however, ye shall have it commanded unto you by me – and it is this: man is something that is to be surpassed.

So live your life of obedience and of war! What matter about long life! What warrior wisheth to be spared!

I spare you not, I love you from my very heart, my brethren in war!

Thus spake Zarathustra.

11 The New Idol

Somewhere there are still peoples and herds, but not with us, my brethren; here there are states.

A state? What is that? Well! open now your ears unto me, for now will I say unto you my word concerning the death of peoples.

A state is called the coldest of all cold monsters. Coldly lieth it also, and this lie creepeth from its mouth: 'I, the state, am the people.'

It is a lie! Creators were they who created peoples, and hung a faith and a love over them: thus they served life.

Destroyers are they who lay snares for many, and call it the state; they hang a sword and a hundred cravings over them.

Where there is still a people, there the state is not understood, but hated as the evil eye, and as sin against laws and customs.

This sign I give unto you: every people speaketh its language of good and evil; this its neighbour understandeth not. Its language hath it devised for itself in laws and customs.

But the state lieth in all languages of good and evil; and whatever it saith it lieth, and whatever it hath it hath stolen.

False is everything in it; with stolen teeth it biteth, the biting one. False are even its bowels.

Confusion of language of good and evil: this sign I give unto you as the sign of the state. Verily, the will to death indicateth this sign! Verily, it beckoneth unto the preachers of death!

Many too many are born; for the superfluous ones was the state devised!

See just how it enticeth them to it, the many-too-many! How it swalloweth and cheweth and recheweth them!

'On earth there is nothing greater than I: it is I who am the regulating finger of God' – thus roareth the monster. And not only the long-eared and short-sighted fall upon their knees!

Ah, even in your ears, ye great souls, it whispereth its gloomy lies! Ah, it findeth out the rich hearts which willingly lavish themselves!

Yea, it findeth you out too, ye conquerors of the old God!

Weary ye became of the conflict, and now your weariness serveth the new idol!

Heroes and honourable ones it would fain set up around it, the new idol! Gladly it basketh in the sunshine of good consciences, the cold monster!

Everything will it give you, if ye worship it, the new idol; thus it purchaseth the lustre of your virtue, and the glance of your proud eyes.

It seeketh to allure by means of you, the many-too-many! Yea, a hellish artifice hath here been devised, a death-horse jingling with the trappings of divine honours!

Yea, a dying for many hath here been devised, which glorifieth itself as life: verily, a hearty service unto all preachers of death!

The state, I call it, where all are poison-drinkers, the good and the bad; the state, where all lose themselves, the good and the bad; the state, where the slow suicide of all – is called 'life'.

Just see these superfluous ones! They steal the works of the inventors and the treasures of the wise. Culture, they call their theft – and everything becometh sickness and trouble unto them!

Just see these superfluous ones! Sick are they always; they vomit their bile and call it a newspaper. They devour one another, and cannot even digest themselves.

Just see these superfluous ones! Wealth they acquire and become poorer thereby. Power they seek for, and above all the lever of power, much money – these impotent ones!

See them clamber, these nimble apes! They clamber over one another, and thus scuffle into the mud and the abyss.

Towards the throne they all strive; it is their madness – as if happiness sat on the throne! Ofttimes sitteth filth on the throne – and ofttimes also the throne on filth.

Madmen they all seem to me, and clambering apes, and too eager. Badly smelleth their idol to me, the cold monster; badly they all smell to me, these idolaters.

My brethren, will ye suffocate in the fumes of their maws and appetites! Better break the windows and jump into the open air!

Do go out of the way of the bad odour! Withdraw from the idolatry of the superfluous!

Do go out of the way of the bad odour! Withdraw from the steam of these human sacrifices!

Open still remaineth the earth for great souls. Empty are still many sites for lone ones and twain ones, around which floateth the odour of tranquil seas.

Open still remaineth a free life for great souls. Verily, he who possesseth little is so much the less possessed: blessed be moderate poverty!

There, where the state ceaseth – there only commenceth the man who is not superfluous: there commenceth the song of the necessary ones, the single and irreplaceable melody.

There, where the state *ceaseth* – pray look thither, my brethren! Do ye not see it, the rainbow and the bridges of the Superman?

Thus spake Zarathustra.

12 *The Flies in the Market-place*

Flee, my friend, into thy solitude! I see thee deafened with the noise of the great men, and stung all over with the stings of the little ones.

Admirably do forest and rock know how to be silent with thee. Resemble again the tree which thou lovest, the broad-branched one – silently and attentively it o'erhangeth the sea.

Where solitude endeth, there beginneth the market-place; and where the market-place beginneth, there beginneth also the noise of the great actors, and the buzzing of the poison-flies.

In the world even the best things are worthless without those who represent them; those representers the people call great men.

Little do the people understand what is great – that is to say, the creating agency. But they have a taste for all representers and actors of great things.

Around the devisers of new values revolveth the world – invisibly it revolveth. But around the actors revolve the people and the glory: such is the course of things.

Spirit hath the actor, but little conscience of the spirit. He believeth always in that wherewith he maketh believe most strongly – in *himself*!

Tomorrow he hath a new belief, and the day after one still newer. Sharp perceptions hath he, like the people, and changeable humours.

To upset – that meaneth with him to prove. To drive mad – that meaneth with him to convince. And blood is counted by him as the best of all arguments.

A truth which only glideth into fine ears he calleth falsehood and trumpery. Verily, he believeth only in Gods that make a great noise in the world!

Full of clattering buffoons is the market-place – and the people glory in their great men! These are for them the masters of the hour.

But the hour presseth them; so they press thee. And also from thee they want Yea or Nay. Alas! Thou wouldst set thy chair betwixt For and Against?

On account of those absolute and impatient ones, be not jealous, thou lover of truth! Never yet did truth cling to the arm of an absolute one.

On account of those abrupt ones, return into thy security; only in the market-place is one assailed by Yea or Nay.

Slow is the experience of all deep fountains: long have they to wait until they know *what* hath fallen into their depths.

Away from the market-place and from fame taketh place all that is great; away from the market-place and from fame have ever dwelt the devisers of new values.

Flee, my friend, into thy solitude; I see thee stung all over by the poisonous flies. Flee thither, where a rough strong breeze bloweth!

Flee into thy solitude! Thou hast lived too close to the small and the pitiable. Flee from their invisible vengeance! Towards thee they have nothing but vengeance.

Raise no longer an arm against them! Innumerable are they, and it is not thy lot to be a fly-flap.

Innumerable are the small and pitiable ones; and of many a proud structure rain-drops and weeds have been the ruin.

Thou art not stone; but already hast thou become hollow by the numerous drops. Thou wilt yet break and burst by the numerous drops.

Exhausted I see thee, by poisonous flies; bleeding I see thee, and torn at a hundred spots; and thy pride will not even upbraid.

Blood they would have from thee in all innocence; blood their bloodless souls crave for – and they sting, therefore, in all innocence.

But thou, profound one, thou sufferest too profoundly even from small wounds; and ere thou hadst recovered, the same poison-worm crawled over thy hand.

Too proud art thou to kill these sweet-tooths. But take care lest it be thy fate to suffer all their poisonous injustice!

They buzz around thee also with their praise: obtrusiveness is their praise. They want to be close to thy skin and thy blood.

They flatter thee, as one flattereth a God or devil; they whimper before thee, as before a God or devil. What doth it come to! Flatterers are they, and whimperers, and nothing more.

Often also do they show themselves to thee as amiable ones. But that hath ever been the prudence of the cowardly. Yea, the cowardly are wise!

They think much about thee with their circumscribed souls – thou art always suspected by them! Whatever is much thought about is at last thought suspicious.

They punish thee for all thy virtues. They pardon thee in their inmost hearts only – for thine errors.

Because thou art gentle and of upright character, thou sayest: 'Blameless are they for their small existence.' But their circumscribed souls think: 'Blamable is all great existence.'

Even when thou art gentle towards them, they still feel themselves despised by thee; and they repay thy beneficence with secret maleficence.

Thy silent pride is always counter to their taste; they rejoice if once thou be humble enough to be frivolous.

What we recognise in a man, we also irritate in him. Therefore be on your guard against the small ones!

In thy presence they feel themselves small, and their baseness gleameth and gloweth against thee in invisible vengeance.

Sawest thou not how often they became dumb when thou approachedst them, and how their energy left them like the smoke of an extinguishing fire?

Yea, my friend, the bad conscience art thou of thy neighbours; for they are unworthy of thee. Therefore they hate thee, and would fain suck thy blood.

Thy neighbours will always be poisonous flies; what is great in thee – that itself must make them more poisonous, and always more fly-like.

Flee, my friend, into thy solitude – and thither, where a rough strong breeze bloweth. It is not thy lot to be a fly-flap.

Thus spake Zarathustra.

13 *Chastity*

I love the forest. It is bad to live in cities; there, there are too many of the lustful.

Is it not better to fall into the hands of a murderer than into the dreams of a lustful woman?

And just look at these men; their eye saith it – they know nothing better on earth than to lie with a woman.

Filth is at the bottom of their souls; and alas, if their filth hath still spirit in it!

Would that ye were perfect – at least as animals! But to animals belongeth innocence.

Do I counsel you to slay your instincts? I counsel you to innocence in your instincts.

Do I counsel you to chastity? Chastity is a virtue with some, but with many almost a vice.

These are continent, to be sure; but doggish lust looketh enviously out of all that they do.

Even into the heights of their virtue and into their cold spirit doth this creature follow them, with its discord.

And how nicely can doggish lust beg for a piece of spirit, when a piece of flesh is denied it!

Ye love tragedies and all that breaketh the heart? But I am distrustful of your doggish lust.

Ye have too cruel eyes, and ye look wantonly towards the sufferers. Hath not your lust just disguised itself and taken the name of fellow-suffering?

And also this parable give I unto you: not a few who meant to cast out their devil, went thereby into the swine themselves.

To whom chastity is difficult, it is to be dissuaded, lest it become the road to hell – to filth and lust of soul.

Do I speak of filthy things? That is not the worst thing for me to do.

Not when the truth is filthy, but when it is shallow, doth the discerning one go unwillingly into its waters.

Verily, there are chaste ones from their very nature; they are gentler of heart, and laugh better and oftener than you.

They laugh also at chastity, and ask: 'What is chastity?

Is chastity not folly? But the folly came unto us, and not we unto it.

We offered that guest harbour and heart; now it dwelleth with us – let it stay as long as it will!'

Thus spake Zarathustra.

14 *The Friend*

'One is always too many about me,' thinketh the anchorite. 'Always once one – that maketh two in the long run.'

I and me are always too earnestly in conversation; how could it be endured if there were not a friend?

The friend of the anchorite is always the third one; the third one is the cork which preventeth the conversation of the two sinking into the depth.

Ah, there are too many depths for all anchorites. Therefore do they long so much for a friend, and for his elevation.

Our faith in others betrayeth wherein we would fain have faith in ourselves. Our longing for a friend is our betrayer.

And often with our love we want merely to overleap envy. And often we attack and make ourselves enemies, to conceal that we are vulnerable.

'Be at least mine enemy!' Thus speaketh the true reverence, which doth not venture to solicit friendship.

If one would have a friend, then must one also be willing to wage war for him; and in order to wage war, one must be *capable* of being an enemy.

One ought still to honour the enemy in one's friend. Canst thou go nigh unto thy friend, and not go over to him?

In one's friend one shall have one's best enemy. Thou shalt be closest unto him with thy heart when thou withstandest him.

Thou wouldst wear no raiment before thy friend? It is in honour of thy friend that thou showest thyself to him as thou art? But he wisheth thee to the devil on that account!

He who maketh no secret of himself shocketh: so much reason have ye to fear nakedness! Aye, if ye were Gods, ye could then be ashamed of clothing!

Thou canst not adorn thyself fine enough for thy friend; for thou shalt be unto him an arrow and a longing for the Superman.

Sawest thou ever thy friend asleep – to know how he looketh? What is usually the countenance of thy friend? It is thine own countenance in a coarse and imperfect mirror.

Sawest thou ever thy friend asleep? Wert thou not dismayed at thy friend looking so? O my friend, man is something that hath to be surpassed.

In divining and keeping silence shall the friend be a master; not everything must thou wish to see. Thy dream shall disclose unto thee what thy friend doth when awake.

Let thy pity be a divining: to know first if thy friend wanteth pity. Perhaps he loveth in thee the unmoved eye, and the look of eternity.

Let thy pity for thy friend be hid under a hard shell; thou shalt bite out a tooth upon it. Thus will it have delicacy and sweetness.

Art thou pure air and solitude and bread and medicine to thy friend? Many a one cannot loosen his own fetters, but is nevertheless his friend's emancipator.

Art thou a slave? Then thou canst not be a friend. Art thou a tyrant? Then thou canst not have friends.

Far too long hath there been a slave and a tyrant concealed in woman. On that account woman is not yet capable of friendship; she knoweth only love.

In woman's love there is injustice and blindness to all she doth not love. And even in woman's conscious love, there is still always surprise and lightning and night, along with the light.

As yet woman is not capable of friendship; women are still cats, and birds. Or at the best, cows.

As yet woman is not capable of friendship. But tell me, ye men, who of you are capable of friendship?

Oh, your poverty, ye men, and your sordidness of soul! As much as ye give to your friend, will I give even to my foe, and will not have become poorer thereby.

There is comradeship; may there be friendship!

Thus spake Zarathustra.

15 *The Thousand and One Goals*

Many lands saw Zarathustra, and many people; thus he discovered the good and bad of many peoples. No greater power did Zarathustra find on earth than good and bad.

No people could live without first valuing; if a people will maintain itself, however, it must not value as its neighbour valueth.

Much that passed for good with one people was regarded with scorn and contempt by another: thus I found it. Much found I here called bad, which was there decked with purple honours.

Never did the one neighbour understand the other; ever did his soul marvel at his neighbour's delusion and wickedness.

A table of excellencies hangeth over every people. Lo, it is the table of their triumphs; lo, it is the voice of their Will to Power.

It is laudable, what they think hard; what is indispensable and hard they call good; and what relieveth in the direst distress, the unique and hardest of all – they extol as holy.

Whatever maketh them rule and conquer and shine, to the dismay and envy of their neighbours, they regard as the high and foremost thing, the test and the meaning of all else.

Verily, my brother, if thou knewest but a people's need, its land, its sky and its neighbour, then wouldst thou divine the law of its surmountings, and why it climbeth up that ladder to its hope.

'Always shalt thou be the foremost and prominent above others; no one shall thy jealous soul love, except a friend': that made the soul of a Greek thrill; thereby went he his way to greatness.

'To speak truth, and be skilful with bow and arrow': so seemed it alike pleasing and hard to the people from whom cometh my name – the name which is alike pleasing and hard to me.

'To honour father and mother, and from the root of the soul to do their will': this table of surmounting hung another people over them, and became powerful and permanent thereby.

'To have fidelity, and for the sake of fidelity to risk honour and blood, even in evil and dangerous courses': teaching itself so, another people mastered itself; and thus mastering itself, became pregnant and heavy with great hopes.

Verily, men have given unto themselves all their good and bad. Verily, they took it not, they found it not, it came not unto them as a voice from heaven.

Values did man only assign to things in order to maintain himself – he created only the significance of things, a human significance! Therefore calleth he himself 'man' – that is, the valuator.

Valuing is creating; hear it, ye creating ones! Valuation itself is the treasure and jewel of the valued things.

Through valuation only is there value; and without valuation the nut of existence would be hollow. Hear it, ye creating ones!

Change of values – that is, change of the creating ones. Always doth he destroy who hath to be a creator.

Creating ones were first of all peoples, and only in late times individuals; verily, the individual himself is still the latest creation.

Peoples once hung over them tables of the good. Love which would rule and love which would obey created for themselves such tables.

Older is the pleasure in the herd than the pleasure in the ego; and as long as the good conscience is for the herd, the bad conscience only saith: ego.

Verily, the crafty ego, the loveless one, that seeketh its advantage in the advantage of many – it is not the origin of the herd, but its ruin.

Loving ones was it always, and creating ones, that created good and bad. Fire of love gloweth in the names of all the virtues, and fire of wrath.

Many lands saw Zarathustra, and many peoples: no greater power did Zarathustra find on earth than the creations of the loving ones – 'good' and 'bad' are they called.

Verily, a prodigy is this power of praising and blaming. Tell me, ye brethren, who will master it for me? Who will put a fetter upon the thousand necks of this animal?

A thousand goals have there been hitherto, for a thousand peoples have there been. Only the fetter for the thousand necks is still lacking; there is lacking the one goal. As yet humanity hath not a goal.

But pray tell me, my brethren; if the goal of humanity be still lacking, is there not also still lacking – humanity itself?

Thus spake Zarathustra.

16 *Neighbour-love*

Ye crowd around your neighbour, and have fine words for it. But I say unto you: your neighbour-love is your bad love of yourselves.

Ye flee unto your neighbour from yourselves, and would fain make a virtue thereof; but I fathom your 'unselfishness'.

The *Thou is* older than the *I*; the *Thou* hath been consecrated, but not yet the *I*: so man presseth nigh unto his neighbour.

Do I advise you to neighbour-love? Rather do I advise you to neighbour-flight and to furthest loves.

Higher than love to your neighbour is love to the furthest and future ones; higher still than love to men is love to things and phantoms.

The phantom that runneth on before thee, my brother, is fairer than thou; why dost thou not give unto it thy flesh and thy bones? But thou fearest, and runnest unto thy neighbour.

Ye cannot endure it with yourselves, and do not love yourselves sufficiently; so ye seek to mislead your neighbour into love, and would fain gild yourselves with his error.

Would that ye could not endure it with any kind of near ones, or their neighbours; then would ye have to create your friend and his overflowing heart out of yourselves.

Ye call in a witness when ye want to speak well of yourselves; and when ye have misled him to think well of you, ye also think well of yourselves.

Not only doth he lie, who speaketh contrary to his knowledge, but more so, he who speaketh contrary to his ignorance. And thus speak ye of yourselves in your intercourse, and belie your neighbour with yourselves.

Thus saith the fool: 'Association with men spoileth the character, especially when one hath none.'

The one goeth to his neighbour because he seeketh himself, and the other because he would fain lose himself. Your bad love to yourselves maketh solitude a prison to you.

The furthest ones are they who pay for your love to the near ones; and when there are but five of you together, a sixth must always die.

I love not your festivals either; too many actors found I there, and even the spectators often behaved like actors.

Not the neighbour do I teach you, but the friend. Let the friend be the festival of the earth to you, and a foretaste of the Superman.

I teach you the friend and his overflowing heart. But one must know how to be a sponge, if one would be loved by overflowing hearts.

I teach you the friend in whom the world standeth complete, a capsule of the good – the creating friend, who hath always a complete world to bestow.

And as the world unrolled itself for him, so rolleth it together again for him in rings, as the growth of good through evil, as the growth of purpose out of chance.

Let the future and the furthest be the motive of thy today; in thy friend shalt thou love the Superman as thy motive.

My brethren, I advise you not to neighbour-love – I advise you to furthest love!

Thus spake Zarathustra.

17 *The Way of the Creating One*

Wouldst thou go into isolation, my brother? Wouldst thou seek the way unto thyself? Tarry yet a little and hearken unto me.

'He who seeketh may easily get lost himself. All isolation is wrong': so say the herd. And long didst thou belong to the herd.

The voice of the herd will still echo in thee. And when thou sayest, 'I have no longer a conscience in common with you', then will it be a plaint and a pain.

Lo, that pain itself did the same conscience produce; and the last gleam of that conscience still gloweth on thine affliction.

But thou wouldst go the way of thine affliction, which is the way unto thyself? Then show me thine authority and thy strength to do so!

Art thou a new strength and a new authority? A first motion? A self-rolling wheel? Canst thou also compel stars to revolve around thee?

Alas, there is so much lusting for loftiness! There are so many convulsions of the ambitions! Show me that thou are not a lusting and ambitious one!

Alas, there are so many great thoughts that do nothing more than the bellows; they inflate, and make emptier than ever.

Free, dost thou call thyself? Thy ruling thought would I hear of, and not that thou hast escaped from a yoke.

Art thou one *entitled* to escape from a yoke? Many a one hath cast away his final worth when he hath cast away his servitude.

Free from what? What doth that matter to Zarathustra! Clearly, however, shall thine eye show unto me: free for *what*?

Canst thou give unto thyself thy bad and thy good, and set up thy will as a law over thee? Canst thou be judge for thyself, and avenger of thy law?

Terrible is aloneness with the judge and avenger of one's own law. Thus is a star projected into desert space, and into the icy breath of aloneness.

Today sufferest thou still from the multitude, thou individual; today hast thou still thy courage unabated, and thy hopes.

But one day will the solitude weary thee; one day will thy pride yield, and thy courage quail. Thou wilt one day cry: 'I am alone!'

One day wilt thou see no longer thy loftiness, and see too closely thy lowliness; thy sublimity itself will frighten thee as a phantom. Thou wilt one day cry: 'All is false!'

There are feelings which seek to slay the lonesome one; if they do not succeed, then must they themselves die! But art thou capable of it – to be a murderer?

Hast thou ever known, my brother, the word 'disdain'? And the anguish of thy justice in being just to those that disdain thee?

Thou forcest many to think differently about thee; that charge they heavily to thine account. Thou camest nigh unto them, and yet wentest past: for that they never forgive thee.

Thou goest beyond them; but the higher thou risest the smaller doth the eye of envy see thee. Most of all, however, is the flying one hated.

'How could ye be just unto me!' must thou say. 'I choose your injustice as my allotted portion.'

Injustice and filth cast they at the lonesome one – but my brother, if thou wouldst be a star, thou must shine for them none the less on that account!

And be on thy guard against the good and just! They would fain crucify those who devise their own virtue – they hate the lonesome ones.

Be on thy guard, also, against holy simplicity! All is unholy to it that is not simple; fain, likewise, would it play with the fire – of the faggot and stake.

And be on thy guard also against the assaults of thy love! Too readily doth the recluse reach his hand to any one who meeteth him.

To many a one mayest thou not give thy hand, but only thy paw; and I wish thy paw also to have claws.

But the worst enemy thou canst meet wilt thou thyself always be; thou waylayest thyself in caverns and forests.

Thou lonesome one, thou goest the way to thyself! And past thyself and thy seven devils leadeth thy way!

A heretic wilt thou be to thyself, and a wizard and a soothsayer, and a fool, and a doubter, and a reprobate,

Ready must thou be to burn thyself in thine own flame; how

couldst thou become new if thou have not first become ashes?

Thou lonesome one, thou goest the way of the creating one; a God wilt thou create for thyself out of thy seven devils!

Thou lonesome one, thou goest the way of the loving one; thou lovest thyself, and on that account despisest thou thyself, as only the loving ones despise.

To create, desireth the loving one, because he despiseth! What knoweth he of love who hath not been obliged to despise just what he loved!

With thy love, go into thine isolation, my brother, and with thy creating; and late only will justice limp after thee.

With my tears, go into thine isolation, my brother. I love him who seeketh to create beyond himself, and thus succumbeth.

Thus spake Zarathustra.

18 Old and Young Women

Why stealest thou along so furtively in the twilight, Zarathustra? And what hidest thou so carefully under thy mantle?

Is it a treasure that hath been given thee? Or a child that hath been born thee? Or goest thou thyself on a thief's errand, thou friend of the evil?

Verily, my brother, said Zarathustra, it is a treasure that hath been given me; it is a little truth which I carry.

But it is naughty, like a young child; and if I hold not its mouth, it screameth too loudly.

As I went on my way alone today, at the hour when the sun declineth, there met me an old woman, and she spake thus unto my soul:

'Much hath Zarathustra spoken also to us women, but never spake he unto us concerning woman.'

And I answered her: 'Concerning woman, one should only talk unto men.'

'Talk also unto me of woman,' said she; 'I am old enough to forget it presently.'

And I obliged the old woman and spake thus unto her:

'Everything in woman is a riddle, and everything in woman hath one solution – it is called pregnancy.

Man is for woman, a means: the purpose is always the child. But what is woman for man?

Two different things wanteth the true man: danger and diversion. Therefore wanteth he woman, as the most dangerous plaything.

Man shall be trained for war, and woman for the recreation of the warrior; all else is folly.

Too sweet fruits – these the warrior liketh not. Therefore liketh he woman; bitter is even the sweetest woman.

Better than man doth woman understand children, but man is more childish than woman.

In the true man there is a child hidden; it wanteth to play. Up then, ye women, and discover the child in man!

A plaything let woman be, pure and fine like the precious stone, illumined with the virtues of a world not yet come.

Let the beam of a star shine in your love! Let your hope say: "May I bear the Superman!"

In your love let there be valour! With your love shall ye assail him who inspireth you with fear!

In your love be your honour! Little doth woman understand otherwise about honour. But let this be your honour: always to love more than ye are loved, and never be the second.

Let man fear woman when she loveth: then maketh she every sacrifice, and everything else she regardeth as worthless.

Let man fear woman when she hateth: for man in his innermost soul is merely evil; woman, however, is mean.

"Whom hateth woman most?" Thus spake the iron to the lodestone: "I hate thee most, because thou attractest, but art too weak to draw unto thee."

The happiness of man is "I will". The happiness of woman is "He will".

"Lo, now hath the world become perfect!" Thus thinketh every woman when she obeyeth with all her love.

Obey, must the woman, and find a depth for her surface. Surface is woman's soul, a mobile, stormy film on shallow water.

Man's soul, however, is deep, its current gusheth in subterranean caverns; woman surmiseth its force, but comprehendeth it not.'

Then answered me the old woman: 'Many fine things hath Zarathustra said, especially for those who are young enough for them.

Strange! Zarathustra knoweth little about woman, and yet he is right about them! Doth this happen because with women nothing is impossible?

And now accept a little truth by way of thanks! I am old enough for it!

Swaddle it up and hold its mouth; otherwise it will scream too loudly, the little truth.'

'Give me, woman, thy little truth!' said I. And thus spake the old woman:

'Thou goest to women? Do not forget thy whip!'

Thus spake Zarathustra.

19 The Bite of the Adder

One day had Zarathustra fallen asleep under a fig-tree, owing to the heat, with his arms over his face. And there came an adder and bit him in the neck, so that Zarathustra screamed with pain. When he had taken his arm from his face he looked at the serpent; and then did it recognise the eyes of Zarathustra, wriggled awkwardly, and tried to get away. Not at all, said Zarathustra. As yet hast thou not received my thanks! Thou hast awakened me in time; my journey is yet long. Thy journey is short, said the adder sadly. My poison is fatal. Zarathustra smiled. When did ever a dragon die of a serpent's poison? said he. But take thy poison back! Thou art not rich enough to present it to me. Then fell the adder again on his neck, and licked his wound.

When Zarathustra once told this to his disciples they asked him: And what, O Zarathustra, is the moral of thy story? And Zarathustra answered them thus:

The destroyer of morality, the good and just call me; my story is immoral.

When, however, ye have an enemy, then return him not good for evil: for that would abash him. But prove that he hath done something good to you.

And rather be angry than abash any one! And when ye are cursed, it pleaseth me not that ye should then desire to bless. Rather curse a little also!

And should a great injustice befall you, then do quickly five small ones besides. Hideous to behold is he on whom injustice presseth alone.

Did ye ever know this? Shared injustice is half justice. And he who can bear it shall take the injustice upon himself!

A small revenge is humaner than no revenge at all. And if the punishment be not also a right and an honour to the transgressor, I do not like your punishing.

Nobler is it to own oneself in the wrong than to establish one's right, especially if one be in the right. Only, one must be rich enough to do so.

I do not like your cold justice; out of the eye of your judges there always glanceth the executioner and his cold steel.

Tell me: where find we justice, which is love with seeing eyes?

Devise me, then, the love which not only beareth all punishment, but also all guilt!

Devise me, then, the justice which acquitteth every one except the judge!

And would ye hear this likewise? To him who seeketh to be just from the heart, even the lie becometh philanthropy.

But how could I be just from the heart! How can I give every one his own! Let this be enough for me: I give unto every one mine own.

Finally, my brethren, guard against doing wrong to any anchorite. How could an anchorite forget! How could he requite!

Like a deep well is an anchorite. Easy is it to throw in a stone; if it should sink to the bottom, however, tell me who will bring it out again?

Guard against injuring the anchorite! If ye have done so, however, well then, kill him also!

Thus spake Zarathustra.

20 Child and Marriage

I have a question for thee alone, my brother: like a sounding-lead cast I this question into thy soul, that I may know its depth.

Thou art young, and desirest child and marriage. But I ask thee: Art thou a man *entitled* to desire a child?

Art thou the victorious one, the self-conqueror, the ruler of thy passions, the master of thy virtues? Thus do I ask thee.

Or doth the animal speak in thy wish, and necessity? Or isolation? Or discord in thee?

I would have thy victory and freedom long for a child. Living monuments shalt thou build to thy victory and emancipation.

Beyond thyself shalt thou build. But first of all must thou be built thyself, rectangular in body and soul.

Not only onward shalt thou propagate thyself, but upward! For that purpose may the garden of marriage help thee!

A higher body shalt thou create, a first movement, a spontaneously rolling wheel – a creating one shalt thou create.

Marriage: so call I the will of the twain to create the one that is more than those who created it. The reverence for one another, as those exercising such a will, call I marriage.

Let this be the significance and the truth of thy marriage. But that which the many-too-many call marriage, those superfluous ones – ah, what shall I call it?

Ah, the poverty of soul in the twain! Ah, the filth of soul in the twain! Ah, the pitiable self-complacency in the twain!

Marriage, they call it all; and they say their marriages are made in heaven.

Well, I do not like it, that heaven of the superfluous! No, I do not like them, those animals tangled in the heavenly toils!

Far from me also be the God who limpeth thither to bless what he hath not matched!

Laugh not at such marriages! What child hath not had reason to weep over its parents?

Worthy did this man seem, and ripe for the meaning of the earth; but when I saw his wife, the earth seemed to me a home for madcaps.

Yea, I would that the earth shook with convulsions when a saint and a goose mate with one another.

This one went forth in quest of truth as a hero, and at last got for himself a small decked-up lie: his marriage he calleth it.

That one was reserved in intercourse and chose choicely. But one time he spoilt his company for all time: his marriage he calleth it.

Another sought a handmaid with the virtues of an angel. But all at once he became the handmaid of a woman, and now would he need also to become an angel.

Careful have I found all buyers, and all of them have astute eyes. But even the astutest of them buyeth his wife in a sack.

Many short follies – that is called love by you. And your marriage putteth an end to many short follies with one long stupidity.

Your love to woman, and woman's love to man – ah, would that it were sympathy for suffering and veiled deities! But generally two animals light on one another.

But even your best love is only an enraptured simile and a painful ardour. It is a torch to light you to loftier paths.

Beyond yourselves shall ye love some day! Then *learn* first of all to love. And on that account ye had to drink the bitter cup of your love.

Bitterness is in the cup even of the best love; thus doth it cause longing for the Superman; thus doth it cause thirst in thee, the creating one!

Thirst in the creating one, arrow and longing for the Superman: tell me, my brother, is this thy will to marriage?

Holy call I such a will, and such a marriage.

Thus spake Zarathustra.

21 *Voluntary Death*

Many die too late, and some die too early. Yet strange soundeth the precept: 'Die at the right time!'

Die at the right time: so teacheth Zarathustra.

To be sure, he who never liveth at the right time, how could he ever die at the right time? Would that he might never be born! Thus do I advise the superfluous ones.

But even the superfluous ones make much ado about their death, and even the hollowest nut wanteth to be cracked.

Every one regardeth dying as a great matter; but as yet death is not a festival. Not yet have people learned to inaugurate the finest festivals.

The consummating death I show unto you, which becometh a stimulus and promise to the living.

His death dieth the consummating one triumphantly, surrounded by hoping and promising ones.

Thus should one learn to die; and there should be no festival at which such a dying one doth not consecrate the oaths of the living!

Thus to die is best; the next best, however, is to die in battle, and sacrifice a great soul.

But to the fighter equally hateful as to the victor, is your grinning death which stealeth nigh like a thief – and yet cometh as master.

My death praise I unto you, the voluntary death which cometh unto me because I want it.

And when shall I want it? He that hath a goal and an heir wanteth death at the right time for the goal and the heir.

And out of reverence for the goal and the heir, he will hang up no more withered wreaths in the sanctuary of life.

Verily, not the rope-makers will I resemble: they lengthen out their cord, and thereby go ever backward.

Many a one, also, waxeth too old for his truths and triumphs; a toothless mouth hath no longer the right to every truth.

And whoever wanteth to have fame, must take leave of honour betimes, and practise the difficult art of – going at the right time.

One must discontinue being feasted upon when one tasteth best; that is known by those who want to be long loved.

Sour apples are there, no doubt, whose lot is to wait until the last day of autumn; and at the same time they become ripe, yellow, and shrivelled.

In some ageth the heart first, and in others the spirit. And some are hoary in youth, but the late young keep long young.

To many men life is a failure; a poison-worm gnaweth at their heart. Then let them see to it that their dying is all the more a success.

Many never become sweet; they rot even in the summer. It is cowardice that holdeth them fast to their branches.

Far too many live, and far too long hang they on their branches. Would that a storm came and shook all this rottenness and worm-eatenness from the tree!

Would that there came preachers of *speedy* death! Those would be the appropriate storms and agitators of the trees of life! But I hear only slow death preached, and patience with all that is 'earthly'.

Ah! ye preach patience with what is earthly? This earthly is it that hath too much patience with you, ye blasphemers!

Verily, too early died that Hebrew whom the preachers of slow death honour; and to many hath it proved a calamity that he died too early.

As yet had he known only tears, and the melancholy of the Hebrews, together with the hatred of the good and just – the Hebrew Jesus: then was he seized with the longing for death.

Had he but remained in the wilderness, and far from the good and just! Then, perhaps, would he have learned to live, and love the earth – and laughter also!

Believe it, my brethren! He died too early; he himself would have disavowed his doctrine had he attained to my age! Noble enough was he to disavow!

But he was still immature. Immaturely loveth the youth, and immaturely also hateth he man and earth. Confined and awkward are still his soul and the wings of his spirit.

But in man there is more of the child than in the youth, and less of melancholy: better understandeth he about life and death.

Free for death, and free in death; a holy Naysayer, when there is no longer time for Yea: thus understandeth he about death and life.

That your dying may not be a reproach to man and the earth, my friends: that do I solicit from the honey of your soul.

In your dying shall your spirit and your virtue still shine like an evening after-glow around the earth; otherwise your dying hath been unsatisfactory.

Thus will I die myself, that ye friends may love the earth more for my sake; and earth will I again become, to have rest in her that bore me.

Verily, a goal had Zarathustra; he threw his ball. Now be ye friends the heirs of my goal; to you throw I the golden ball.

Best of all, do I see you, my friends, throw the golden ball! And so tarry I still a little while on the earth – pardon me for it!

Thus spake Zarathustra.

22 *The Bestowing Virtue*

1

When Zarathustra had taken leave of the town to which his heart was attached, the name of which is 'The Pied Cow', there followed him many people who called themselves his disciples, and kept him company. Thus came they to a cross-road. Then Zarathustra told them that he now wanted to go alone; for he was fond of going alone. His disciples, however, presented him at his departure with a staff, on the golden handle of which a serpent twined round the sun. Zarathustra rejoiced on account of the staff, and supported himself thereon; then spake he thus to his disciples:

Tell me, pray: how came gold to the highest value? Because it is uncommon, and unprofiting, and beaming, and soft in lustre; it always bestoweth itself.

Only as image of the highest virtue came gold to the highest value. Goldlike beameth the glance of the bestower. Gold-lustre maketh peace between moon and sun.

Uncommon is the highest virtue, and unprofiting; beaming is it, and soft of lustre: a bestowing virtue is the highest virtue.

Verily, I divine you well, my disciples; ye strive like me for the bestowing virtue. What should ye have in common with cats and wolves?

It is your thirst to become sacrifices and gifts yourselves; and therefore have ye the thirst to accumulate all riches in your soul.

Insatiably striveth your soul for treasures and jewels, because your virtue is insatiable in desiring to bestow.

Ye constrain all things to flow towards you and into you, so that they shall flow back again out of your fountain as the gifts of your love.

Verily, an appropriator of all values must such bestowing love become; but healthy and holy call I this selfishness.

Another selfishness is there, an all-too-poor and hungry kind, which would always steal – the selfishness of the sick, the sickly selfishness.

With the eye of the thief it looketh upon all that is lustrous; with the craving of hunger it measureth him who hath abundance; and ever doth it prowl round the tables of bestowers.

Sickness speaketh in such craving, and invisible degeneration; of a sickly body speaketh the larcenous craving of this selfishness.

Tell me, my brother, what do we think bad, and worst of all? Is it not *degeneration*? And we always suspect degeneration when the bestowing soul is lacking.

Upward goeth our course from genera on to super-genera. But a horror to us is the degenerating sense, which saith: 'All for myself.'

Upward soareth our sense: thus is it a simile of our body, a simile of an elevation. Such similes of elevations are the names of the virtues.

Thus goeth the body through history, a becomer and fighter. And the spirit – what is it to the body? The herald of its fights and victories, its companion and echo.

Similes are all names of good and evil; they do not speak out, they only hint. A fool who seeketh knowledge from them!

Give heed, my brethren, to every hour when your spirit would speak in similes: there is the origin of your virtue.

Elevated is then your body, and raised up; with its delight enraptureth it the spirit, so that it becometh creator, and valuer, and lover, and everything's benefactor.

When your heart overfloweth broad and full like the river, a blessing and a danger to the lowlanders, there is the origin of your virtue.

When ye are exalted above praise and blame, and your will would command all things, as a loving one's will, there is the origin of your virtue. When ye despise pleasant things, and the effeminate couch, and cannot couch far enough from the effeminate, there is the origin of your virtue.

When ye are willers of one will, and when that change of every need is needful to you, there is the origin of your virtue.

Verily, a new good and evil is it! Verily, a new deep murmuring, and the voice of a new fountain!

Power is it, this new virtue; a ruling thought is it, and around it a subtle soul: a golden sun, with the serpent of knowledge around it.

2

Here paused Zarathustra awhile, and looked lovingly on his disciples. Then he continued to speak thus – and his voice had changed:

Remain true to the earth, my brethren, with the power of your virtue! Let your bestowing love and your knowledge be devoted to be the meaning of the earth! Thus do I pray and conjure you.

Let it not fly away from the earthly and beat against eternal walls with its wings! Ah, there hath always been so much flown-away virtue!

Lead, like me, the flown-away virtue back to the earth – yea, back to body and life, that it may give to the earth its meaning, a human meaning!

A hundred times hitherto hath spirit as well as virtue flown away and blundered. Alas, in our body dwelleth still all this delusion and blundering! Body and will hath it there become.

A hundred times hitherto hath spirit as well as virtue attempted and erred. Yea, an attempt hath man been. Alas, much ignorance and error hath become embodied in us!

Not only the rationality of millenniums – also their madness breaketh out in us. Dangerous is it to be an heir.

Still fight we step by step with the giant Chance, and over all mankind hath hitherto ruled nonsense, the lack-of-sense.

Let your spirit and your virtue be devoted to the sense of the earth, my brethren; let the value of everything be determined anew by you! Therefore shall ye be fighters! Therefore shall ye be creators!

Intelligently doth the body purify itself; attempting with intelligence it exalteth itself; to the discerners all impulses sanctify themselves; to the exalted the soul becometh joyful.

Physician, heal thyself; then wilt thou also heal thy patient. Let it be his best cure to see with his eyes him who maketh himself whole.

A thousand paths are there which have never yet been trodden; a thousand salubrities and hidden islands of life. Unexhausted and undiscovered is still man and man's world.

Awake and hearken, ye lonesome ones! From the future come winds with stealthy pinions, and to fine ears good tidings are proclaimed.

Ye lonesome ones of today, ye seceding ones, ye shall one day be a people; out of you who have chosen yourselves shall a chosen people arise – and out of it the Superman.

Verily, a place of healing shall the earth become! And already is a new odour diffused around it, a salvation-bringing odour – and a new hope!

3

When Zarathustra had spoken these words, he paused, like one who had not said his last word; and long did he balance the staff doubtfully in his hand. At last he spake thus – and his voice had changed:

I now go alone, my disciples! Ye also now go away, and alone! So will I have it.

Verily I advise you: depart from me, and guard yourselves against Zarathustra! And better still: be ashamed of him! Perhaps he hath deceived you.

The man of knowledge must be able not only to love his enemies, but also to hate his friends.

One requiteth a teacher badly if one remain merely a scholar. And why will ye not pluck at my wreath?

Ye venerate me; but what if your veneration should some day collapse? Take heed lest a statue crush you!

Ye say ye believe in Zarathustra? But of what account is Zarathustra! Ye are my believers; but of what account are all believers!

Ye had not yet sought yourselves: then did ye find me. So do all believers; therefore all belief is of so little account.

Now do I bid you lose me and find yourselves; and only when ye have all denied me will I return unto you.

Verily, with other eyes, my brethren, shall I then seek my lost ones; with another love shall I then love you.

And once again shall ye have become friends unto me, and children of one hope: then will I be with you for the third time, to celebrate the great noontide with you.

And it is the great noontide, when man is in the middle of his course between animal and Superman, and celebrateth his advance to the evening as his highest hope; for it is the advance to a new morning.

At such time will the down-goer bless himself, that he should be an over-goer; and the sun of his knowledge will be at noontide.

'*Dead are all the Gods: now do we desire the Superman to live.*' Let this be our final will at the great noontide!

Thus spake Zarathustra.

THUS SPAKE ZARATHUSTRA

SECOND PART

– and only when ye have all denied me will I return unto you.

Verily, with other eyes, my brethren, shall I then seek my lost ones; with another love shall I then love you.

ZARATHUSTRA I, *22 The Bestowing Virtue*

23 *The Child with the Mirror*

After this Zarathustra returned again into the mountains to the solitude of his cave, and withdrew himself from men, waiting like a sower who hath scattered his seed. His soul, however, became impatient and full of longing for those whom he loved, because he had still much to give them. For this is hardest of all: to close the open hand out of love, and keep modest as a giver.

Thus passed with the lonesome one months and years; his wisdom meanwhile increased, and caused him pain by its abundance.

One morning, however, he awoke ere the rosy dawn, and having meditated long on his couch, at last spake thus to his heart:

Why did I startle in my dream, so that I awoke? Did not a child come to me, carrying a mirror?

'O Zarathustra,' said the child unto me, 'look at thyself in the mirror!'

But when I looked into the mirror, I shrieked, and my heart throbbed; for not myself did I see therein, but a devil's grimace and derision.

Verily, all too well do I understand the dream's portent and monition: my *doctrine* is in danger; tares want to be called wheat!

Mine enemies have grown powerful and have disfigured the likeness of my doctrine, so that my dearest ones have to blush for the gifts that I gave them.

Lost are my friends; the hour hath come for me to seek my lost ones!

With these words Zarathustra started up – not however like a person in anguish seeking relief, but rather like a seer and a singer whom the spirit inspireth. With amazement did his eagle and serpent gaze upon him; for a coming bliss overspread his countenance like the rosy dawn.

What hath happened unto me, mine animals – said Zarathustra. Am I not transformed? Hath not bliss come unto me like a whirlwind?

Foolish is my happiness, and foolish things will it speak; it is still too young – so have patience with it!

Wounded am I by my happiness; all sufferers shall be physicians unto me!

To my friends can I again go down, and also to mine enemies! Zarathustra can again speak and bestow, and show his best love to his loved ones!

My impatient love overfloweth in streams – down towards sunrise and sunset. Out of silent mountains and storms of affliction rusheth my soul into the valleys.

Too long have I longed and looked into the distance. Too long hath solitude possessed me; thus have I unlearned to keep silence.

Utterance have I become altogether, and the brawling of a brook from high rocks; downward into the valleys will I hurl my speech.

And let the stream of my love sweep into unfrequented channels! How should a stream not finally find its way to the sea!

Forsooth, there is a lake in me, sequestered and self-sufficing; but the stream of my love beareth this along with it, down – to the sea!

New paths do I tread, a new speech cometh unto me; tired have I become – like all creators – of the old tongues. No longer will my spirit walk on worn-out soles.

Too slowly runneth all speaking for me; into thy chariot, O storm, do I leap! And even thee will I whip with my spite!

Like a cry and an huzza will I traverse wide seas, till I find the Happy Isles where my friends sojourn –

And mine enemies amongst them! How I now love every one unto whom I may but speak! Even mine enemies pertain to my bliss.

And when I want to mount my wildest horse, then doth my spear always help me up best: it is my foot's ever ready servant –

The spear which I hurl at mine enemies! How grateful am I to mine enemies that I may at last hurl it!

Too great hath been the tension of my cloud; 'twixt laughters of lightnings will I cast hail-showers into the depths.

Violently will my breast then heave; violently will it blow its storm over the mountains: thus cometh its assuagement.

Verily, like a storm cometh my happiness and my freedom! But mine enemies shall think that *the evil one* roareth over their heads.

Yea, ye also, my friends, will be alarmed by my wild wisdom;

and perhaps ye will flee therefrom, along with mine enemies.

Ah, that I knew how to lure you back with shepherds' flutes! Ah, that my lioness wisdom would learn to roar softly! And much have we already learned with one another!

My wild wisdom became pregnant on the lonesome mountains; on the rough stones did she bear the youngest of her young.

Now runneth she foolishly in the arid wilderness, and seeketh and seeketh the soft sward – mine old, wild wisdom!

On the soft sward of your hearts, my friends – on your love would she fain couch her dearest one!

Thus spake Zarathustra.

24 *In the Happy Isles*

The figs fall from the trees, they are good and sweet; and in falling the red skins of them break. A north wind am I to ripe figs.

Thus, like figs, do these doctrines fall for you, my friends; imbibe now their juice and their sweet substance! It is autumn all around, and clear sky, and afternoon.

Lo, what fulness is around us! And out of the midst of superabundance, it is delightful to look out upon distant seas.

Once did people say God, when they looked out upon distant seas; now, however, have I taught you to say, Superman.

God is a conjecture; but I do not wish your conjecturing to reach beyond your creating will.

Could ye *create* a God? Then I pray you, be silent about all Gods! But ye could well create the Superman.

Not perhaps ye yourselves, my brethren! But into fathers and forefathers of the Superman could ye transform yourselves; and let that be your best creating!

God is a conjecture: but I should like your conjecturing restricted to the conceivable.

Could ye *conceive* a God? But let this mean Will to Truth unto you, that everything be transformed into the humanly conceivable, the humanly visible, the humanly sensible! Your own discernment shall ye follow out to the end!

And what ye have called the world shall but be created by you; your reason, your likeness, your will, your love, shall it itself become! And verily, for your bliss, ye discerning ones!

And how would ye endure life without that hope, ye discerning ones? Neither in the inconceivable could ye have been born, nor in the irrational.

But that I may reveal my heart entirely unto you, my friends: *if* there were Gods, how could I endure to be no God! *Therefore* there are no Gods.

Yea, I have drawn the conclusion; now, however, doth it draw me.

God is a conjecture; but who could drink all the bitterness of this conjecture without dying? Shall his faith be taken from the creating one, and from the eagle his flights into eagle-heights?

God is a thought – it maketh all the straight crooked, and all that standeth reel. What? Time would be gone, and all the perishable would be but a lie?

To think this is giddiness and vertigo to human limbs, and even vomiting to the stomach; verily, the reeling sickness do I call it, to conjecture such a thing.

Evil do I call it and misanthropic, all that teaching about the one, and the plenum, and the unmoved, and the sufficient and the imperishable!

All the imperishable – that's but a simile, and the poets lie too much.

But of time and of becoming shall the best similes speak; a praise shall they be, and a justification of all perishableness!

Creating – that is the great salvation from suffering, and life's alleviation. But for the creator to appear, suffering itself is needed, and much transformation.

Yea, much bitter dying must there be in your life, ye creators! Thus are ye advocates and justifiers of all perishableness.

For the creator himself to be the new-born child, he must also be willing to be the child-bearer, and endure the pangs of the child-bearer.

Verily, through a hundred souls went I my way, and through a hundred cradles and birth-throes. Many a farewell have I taken; I know the heart-breaking last hours.

But so willeth my creating Will, my fate. Or, to tell you it more candidly: just such a fate – willeth my Will.

All *feeling* suffereth in me, and is in prison; but my *willing* ever cometh to me as mine emancipator and comforter.

Willing emancipateth: that is the true doctrine of will and emancipation – so teacheth you Zarathustra.

No longer willing, and no longer valuing, and no longer creating! Ah, that that great debility may ever be far from me!

And also in discerning do I feel only my will's procreating and evolving delight; and if there be innocence in my knowledge, it is because there is will to procreation in it.

Away from God and Gods did this will allure me; what would there be to create if there were – Gods!

But to man doth it ever impel me anew, my fervent creative will; thus impelleth it the hammer to the stone.

Ah, ye men, within the stone slumbereth an image for me, the image of my visions! Ah, that it should slumber in the hardest, ugliest stone!

Now rageth my hammer ruthlessly against its prison. From the stone fly the fragments: what's that to me?

I will complete it: for a shadow came unto me – the stillest and lightest of all things once came unto me!

The beauty of the Superman came unto me as a shadow. Ah, my brethren! Of what account now are – the Gods to me!

Thus spake Zarathustra.

25 *The Pitiful*

My friends, there hath arisen a satire on your friend: 'Behold Zarathustra! Walketh he not amongst us as if amongst animals?'

But it is better said in this wise: 'The discerning one walketh amongst men *as* amongst animals.'

Man himself is to the discerning one – the animal with red cheeks.

How hath that happened unto him? Is it not because he hath had to be ashamed too oft?

O my friends! Thus speaketh the discerning one: shame, shame, shame – that is the history of man!

And on that account doth the noble one enjoin upon himself not to abash; bashfulness doth he enjoin on himself in presence of all sufferers.

Verily, I like them not, the merciful ones, whose bliss is in their pity; too destitute are they of bashfulness.

If I must be pitiful, I dislike to be called so; and if I be so, it is preferably at a distance.

Preferably also do I shroud my head, and flee, before being recognised; and thus do I bid you do, my friends!

May my destiny ever lead unafflicted ones like you across my path, and those with whom I may have hope and repast and honey in common!

Verily, I have done this and that for the afflicted; but something better did I always seem to do when I had learned to enjoy myself better.

Since humanity came into being, man hath enjoyed himself too little: that alone, my brethren, is our original sin!

And when we learn better to enjoy ourselves, then do we unlearn best to give pain unto others, and to contrive pain.

Therefore do I wash the hand that hath helped the sufferer; therefore do I wipe also my soul.

For in seeing the sufferer suffering – thereof was I ashamed on account of his shame; and in helping him, sorely did I wound his pride.

Great obligations do not make grateful, but revengeful; and when a small kindness is not forgotten, it becometh a gnawing worm.

'Be shy in accepting! Distinguish by accepting!' Thus do I advise those who have naught to bestow.

I, however, am a bestower; willingly do I bestow as friend to friends. Strangers, however, and the poor, may pluck for themselves the fruit from my tree: thus doth it cause less shame.

Beggars, however, one should entirely do away with! Verily, it annoyeth one to give unto them, and it annoyeth one not to give unto them.

And likewise sinners and bad consciences! Believe me, my friends: the sting of conscience teacheth one to sting.

The worst things, however, are the petty thoughts. Verily, better to have done evilly than to have thought pettily!

To be sure, ye say: 'The delight in petty evils spareth one many a great evil deed.' But here one should not wish to be sparing.

Like a boil is the evil deed: it itcheth and irritateth and breaketh forth – it speaketh honourably.

'Behold, I am disease,' saith the evil deed: that is its honourableness.

But like infection is the petty thought; it creepeth, and hideth, and wanteth to be nowhere – until the whole body is decayed and withered by the petty infection.

To him however, who is possessed of a devil, I would whisper this word in the ear: 'Better for thee to rear up thy devil! Even for thee there is still a path to greatness!'

Ah my brethren! One knoweth a little too much about every one! And many a one becometh transparent to us, but still we can by no means penetrate him.

It is difficult to live among men, because silence is so difficult.

And not to him who is offensive to us are we most unfair, but to him who doth not concern us at all.

If, however, thou hast a suffering friend, then be a testing-place for his suffering. Like a hard bed, however, a camp-bed: thus wilt thou serve him best.

And if a friend doth thee wrong, then say: 'I forgive thee what thou hast done unto me; that thou hast done it unto *thyself*, however – how could I forgive that!'

Thus speaketh all great love: it surpasseth even forgiveness and pity.

One should hold fast one's heart; for when one letteth it go, how quickly doth one's head run away!

Ah, where in the world have there been greater follies than with the pitiful? And what in the world hath caused more suffering than the follies of the pitiful?

Woe unto all loving ones who have not an elevation which is above their pity!

Thus spake the devil unto me, once on a time: 'Even God hath his hell: it is his love for man.'

And lately, did I hear him say these words: 'God is dead: of his pity for man hath God died.'

So be ye warned against pity; *from thence* there yet cometh unto men a heavy cloud! Verily, I understand weather-signs!

But attend also to this word: all great love is above all its pity; for it seeketh – to create what is loved!

'Myself do I offer unto my love, *and my neighbour as myself*' – such is the language of all creators.

All creators, however, are hard.

Thus spake Zarathustra.

26 The Priests

And one day Zarathustra made a sign to his disciples and spake these words unto them:

Here are priests; but although they are mine enemies pass them quietly and with sleeping swords!

Even among them there are heroes; many of them have suffered too much – so they want to make others suffer.

Bad enemies are they; nothing is more revengeful than their meekness. And readily doth he soil himself who toucheth them.

But my blood is related to theirs; and I want withal to see my blood honoured in theirs.

And when they had passed, a pain attacked Zarathustra; but not long had he struggled with the pain, when he began to speak thus:

It moveth my heart for those priests. They also go against my taste; but that is the smallest matter unto me, since I am among men.

But I suffer and have suffered with them: prisoners are they unto me, and stigmatised ones. He whom they call Saviour put them in fetters –

In fetters of false values and fatuous words! Oh, that someone would save them from their Saviour!

On an isle they once thought they had landed, when the sea tossed them about; but behold, it was a slumbering monster!

False values and fatuous words: these are the worst monsters for mortals – long slumbereth and waiteth the fate that is in them.

But at last it cometh, and awaketh and devoureth and engulfeth whatever hath built tabernacles upon it.

Oh, just look at those tabernacles which those priests have built themselves! Churches, they call their sweet-smelling caves!

Oh, that falsified light, that mustified air! Where the soul – may not fly aloft to its height!

But so enjoineth their belief: 'On your knees, up the stair, ye sinners!'

Verily, rather would I see a shameless one than the distorted eyes of their shame and devotion!

Who created for themselves such caves and penitence-stairs? Was it not those who sought to conceal themselves, and were ashamed under the clear sky?

And only when the clear sky looketh again through ruined roofs, and down upon grass and red poppies on ruined walls – will I again turn my heart to the seats of this God.

They called God that which opposed and afflicted them; and verily, there was much hero-spirit in their worship!

And they knew not how to love their God otherwise than by nailing men to the cross!

As corpses they thought to live; in black draped they their corpses; even in their talk do I still feel the evil flavour of charnel-houses.

And he who liveth nigh unto them liveth nigh unto black pools, wherein the toad singeth his song with sweet gravity.

Better songs would they have to sing for me to believe in their Saviour; more like saved ones would his disciples have to appear unto me!

Naked would I like to see them; for beauty alone should preach penitence. But whom would that disguised affliction convince!

Verily, their Saviours themselves came not from freedom and freedom's seventh heaven! Verily, they themselves never trod the carpets of knowledge !

Of defects did the spirit of those Saviours consist; but into every defect had they put their illusion, their stopgap, which they called God.

In their pity was their spirit drowned; and when they swelled and o'erswelled with pity, there always floated to the surface a great folly.

Eagerly and with shouts drove they their flock over their foot-bridge; as if there were but one foot-bridge to the future! Verily, those shepherds also were still of the flock!

Small spirits and spacious souls had those shepherds; but, my brethren, what small domains have even the most spacious souls hitherto been!

Characters of blood did they write on the way they went, and their folly taught that truth is proved by blood.

But blood is the very worst witness to truth; blood tainteth the purest teaching, and turneth it into delusion and hatred of heart.

And when a person goeth through fire for his teaching – what doth that prove! It is more, verily, when out of one's own burning cometh one's own teaching!

Sultry heart and cold head; where these meet, there ariseth the blusterer, the 'Saviour'.

Greater ones, verily, have there been, and higher-born ones, than those whom the people call Saviours, those rapturous blusterers!

And by still greater ones than any of the Saviours must ye be saved, my brethren, if ye would find the way to freedom!

Never yet hath there been a Superman. Naked have I seen both of them, the greatest man and the smallest man –

All-too-similar are they still to each other. Verily, even the greatest found I – all-too-human!

Thus spake Zarathustra.

27 The Virtuous

With thunder and heavenly fireworks must one speak to indolent and somnolent senses.

But beauty's voice speaketh gently; it appealeth only to the most awakened souls.

Gently vibrated and laughed unto me today my buckler; it was beauty's holy laughing and thrilling.

At you, ye virtuous ones, laughed my beauty today. And thus came its voice unto me: 'They want – to be paid besides!'

Ye want to be paid besides, ye virtuous ones! Ye want reward for virtue, and heaven for earth, and eternity for your today?

And now ye upbraid me for teaching that there is no reward-giver, nor paymaster? And verily, I do not even teach that virtue is its own reward.

Ah, this is my sorrow: into the basis of things have reward and punishment been insinuated – and now even into the basis of your souls, ye virtuous ones!

But like the snout of the boar shall my word grub up the basis of your souls; a ploughshare will I be called by you.

All the secrets of your heart shall be brought to light; and when ye lie in the sun, grubbed up and broken, then will also your falsehood be separated from your truth.

For this is your truth: ye are *too pure* for the filth of the words vengeance, punishment, recompense, retribution.

Ye love your virtue as a mother loveth her child; but when did one hear of a mother wanting to be paid for her love?

It is your dearest Self, your virtue. The ring's thirst is in you: to reach itself again struggleth every ring, and turneth itself.

And like the star that goeth out, so is every work of your virtue: ever is its light on its way and travelling – and when will it cease to be on its way?

Thus is the light of your virtue still on its way, even when its work is done. Be it forgotten and dead, still its ray of light liveth and travelleth.

That your virtue is your Self, and not an outward thing, a skin, or a cloak: that is the truth from the basis of your souls, ye virtuous ones!

But sure enough there are those to whom virtue meaneth writhing under the lash; and ye have hearkened too much unto their crying!

And others are there who call virtue the slothfulness of their vices; and when once their hatred and jealousy relax the limbs, their 'justice' becometh lively and rubbeth its sleepy eyes.

And others are there who are drawn downwards; their devils draw them. But the more they sink, the more ardently gloweth their eye, and the longing for their God.

Ah! their crying also hath reached your ears, ye virtuous ones: 'What I am *not* – that, that is God to me, and virtue.

And others are there who go along heavily and creakingly, like carts taking stones downhill; they talk much of dignity and virtue – their drag they call virtue!

And others are there who are like eight-day clocks when wound up; they tick, and want people to call ticking – virtue.

Verily, in those have I mine amusement: wherever I find such clocks I shall wind them up with my mockery, and they shall even whirr thereby!

And others are proud of their modicum of righteousness, and for the sake of it do violence to all things, so that the world is drowned in their unrighteousness.

Ah, how ineptly cometh the word 'virtue' out of their mouth! And when they say: 'I am just', it always soundeth like: 'I am just – revenged!'

With their virtues they want to scratch out the eyes of their enemies; and they elevate themselves only that they may lower others.

And again there are those who sit in their swamp, and speak thus from among the bulrushes: 'Virtue – that is to sit quietly in the swamp.

We bite no one, and go out of the way of him who would bite; and in all matters we have the opinion that is given us.'

And again there are those who love attitudes, and think that virtue is a sort of attitude.

Their knees continually adore, and their hands are eulogies of virtue, but their heart knoweth naught thereof.

And again there are those who regard it as virtue to say: 'Virtue is necessary'; but after all they believe only that policemen are necessary.

And many a one who cannot see men's loftiness, calleth it virtue to see their baseness far too well: thus calleth he his evil eye virtue.

And some want to be edified and raised up, and call it virtue; and others want to be cast down – and likewise call it virtue.

And thus do almost all think that they participate in virtue; and at least every one claimeth to be an authority on 'good' and 'evil'.

But Zarathustra came not to say unto all those liars and fools: 'What do ye know of virtue! What *could* ye know of virtue!'

But that ye, my friends, might become weary of the old words which ye have learned from the fools and liars;

That ye might become weary of the words 'reward', 'retribution', 'punishment', 'righteous vengeance';

That ye might become weary of saying: 'That an action is good is because it is unselfish.'

Ah! my friends! That *your* very Self be in your action, as the mother is in the child: let that be *your* formula of virtue!

Verily, I have taken from you a hundred formulae and your virtue's favourite playthings; and now ye upbraid me, as children upbraid.

They played by the sea – then came there a wave and swept their playthings into the deep; and now do they cry.

But the same wave shall bring them new playthings, and spread before them new speckled shells!

Thus will they be comforted; and like them shall ye also, my friends, have your comforting – and new speckled shells!

Thus spake Zarathustra.

28 *The Rabble*

Life is a well of delight; but where the rabble also drink, there all fountains are poisoned.

To everything cleanly am I well disposed; but I hate to see the grinning mouths and the thirst of the unclean.

They cast their eye down into the fountain; and now glanceth up to me their odious smile out of the fountain.

The holy water have they poisoned with their lustfulness; and when they called their filthy dreams delight, then poisoned they also the words.

Indignant becometh the flame when they put their damp hearts to the fire; the spirit itself bubbleth and smoketh when the rabble approach the fire.

Mawkish and over-mellow becometh the fruit in their hands; unsteady, and withered at the top, doth their look make the fruit-tree.

And many a one who hath turned away from life, hath only turned away from the rabble; he hated to share with them fountain, flame and fruit.

And many a one who hath gone into the wilderness and suffered thirst with beasts of prey, disliked only to sit at the cistern with filthy camel-drivers.

And many a one who hath come along as a destroyer, and as a hailstorm to all cornfields, wanted merely to put his foot into the jaws of the rabble, and thus stop their throat.

And it is not the mouthful which hath most choked me, to know that life itself requireth enmity and death and torture-crosses –

But I asked once, and suffocated almost with my question: What? Is the rabble also *necessary* for life?

Are poisoned fountains necessary, and stinking fires, and filthy dreams, and maggots in the bread of life?

Not my hatred, but my loathing, gnawed hungrily at my life! Ah, ofttimes became I weary of spirit, when I found even the rabble spiritual!

And on the rulers turned I my back, when I saw what they now call ruling: to traffic and bargain for power with the rabble!

Amongst peoples of a strange language did I dwell, with stopped ears, so that the language of their trafficking might remain strange unto me, and their bargaining for power.

And holding my nose, I went morosely through all yesterdays and todays: verily, badly smell all yesterdays and todays of the scribbling rabble!

Like a cripple become deaf, and blind, and dumb – thus have I lived long, that I might not live with the power-rabble, the scribe-rabble and the pleasure-rabble.

Toilsomely did my spirit mount stairs, and cautiously; alms of delight were its refreshment; on the staff did life creep along with the blind one.

What hath happened unto me? How have I freed myself from loathing? Who hath rejuvenated mine eye? How have I flown to the height where no rabble any longer sit at the wells?

Did my loathing itself create for me wings and fountain-divining powers? Verily, to the loftiest height had I to fly, to find again the well of delight!

Oh, I have found it, my brethren! Here on the loftiest height bubbleth up for me the well of delight! And there is a life at whose waters none of the rabble drink with me!

Almost too violently dost thou flow for me, thou fountain of delight! And often emptiest thou the goblet again, in wanting to fill it!

And yet must I learn to approach thee more modestly; far too violently doth my heart still flow towards thee –

My heart on which my summer burneth, my short, hot, melancholy, over-happy summer: how my summer heart longeth for thy coolness!

Past, the lingering distress of my spring! Past, the wickedness of my snowflakes in June! Summer have I become entirely, and summer-noontide!

A summer on the loftiest height, with cold fountains and blissful stillness; oh, come, my friends, that the stillness may become more blissful!

For this is *our* height and our home; too high and steep do we here dwell for all uncleanly ones and their thirst.

Cast but your pure eyes into the well of my delight, my friends! How could it become turbid thereby! It shall laugh back to you with *its* purity.

On the tree of the future build we our nest; eagles shall bring us lone ones food in their beaks!

Verily, no food of which the impure could be fellow-partakers! Fire would they think they devoured, and burn their mouths!

Verily, no abodes do we here keep ready for the impure! An ice-cave to their bodies would our happiness be, and to their spirits!

And as strong winds will we live above them, neighbours to the eagles, neighbours to the snow, neighbours to the sun: thus live the strong winds.

And like a wind will I one day blow amongst them, and with my spirit take the breath from their spirit: thus willeth my future.

Verily, a strong wind is Zarathustra to all low places; and this counsel counselleth he to his enemies, and to whatever spitteth and speweth: 'Take care not to spit *against* the wind!'

Thus spake Zarathustra.

29 *The Tarantulas*

Lo, this is the tarantula's den! Would'st thou see the tarantula itself? Here hangeth its web: touch this, so that it may tremble.

Cometh the tarantula willingly: Welcome, tarantula! Black on thy back is thy triangle and symbol; and I know also what is in thy soul.

Revenge is in thy soul: wherever thou bitest, there ariseth black scab; with revenge thy poison maketh the soul giddy!

Thus do I speak unto you in parable, ye who make the soul giddy, ye preachers of *equality*! Tarantulas are ye unto me, and secretly revengeful ones!

But I will soon bring your hiding-places to the light; therefore do I laugh in your face my laughter of the height.

Therefore do I tear at your web, that your rage may lure you out of your den of lies, and that your revenge may leap forth from behind your word 'justice'.

Because, *for man to be redeemed from revenge* – that is for me the bridge to the highest hope, and a rainbow after long storms.

Otherwise, however, would the tarantulas have it. 'Let it be very justice for the world to become full of the storms of our vengeance' – thus do they talk to one another.

'Vengeance will we use, and insult, against all who are not like us' – thus do the tarantula-hearts pledge themselves.

'And "Will to Equality" – that itself shall henceforth be the name of virtue; and against all that hath power will we raise an outcry!'

Ye preachers of equality, the tyrant-frenzy of impotence crieth thus in you for 'equality': your most secret tyrant-longings disguise themselves thus in virtue-words!

Fretted conceit and suppressed envy – perhaps your fathers' conceit and envy: in you break they forth as flame and frenzy of vengeance.

What the father hath hid cometh out in the son; and oft have I found the son the father's revealed secret.

Inspired ones they resemble; yet it is not the heart that inspireth them – but vengeance. And when they become subtle and cold, it is not spirit, but envy, that maketh them so.

Their jealousy leadeth them also into thinkers' paths; and this is the sign of their jealousy – they always go too far, so that their fatigue hath at last to go to sleep on the snow.

In all their lamentations soundeth vengeance, in all their eulogies is maleficence; and being judge seemeth to them bliss.

But thus do I counsel you, my friends: distrust all in whom the impulse to punish is powerful!

They are people of bad race and lineage; out of their countenances peer the hangman and the sleuth-hound.

Distrust all those who talk much of their justice! Verily, in their souls not only honey is lacking.

And when they call themselves 'the good and just', forget not that for them to be Pharisees, nothing is lacking but – power!

My friends, I will not be mixed up and confounded with others.

There are those who preach my doctrine of life, and are at the same time preachers of equality, and tarantulas.

That they speak in favour of life, though they sit in their den, these poison-spiders, and withdrawn from life – is because they would thereby do injury.

To those would they thereby do injury who have power at present; for with those the preaching of death is still most at home.

Were it otherwise, then would the tarantulas teach otherwise; and they themselves were formerly the best world-maligners and heretic-burners.

With these preachers of equality will I not be mixed up and confounded. For thus speaketh justice *unto me:* 'Men are not equal.'

And neither shall they become so! What would be my love to the Superman, if I spake otherwise?

On a thousand bridges and piers shall they throng to the future, and always shall there be more war and inequality among them: thus doth my great love make me speak!

Inventors of figures and phantoms shall they be in their hostilities; and with those figures and phantoms shall they yet fight with each other the supreme fight!

Good and evil, and rich and poor, and high and low, and all names of values: weapons shall they be, and sounding signs, that life must again and again surpass itself!

Aloft will it build itself with columns and stairs – life itself; into remote distances would it gaze, and out towards blissful beauties – *therefore* doth it require elevation!

And because it requireth elevation, therefore doth it require steps, and variance of steps and climbers! To rise striveth life, and in rising to surpass itself.

And just behold, my friends! Here where the tarantula's den is, riseth aloft an ancient temple's ruins – just behold it with enlightened eyes!

Verily, he who here towered aloft his thoughts in stone, knew as well as the wisest ones about the secret of life!

That there is struggle and inequality even in beauty, and war for power and supremacy: that doth he here teach us in the plainest parable.

How divinely do vault and arch here contrast in the struggle; how with light and shade they strive against each other, the divinely striving ones –

Thus, steadfast and beautiful, let us also be enemies, my friends! Divinely will we strive *against* one another!

Alas! There hath the tarantula bit me myself, mine old enemy! Divinely steadfast and beautiful, it hath bit me on the finger!

'Punishment must there be, and justice' – so thinketh it; 'not gratuitously shall he here sing songs in honour of enmity!'

Yea, it hath revenged itself! And alas, now will it make my soul also dizzy with revenge!

That I may *not* turn dizzy, however, bind me fast, my friends, to this pillar! Rather will I be a pillar-saint than a whirl of vengeance!

Verily, no cyclone or whirlwind is Zarathustra; and if he be a dancer, he is not at all a tarantula-dancer!

Thus spake Zarathustra.

30 *The Famous Wise Ones*

The people have ye served and the people's superstition – not the truth – all ye famous wise ones! And just on that account did they pay you reverence.

And on that account also did they tolerate your unbelief, because it was a pleasantry and a by-path for the people. Thus doth the master give free scope to his slaves, and even enjoyeth their presumptuousness.

But he who is hated by the people, as the wolf by the dogs – is the free spirit, the enemy of fetters, the non-adorer, the dweller in the woods.

To hunt him out of his lair – that was always called 'sense of right' by the people; on him do they still hound their sharpest-toothed dogs.

'For there the truth is, where the people are! Woe, woe to the seeking ones!' Thus hath it echoed through all time.

Your people would ye justify in their reverence: that called ye 'Will to Truth', ye famous wise ones!

And your heart hath always said to itself: 'From the people have I come; from thence came to me also the voice of God.'

Stiff-necked and artful, like the ass, have ye always been, as the advocates of the people.

And many a powerful one who wanted to run well with the people, hath harnessed in front of his horses – a donkey, a famous wise man.

And now, ye famous wise ones, I would have you finally throw off entirely the skin of the lion!

The skin of the beast of prey, the speckled skin, and the dishevelled locks of the investigator, the searcher, and the conqueror!

Ah, for me to learn to believe in your 'conscientiousness', ye would first have to break your venerating will.

Conscientious – so call I him who goeth into God-forsaken wildernesses, and hath broken his venerating heart.

In the yellow sands and burnt by the sun, he doubtless peereth thirstily at the isles rich in fountains, where life reposeth under shady trees.

But his thirst doth not persuade him to become like those comfortable ones; for where there are oases, there are also idols.

Hungry, fierce, lonesome, God-forsaken: so doth the lion-will wish itself.

Free from the happiness of slaves, redeemed from deities and adorations, fearless and fear-inspiring, grand and lonesome: so is the will of the conscientious.

In the wilderness have ever dwelt the conscientious, the free spirits, as lords of the wilderness; but in the cities dwell the well-foddered, famous wise ones – the draught-beasts.

For always do they draw, as asses – the *people's* carts!

Not that I on that account upbraid them; but serving ones do they remain, and harnessed ones, even though they glitter in golden harness.

And often have they been good servants and worthy of their hire. For thus saith virtue: 'If thou must be a servant, seek him unto whom thy service is most useful!

The spirit and virtue of thy master shall advance by thou being his servant: thus wilt thou thyself advance with his spirit and virtue!'

And verily, ye famous wise ones, ye servants of the people! Ye yourselves have advanced with the people's spirit and virtue – and the people by you! To your honour do I say it!

But the people ye remain for me, even with your virtues, the people with purblind eyes – the people who know not what *spirit* is!

Spirit is life which itself cutteth into life; by its own torture doth it increase its own knowledge – did ye know that before?

And the spirit's happiness is this: to be anointed and consecrated with tears as a sacrificial victim – did ye know that before?

And the blindness of the blind one, and his seeking and groping, shall yet testify to the power of the sun into which he hath gazed – did ye know that before?

And with mountains shall the discerning one learn to *build*! It is a small thing for the spirit to remove mountains – did ye know that before?

Ye know only the sparks of the spirit; but ye do not see the anvil which it is, and the cruelty of its hammer!

Verily, ye know not the spirit's pride! But still less could ye endure the spirit's humility, should it ever want to speak!

And never yet could ye cast your spirit into a pit of snow; ye are not hot enough for that! Thus are ye unaware, also, of the delight of its coldness.

In all respects, however, ye make too familiar with the spirit; and out of wisdom have ye often made an almshouse and a hospital for bad poets.

Ye are not eagles: thus have ye never experienced the happiness of the alarm of the spirit. And he who is not a bird should not camp above abysses.

Ye seem to me lukewarm ones; but coldly floweth all deep knowledge. Ice-cold are the innermost wells of the spirit, a refreshment to hot hands and handlers.

Respectable do ye there stand, and stiff, and with straight backs, ye famous wise ones! No strong wind or will impelleth you.

Have ye ne'er seen a sail crossing the sea, rounded and inflated, and trembling with the violence of the wind?

Like the sail trembling with the violence of the spirit, doth my wisdom cross the sea – my wild wisdom!

But ye servants of the people, ye famous wise ones – how *could* ye go with me!

Thus spake Zarathustra.

31 The Night-song

'Tis night: now do all gushing fountains speak louder. And my soul also is a gushing fountain.

'Tis night: now only do all songs of the loving ones awake. And my soul also is the song of a loving one.

Something unappeased, unappeasable, is within me; it longeth to find expression. A craving for love is within me, which speaketh itself the language of love.

Light am I; ah, that I were night! But it is my lonesomeness to be begirt with light!

Ah, that I were dark and nightly! How would I suck at the breasts of light!

And you yourselves would I bless, ye twinkling starlets and glow-worms aloft – and would rejoice in the gifts of your light.

But I live in mine own light; I drink again into myself the flames that break forth from me.

I know not the happiness of the receiver; and oft have I dreamt that stealing must be more blessed than receiving.

It is my poverty that my hand never ceaseth bestowing; it is mine envy that I see waiting eyes and the brightened nights of longing.

Oh, the misery of all bestowers! Oh, the darkening of my sun! Oh, the craving to crave! Oh, the violent hunger in satiety!

They take from me; but do I yet touch their soul? There is a gap 'twixt giving and receiving; and the smallest gap hath finally to be bridged over.

A hunger ariseth out of my beauty: I should like to injure those I illumine; I should like to rob those I have gifted – thus do I hunger for wickedness.

Withdrawing my hand when another hand already stretcheth out to it; hesitating like the cascade, which hesitateth even in its leap – thus do I hunger for wickedness!

Such revenge doth mine abundance think of; such mischief welleth out of my lonesomeness.

My happiness in bestowing died in bestowing; my virtue became weary of itself by its abundance!

He who ever bestoweth is in danger of losing his shame; to him who ever dispenseth, the hand and heart become callous by very dispensing.

Mine eye no longer overfloweth for the shame of suppliants; my hand hath become too hard for the trembling of filled hands.

Whence have gone the tears of mine eye, and the down of my heart? Oh, the lonesomeness of all bestowers! Oh, the silence of all shining ones!

Many suns circle in desert space: to all that is dark do they speak with their light – but to me they are silent.

Oh, this is the hostility of light to the shining one: unpityingly doth it pursue its course.

Unfair to the shining one in its innermost heart, cold to the suns – thus travelleth every sun.

Like a storm do the suns pursue their courses: that is their travelling. Their inexorable will do they follow: that is their coldness.

Oh, ye only is it, ye dark, nightly ones, that extract warmth from the shining ones! Oh, ye only drink milk and refreshment from the light's udders!

Ah, there is ice around me; my hand burneth with the iciness! Ah, there is thirst in me; it panteth after your thirst!

'Tis night; alas, that I have to be light! And thirst for the nightly! And lonesomeness!

'Tis night; now doth my longing break forth in me as a fountain – for speech do I long.

'Tis night; now do all gushing fountains speak louder. And my soul also is a gushing fountain.

'Tis night; now do all songs of loving ones awake. And my soul also is the song of a loving one.

Thus sang Zarathustra.

32 *The Dance-song*

One evening went Zarathustra and his disciples through the forest; and when he sought for a well, lo, he lighted upon a green meadow peacefully surrounded with trees and bushes, where maidens were dancing together. As soon as the maidens recognised Zarathustra, they ceased dancing; Zarathustra, however, approached them with friendly mien and spake these words:

Cease not your dancing, ye lovely maidens! No game-spoiler hath come to you with evil eye, no enemy of maidens.

God's advocate am I with the devil; he, however, is the spirit of gravity. How could I, ye light-footed ones, be hostile to divine dances? Or to maidens' feet with fine ankles?

To be sure, I am a forest, and a night of dark trees; but he who is not afraid of my darkness will find banks full of roses under my cypresses.

And even the little God may he find, who is dearest to maidens; beside the well lieth he quietly, with closed eyes.

Verily, in broad daylight did he fall asleep, the sluggard! Had he perhaps chased butterflies too much?

Upbraid me not, ye beautiful dancers, when I chasten the little God somewhat! He will cry, certainly, and weep – but he is laughable even when weeping!

And with tears in his eyes shall he ask you for a dance; and I myself will sing a song to his dance –

A dance-song and satire on the spirit of gravity my supremest, most powerful devil, who is said to be 'lord of the world'.

And this is the song that Zarathustra sang when Cupid and the maidens danced together:

Of late did I gaze into thine eye, O Life! And into the
  unfathomable did I there seem to sink.
But thou pulledst me out with a golden angle; derisively
  didst thou laugh when I called thee unfathomable.
'Such is the language of all fish,' saidst thou; 'what *they* do not
  fathom is unfathomable.

But changeable am I only, and wild, and altogether a woman – and no virtuous one:

Though I be called by you men the "profound one", or the "faithful one", "the eternal one", "the mysterious one".

But ye men endow us always with your own virtues – alas, ye virtuous ones!'

Thus did she laugh, the unbelievable one; but never do I believe her and her laughter, when she speaketh evil of herself.

And when I talked face to face with my wild Wisdom, she said to me angrily: 'Thou willest, thou cravest, thou lovest; on that account alone dost thou *praise* Life!'

Then had I almost answered indignantly and told the truth to the angry one; and one cannot answer more indignantly than when one 'telleth the truth' to one's Wisdom.

For thus do things stand with us three. In my heart do I love only Life – and verily, most when I hate her!

But that I am fond of Wisdom, and often too fond, is because she remindeth me very strongly of Life!

She hath her eye, her laugh, and even her golden angle-rod; am I responsible for it that both are so alike?

And when once Life asked me: 'Who is she then, this Wisdom?' Then said I eagerly: 'Ah, yes! Wisdom!

One thirsteth for her and is not satisfied, one looketh through veils, one graspeth through nets.

Is she beautiful? What do I know! But the oldest carps are still lured by her.

Changeable is she, and wayward; often have I seen her bite her lip, and pass the comb against the grain of her hair.

Perhaps she is wicked and false, and altogether a woman; but when she speaketh ill of herself, just then doth she seduce most.'

When I had said this unto Life, then laughed she maliciously, and shut her eyes. 'Of whom dost thou speak?' said she. 'Perhaps of me?

And if thou wert right – is it proper to say *that* in such wise to my face! But now, pray, speak also of thy Wisdom!'

Ah, and now hast thou again opened thine eyes, O beloved Life! And into the unfathomable have I again seemed to sink.

Thus sang Zarathustra. But when the dance was over and the maidens had departed, he became sad.

The sun hath been long set, said he at last. The meadow is damp, and from the forest cometh coolness.

An unknown presence is about me, and gazeth thoughtfully. What! Thou livest still, Zarathustra?

Why? Wherefore? Whereby? Whither? Where? How? Is it not folly still to live?

Ah, my friends; the evening is it which thus interrogateth in me. Forgive me my sadness!

Evening hath come on; forgive me that evening hath come on!

Thus sang Zarathustra.

33 *The Grave-song*

'Yonder is the grave-island, the silent isle; yonder also are the graves of my youth. Thither will I carry an evergreen wreath of life.'

Resolving thus in my heart, did I sail o'er the sea.

Oh, ye sights and scenes of my youth! Oh, all ye gleams of love, ye divine fleeting gleams! How could ye perish so soon for me! I think of you today as my dead ones.

From you, my dearest dead ones, cometh unto me a sweet savour, heart-opening and melting. Verily, it convulseth and openeth the heart of the lone seafarer.

Still am I the richest and most to be envied – I, the lonesomest one! For I *have possessed you*, and ye possess me still. Tell me: to whom hath there ever fallen such rosy apples from the tree as have fallen unto me?

Still am I your love's heir and heritage, blooming to your memory with many-hued, wild-growing virtues, O ye dearest ones!

Ah, we were made to remain nigh unto each other, ye kindly strange marvels; and not like timid birds did ye come to me and my longing – nay, but as trusting ones to a trusting one!

Yea, made for faithfulness, like me, and for fond eternities, must I now name you by your faithlessness, ye divine glances and fleeting gleams: no other name have I yet learnt.

Verily, too early did ye die for me, ye fugitives. Yet did ye not flee from me, nor did I flee from you; innocent are we to each other in our faithlessness.

To kill *me* did they strangle you, ye singing birds of my hopes! Yea, at you, ye dearest ones, did malice ever shoot its arrows – to hit my heart!

And they hit it! Because ye were always my dearest, my possession and my possessedness: *on that account* had ye to die young, and far too early!

At my most vulnerable point did they shoot the arrow – namely, at you, whose skin is like down – or more like the smile that dieth at a glance!

But this word will I say unto mine enemies: What is all manslaughter in comparison with what ye have done unto me!

Worse evil did ye do unto me than all manslaughter; the irretrievable did ye take from me: thus do I speak unto you, mine enemies!

Slew ye not my youth's visions and dearest marvels! My playmates took ye from me, the blessed spirits! To their memory do I deposit this wreath and this curse.

This curse upon you, mine enemies! Have ye not made mine eternal short, as a tone dieth away in a cold night! Scarcely, as the twinkle of divine eyes, did it come to me – as a fleeting gleam!

Thus spake once in a happy hour my purity: 'Divine shall everything be unto me.'

Then did ye haunt me with foul phantoms; ah, whither hath that happy hour now fled!

'All days shall be holy unto me' – so spake once the wisdom of my youth: verily, the language of a joyous wisdom!

But then did ye enemies steal my nights, and sold them to sleepless torture; ah, whither hath that joyous wisdom now fled?

Once did I long for happy auspices; then did ye lead an owl-monster across my path, an adverse sign. Ah, whither did my tender longing then flee?

All loathing did I once vow to renounce: then did ye change my nigh ones and nearest ones into ulcerations. Ah, whither did my noblest vow then flee?

As a blind one did I once walk in blessed ways; then did ye cast filth on the blind one's course, and now is he disgusted with the old footpath.

And when I performed my hardest task, and celebrated the triumph of my victories, then did ye make those who loved me call out that I then grieved them most.

Verily, it was always your doing: ye embittered to me my best honey, and the diligence of my best bees.

To my charity have ye ever sent the most impudent beggars; around my sympathy have ye ever crowded the incurably shameless. Thus have ye wounded the faith of my virtue.

And when I offered my holiest as a sacrifice, immediately did your 'piety' put its fatter gifts beside it: so that my holiest suffocated in the fumes of your fat.

And once did I want to dance as I had never yet danced; beyond all heavens did I want to dance. Then did ye seduce my favourite minstrel.

And now hath he struck up an awful, melancholy air; alas, he tooted as a mournful horn to mine ear!

Murderous minstrel, instrument of evil, most innocent instrument! Already did I stand prepared for the best dance; then didst thou slay my rapture with thy tones!

Only in the dance do I know how to speak the parable of the highest things – and now hath my grandest parable remained unspoken in my limbs!

Unspoken and unrealised hath my highest hope remained! And there have perished for me all the visions and consolations of my youth!

How did I ever bear it? How did I survive and surmount such wounds? How did my soul rise again out of those sepulchres?

Yea, something invulnerable, unburiable is with me, something that would rend rocks asunder: it is called my *Will*. Silently doth it proceed, and unchanged throughout the years.

Its course will it go upon my feet, mine old Will; hard of heart is its nature and invulnerable.

Invulnerable am I only in my heel. Ever livest thou there, and art like thyself, thou most patient one! Ever hast thou burst all shackles of the tomb!

In thee still liveth also the unrealisedness of my youth; and as life and youth sittest thou here hopeful on the yellow ruins of graves.

Yea, thou art still for me the demolisher of all graves. Hail to thee, my Will! And only where there are graves are there resurrections.

Thus sang Zarathustra.

34 Self-surpassing

'Will to Truth' do ye call it, ye wisest ones, that which impelleth you and maketh you ardent?

Will for the thinkableness of all being: thus do I call your will!

All being would ye *make* thinkable: for ye doubt with good reason whether it be already thinkable.

But it shall accommodate and bend itself to you! So willeth your will. Smooth shall it become and subject to the spirit, as its mirror and reflection.

That is your entire will, ye wisest ones, as a Will to Power; and even when ye speak of good and evil, and of estimates of value.

Ye would still create a world before which ye can bow the knee: such is your ultimate hope and ecstasy.

The ignorant, to be sure, the people – they are like a river on which a boat floateth along; and in the boat sit the the estimates of value, solemn and disguised.

Your will and your valuations have ye put on the river of becoming; it betrayeth unto me an old Will to Power, what is believed by the people as good and evil.

It was ye, ye wisest ones, who put such guests in this boat, and gave them pomp and proud names – ye and your ruling Will!

Onward the river now carrieth your boat: it must carry it. A small matter if the rough wave foameth and angrily resisteth its keel!

It is not the river that is your danger and the end of your good and evil, ye wisest ones: but that Will itself, the Will to Power – the unexhausted, procreating life-will.

But that ye may understand my gospel of good and evil, for that purpose will I tell you my gospel of life, and of the nature of all living things.

The living thing did I follow; I walked in the broadest and narrowest paths to learn its nature.

With a hundred-faced mirror did I catch its glance when its mouth was shut, so that its eye might speak unto me. And its eye spake unto me.

But wherever I found living things, there heard I also the language of obedience. All living things are obeying things.

And this heard I secondly: whatever cannot obey itself, is commanded. Such is the nature of living things.

This, however, is the third thing which I heard – namely, that commanding is more difficult than obeying. And not only because the commander beareth the burden of all obeyers, and because this burden readily crusheth him –

An attempt and a risk seemed all commanding unto me; and whenever it commandeth, the living thing risketh itself thereby.

Yea, even when it commandeth itself, then also must it atone for its commanding. Of its own law must it become the judge and avenger and victim.

How doth this happen! So did I ask myself. What persuadeth the living thing to obey, and command, and even be obedient in commanding?

Hearken now unto my word, ye wisest ones! Test it seriously, whether I have crept into the heart of life itself, and into the roots of its heart!

Wherever I found a living thing, there found I Will to Power; and even in the will of the servant found I the will to be master.

That to the stronger the weaker shall serve – thereto persuadeth he his will who would be master over a still weaker one. That delight alone he is unwilling to forego.

And as the lesser surrendereth himself to the greater that he may have delight and power over the least of all, so doth even the greatest surrender himself, and staketh – life, for the sake of power.

It is the surrender of the greatest to run risk and danger, and play dice for death.

And where there is sacrifice and service and love-glances, there also is the will to be master. By by-ways doth the weaker then slink into the fortress, and into the heart of the mightier one – and there stealeth power.

And this secret spake Life herself unto me: 'Behold,' said she, 'I am that *which must ever surpass itself.*

To be sure, ye call it will to procreation, or impulse towards a goal, towards the higher, remoter, more manifold: but all that is one and the same secret.

Rather would I succumb than disown this one thing; and verily, where there is succumbing and leaf-falling, lo, there doth Life sacrifice itself – for power!

That I have to be struggle, and becoming, and purpose, and cross-purpose – ah, he who divineth my will, divineth well also on what *crooked* paths it hath to tread!

Whatever I create, and however much I love it – soon must I be adverse to it, and to my love: so willeth my will.

And even thou, discerning one, art only a path and footstep of my will; verily, my Will to Power walketh even on the feet of thy Will to Truth!

He certainly did not hit the truth who shot at it the formula "Will to Existence"; that will – doth not exist!

For what is not, cannot will; that, however, which is in existence – how could it still strive for existence!

Only where there is life is there also will: not, however, Will to Life, but – so teach I thee – Will to Power!

Much is reckoned higher than life itself by the living one; but out of the very reckoning speaketh – the Will to Power!'

Thus did Life once teach me; and thereby, ye wisest ones, do I solve you the riddle of your hearts.

Verily, I say unto you: good and evil which would be everlasting – it doth not exist! Of its own accord must it ever surpass itself anew.

With your values and formulae of good and evil ye exercise power, ye valuing ones; and that is your secret love, and the sparkling, trembling, and overflowing of your souls.

But a stronger power groweth out of your values, and a new surpassing; by it breaketh egg and egg-shell.

And he who hath to be a creator in good and evil – verily, he hath first to be a destroyer, and break values in pieces.

Thus doth the greatest evil pertain to the greatest good: that, however, is the creating good.

Let us *speak* thereof, ye wisest ones, even though it be bad. To be silent is worse; all suppressed truths become poisonous.

And let everything break up which – can break up by our truths! Many a house is still to be built!

Thus spake Zarathustra.

35 The Sublime Ones

Calm is the bottom of my sea; who would guess that it hideth droll monsters!

Unmoved is my depth; but it sparkleth with swimming enigmas and laughters.

A sublime one saw I today, a solemn one, a penitent of the spirit. Oh, how my soul laughed at his ugliness!

With up-raised breast, and like those who draw in their breath: thus did he stand, the sublime one, and in silence.

O'erhung with ugly truths, the spoil of his hunting, and rich in torn raiment; many thorns also hung on him – but I saw no rose.

Not yet had he learned laughing and beauty. Gloomy did this hunter return from the forest of knowledge.

From the fight with wild beasts returned he home; but even yet a wild beast gazeth out of his seriousness – an unconquered wild beast!

As a tiger doth he ever stand, on the point of springing, but I do not like those strained souls; ungracious is my taste towards all those self-engrossed ones.

And ye tell me, friends, that there is to be no dispute about taste and tasting? But all life is a dispute about taste and tasting!

Taste: that is weight at the same time, and scales and weigher; and alas, for every living thing that would live without dispute about weight and scales and weigher!

Should he become weary of his sublimeness, this sublime one, then only will his beauty begin – and then only will I taste him and find him savoury.

And only when he turneth away from himself will he o'erleap his own shadow – and verily, into *his* sun.

Far too long did he sit in the shade; the cheeks of the penitent of the spirit became pale. He almost starved on his expectations.

Contempt is still in his eye, and loathing hideth in his mouth. To be sure, he now resteth, but he hath not yet taken rest in the sunshine.

As the ox ought he to do; and his happiness should smell of the earth, and not of contempt for the earth.

As a white ox would I like to see him, which snorting and lowing, walketh before the plough-share; and his lowing should also laud all that is earthly!

Dark is still his countenance; the shadow of his hand danceth upon it. O'ershadowed is still the sense of his eye.

His deed itself is still the shadow upon him; his doing obscureth the doer. Not yet hath he overcome his deed.

To be sure, I love in him the shoulders of the ox: but now do I want to see also the eye of the angel.

Also his hero-will hath he still to unlearn; an exalted one shall he be, and not only a sublime one – the ether itself should raise him, the will-less one!

He hath subdued monsters, he hath solved enigmas. But he should also redeem his monsters and enigmas; into heavenly children should he transform them.

As yet hath his knowledge not learned to smile, and to be without jealousy; as yet hath his gushing passion not become calm in beauty.

Verily, not in satiety shall his longing cease and disappear, but in beauty! Gracefulness belongeth to the munificence of the magnanimous.

His arm across his head: thus should the hero repose; thus should he also surmount his repose.

But precisely to the hero is *beauty* the hardest thing of all. Unattainable is beauty by all ardent wills.

A little more, a little less: precisely this is much here, it is the most here.

To stand with relaxed muscles and with unharnessed will: that is the hardest for all of you, ye sublime ones!

When power becometh gracious and descendeth into the visible – I call such condescension beauty.

And from no one do I want beauty so much as from thee, thou powerful one; let thy goodness be thy last self-conquest.

All evil do I accredit to thee; therefore do I desire of thee the good.

Verily, I have often laughed at the weaklings who think themselves good because they have crippled paws!

The virtue of the pillar shalt thou strive after; more beautiful doth it ever become, and more graceful – but internally harder and more sustaining – the higher it riseth.

Yea, thou sublime one, one day shalt thou also be beautiful, and hold up the mirror to thine own beauty.

Then will thy soul thrill with divine desires; and there will be adoration even in thy vanity!

For this is the secret of the soul: when the hero hath abandoned it, then only approacheth it in dreams – the superhero.

Thus spake Zarathustra.

36 *The Land of Culture*

Too far did I fly into the future: a horror seized upon me.

And when I looked around me, lo, there time was my sole contemporary!

Then did I fly backwards, homewards – and always faster. Thus did I come unto you, ye present-day men, and into the land of culture.

For the first time brought I an eye to see you, and good desire; verily, with longing in my heart did I come.

But how did it turn out with me? Although so alarmed – I had yet to laugh! Never did mine eye see anything so motley-coloured!

I laughed and laughed, while my foot still trembled, and my heart as well. 'Here forsooth, is the home of all the paintpots,' said I.

With fifty patches painted on faces and limbs – so sat ye there to mine astonishment, ye present-day men!

And with fifty mirrors around you, which flattered your play of colours, and repeated it!

Verily, ye could wear no better masks, ye present-day men, than your own faces! Who could – *recognise you*!

Written all over with the characters of the past, and these characters also pencilled over with new characters – thus have ye concealed yourselves well from all decipherers!

And though one be a trier of the reins, who still believeth that ye have reins? Out of colours ye seem to be baked, and out of glued scraps.

All times and peoples gaze divers-coloured out of your veils; all customs and beliefs speak divers-coloured out of your gestures.

He who would strip you of veils and wrappers, and paints and gestures, would just have enough left to scare the crows.

Verily, I myself am the scared crow that once saw you naked, and without paint; and I flew away when the skeleton ogled at me.

Rather would I be a day-labourer in the nether-world and among the shades of the by-gone! Fatter and fuller than ye, are forsooth the nether-worldlings!

This, yea this, is bitterness to my bowels, that I can neither endure you naked nor clothed, ye present-day men!

All that is unhomelike in the future, and whatever maketh strayed birds shiver, is verily more homelike and familiar than your 'reality'.

For thus speak ye: 'Real are we wholly, and without faith and superstition': thus do ye plume yourselves – alas! even without plumes!

Indeed, how would ye be *able* to believe, ye divers-coloured ones – ye who are pictures of all that hath ever been believed!

Perambulating refutations are ye, of belief itself, and a dislocation of all thought. *Untrustworthy ones*: thus do I call you, ye real ones!

All periods prate against one another in your spirits; and the dreams and pratings of all periods were even more real than your awakeness!

Unfruitful are ye: *therefore* do ye lack belief. But he who had to create, had always his presaging dreams and astral premonitions – and believed in believing!

Half-open doors are ye, at which grave-diggers wait. And this is *your* reality: 'Everything deserveth to perish.'

Alas, how ye stand there before me, ye unfruitful ones; how lean your ribs! And many of you surely have had knowledge thereof.

Many a one hath said: 'There hath surely a God filched something from me secretly whilst I slept? Verily, enough to make a girl for himself therefrom!

Amazing is the poverty of my ribs!' Thus hath spoken many a present-day man.

Yea, ye are laughable unto me, ye present day men! And especially when ye marvel at yourselves!

And woe unto me if I could not laugh at your marvelling, and had to swallow all that is repugnant in your platters!

As it is, however, I will make lighter of you, since I have to carry *what is heavy*; and what matter if beetles and maybugs also alight on my load!

Verily, it shall not on that account become heavier to me! And not from you, ye present-day men, shall my great weariness arise.

Ah, whither shall I now ascend with my longing! From all mountains do I look out for fatherlands and motherlands.

But a home have I found nowhere; unsettled am I in all cities, and decamping at all gates.

Alien to me, and a mockery, are the present-day men to whom of late my heart impelled me; and exiled am I from fatherlands and motherlands.

Thus do I love only my *children's land*, the undiscovered in the remotest sea; for it do I bid my sails search and search.

Unto my children will I make amends for being the child of my fathers; and unto all the future – for *this* present-day!

Thus spake Zarathustra.

37 *Immaculate Perception*

When yester-eve the moon arose, then did I fancy it about to bear a sun: so broad and teeming did it lie on the horizon.

But it was a liar with its pregnancy; and sooner will I believe in the man in the moon than in the woman.

To be sure, little of a man is he also, that timid night-reveller. Verily, with a bad conscience doth he stalk over the roofs.

For he is covetous and jealous, the monk in the moon; covetous of the earth, and all the joys of lovers.

Nay, I like him not, that tom-cat on the roofs! Hateful unto me are all that slink around half-closed windows!

Piously and silently doth he stalk along on the star-carpets – but I like no light-treading human feet, on which not even a spur jingleth.

Every honest one's step speaketh; the cat however, stealeth along over the ground. Lo, cat-like doth the moon come along, and dishonestly.

This parable speak I unto you sentimental dissemblers, unto you, the 'pure discerners!' You do I call – covetous ones!

Also ye love the earth, and the earthly: I have divined you well! But shame is in your love, and a bad conscience – ye are like the moon!

To despise the earthly hath your spirit been persuaded, but not your bowels; these, however, are the strongest in you!

And now is your spirit ashamed to be at the service of your bowels, and goeth by-ways and lying ways to escape its own shame.

'That would be the highest thing for me' – so saith your lying spirit unto itself – 'to gaze upon life without desire, and not like the dog, with hanging-out tongue;

To be happy in gazing; with dead will, free from the grip and greed of selfishness – cold and ashy-grey all over, but with intoxicated moon-eyes!

That would be the dearest thing to me' – thus doth the seduced one seduce himself – 'to love the earth as the moon loveth it, and with the eye only to feel its beauty.

And this do I call *immaculate* perception of all things: to want nothing else from them, but to be allowed to lie before them as a mirror with a hundred facets.'

Oh, ye sentimental dissemblers, ye covetous ones! Ye lack innocence in your desire; and now do ye defame desiring on that account!

Verily, not as creators, as procreators or as jubilators do ye love the earth!

Where is innocence? Where there is will to procreation. And he who seeketh to create beyond himself, hath for me the purest will.

Where is beauty? Where I *must will* with my whole Will; where I will love and perish, that an image may not remain merely an image.

Loving and perishing: these have rhymed from eternity. Will to love: that is to be ready also for death. Thus do I speak unto you cowards!

But now doth your emasculated ogling profess to be 'contemplation'! And that which can be examined with cowardly eyes is to be christened 'beautiful'! Oh, ye violators of noble names!

But it shall be your curse, ye immaculate ones, ye pure discerners, that ye shall never bring forth, even though ye lie broad and teeming on the horizon!

Verily, ye fill your mouth with noble words; and we are to believe that your heart overfloweth, ye cozeners?

But my words are poor, contemptible, stammering words; gladly do I pick up what falleth from the table at your repasts.

Yet still can I say therewith the truth – to dissemblers! Yea, my fish-bones, shells and prickly leaves shall – tickle the noses of dissemblers!

Bad air is always about you and your repasts; your lascivious thoughts, your lies and secrets are indeed in the air!

Dare only to believe in yourselves – in yourselves and in your inward parts! He who doth not believe in himself always lieth.

A God's mask have ye hung in front of you, ye 'pure ones'; into a God's mask hath your execrable coiling snake crawled.

Verily ye deceive, ye 'contemplative ones'! Even Zarathustra was once the dupe of your godlike exterior; he did not divine the serpent's coil with which it was stuffed.

A God's soul I once thought I saw playing in your games, ye

pure discerners! No better arts did I once dream of than your arts!

Serpents' filth and evil odour, the distance concealed from me; and that a lizard's craft prowled thereabouts lasciviously.

But I came *nigh* unto you; then came to me the day – and now cometh it to you – at an end is the moon's love affair!

See there! Surprised and pale doth it stand – before the rosy dawn!

For already she cometh, the glowing one – *her* love to the earth cometh! Innocence and creative desire is all solar love!

See there, how she cometh impatiently over the sea! Do ye not feel the thirst and the hot breath of her love?

At the sea would she suck, and drink its depths to her height: now riseth the desire of the sea with its thousand breasts.

Kissed and sucked *would* it be by the thirst of the sun; vapour *would* it become, and height, and path of light, and light itself!

Verily, like the sun do I love life, and all deep seas.

And this meaneth *to me* knowledge: all that is deep shall ascend – to my height!

Thus spake Zarathustra.

38 Scholars

When I lay asleep, then did a sheep eat at the ivy-wreath on my head – it ate, and said thereby: 'Zarathustra is no longer a scholar.'

It said this, and went away clumsily and proudly. A child told it to me.

I like to lie here where the children play, beside the ruined wall, among thistles and red poppies.

A scholar am I still to the children, and also to the thistles and red poppies. Innocent are they, even in their wickedness.

But to the sheep I am no longer a scholar: so willeth my lot – blessings upon it!

For this is the truth: I have departed from the house of the scholars, and the door have I also slammed behind me.

Too long did my soul sit hungry at their table; not like them have I got the knack of investigating, as the knack of nut-cracking.

Freedom do I love, and the air over fresh soil; rather would I sleep on ox-skins than on their honours and dignities.

I am too hot and scorched with mine own thought; often is it ready to take away my breath. Then have I to go into the open air, and away from all dusty rooms.

But they sit cool in the cool shade; they want in everything to be merely spectators, and they avoid sitting where the sun burneth on the steps.

Like those who stand in the street and gape at the passers-by: thus do they also wait, and gape at the thoughts which others have thought.

Should one lay hold of them, then do they raise a dust like flour-sacks – and involuntarily; but who would divine that their dust came from corn, and from the yellow delight of the summer fields?

When they give themselves out as wise, then do their petty sayings and truths chill me; in their wisdom there is often an odour as if it came from the swamp; and verily, I have even heard the frog croak in it!

Clever are they – they have dexterous fingers: what doth my simplicity pretend to beside their multiplicity! All threading and knitting and weaving do their fingers understand: thus do they make the hose of the spirit!

Good clockworks are they; only be careful to wind them up properly! Then do they indicate the hour without mistake, and make a modest noise thereby.

Like millstones do they work, and like pestles: throw only seed-corn unto them! They know well how to grind corn small, and make white dust out of it.

They keep a sharp eye on one another, and do not trust each other the best. Ingenious in little artifices, they wait for those whose knowledge walketh on lame feet – like spiders do they wait.

I saw them always prepare their poison with precaution; and always did they put glass gloves on their fingers in doing so.

They also know how to play with false dice; and so eagerly did I find them playing that they perspired thereby.

We are alien to each other, and their virtues are even more repugnant to my taste than their falsehoods and false dice.

And when I lived with them, then did I live above them. Therefore did they take a dislike to me.

They want to hear nothing of any one walking above their heads; and so they put wood and earth and rubbish betwixt me and their heads.

Thus did they deafen the sound of my tread; and least have I hitherto been heard by the most learned.

All mankind's faults and weaknesses did they put betwixt themselves and me – they call it 'false ceiling' in their houses.

But nevertheless I walk with my thoughts *above* their heads; and even should I walk on mine own errors, still would I be above them and their heads.

For men are *not* equal: so speaketh justice. And what I will, *they* may not will!

Thus spake Zarathustra.

39 Poets

Since I have known the body better, said Zarathustra to one of his disciples, the spirit hath only been to me symbolically spirit; and all the 'imperishable' – that is also but a simile.

So have I heard thee say once before, answered the disciple, and then thou addedst: 'But the poets lie too much.' Why didst thou say that the poets lie too much?

Why? said Zarathustra. Thou askest why? I do not belong to those who may be asked after their Why.

Is my experience but of yesterday? It is long ago that I experienced the reasons for mine opinions.

Should I not have to be a cask of memory, if I also wanted to have my reasons with me?

It is already too much for me even to retain mine opinions; and many a bird flieth away.

And sometimes also do I find a fugitive creature in my dovecote, which is alien to me, and trembleth when I lay my hand upon it.

But what did Zarathustra once say unto thee? That the poets lie too much? But Zarathustra also is a poet.

Believest thou that he there spake the truth? Why dost thou believe it?

The disciple answered: I believe in Zarathustra. But Zarathustra shook his head and smiled.

Belief doth not sanctify me, said he, least of all the belief in myself.

But granting that someone did say in all seriousness that the poets lie too much: he was right – *we* do lie too much.

We also know too little, and are bad learners; so we are obliged to lie.

And which of us poets hath not adulterated his wine? Many a poisonous hotchpotch hath evolved in our cellars; many an indescribable thing hath there been done.

And because we know little, therefore are we pleased from the heart with the poor in spirit, especially when they are young women!

And even of those things are we desirous, which old women tell one another in the evening. This do we call the eternally feminine in us.

And as if there were a special secret access to knowledge, which *choketh up* for those who learn anything, so do we believe in the people and in their 'wisdom'.

This, however, do all poets believe: that whoever pricketh up his ears when lying in the grass or on lonely slopes, learneth something of the things that are betwixt heaven and earth.

And if there come unto them tender emotions, then do the poets always think that nature herself is in love with them;

And that she stealeth to their ear to whisper secrets into it, and amorous flatteries: of this do they plume and pride themselves, before all mortals!

Ah, there are so many things betwixt heaven and earth of which only the poets have dreamed!

And especially *above* the heavens: for all Gods are poet-symbolisations, poet-sophistications!

Verily, ever are we drawn aloft – that is, to the realm of the clouds: on these do we set our gaudy puppets, and then call them Gods and Supermen –

Are not they light enough for those chairs – all these Gods and Supermen?

Ah, how I am weary of all the inadequate that is insisted on as actual! Ah, how I am weary of the poets!

When Zarathustra so spake, his disciple resented it, but was silent. And Zarathustra also was silent; and his eye directed itself inwardly, as if it gazed into the far distance. At last he sighed and drew breath –

I am of today and heretofore, said he thereupon; but something is in me that is of the morrow, and the day following, and the hereafter.

I became weary of the poets, of the old and of the new; superficial are they all unto me, and shallow seas.

They did not think sufficiently into the depth; therefore their feeling did not reach to the bottom.

Some sensation of voluptuousness and some sensation of tedium: these have as yet been their best contemplation.

Ghost-breathing and ghost-whisking, seemeth to me all the jingle-jangling of their harps; what have they known hitherto of the fervour of tones!

They are also not pure enough for me; they all muddy their water that it may seem deep.

And fain would they thereby prove themselves reconcilers: but mediaries and mixers are they unto me, and half-and-half, and impure!

Ah, I cast indeed my net into their sea, and meant to catch good fish; but always did I draw up the head of some ancient God.

Thus did the sea give a stone to the hungry one. And they themselves may well originate from the sea.

Certainly, one findeth pearls in them; thereby they are the more like hard molluscs. And instead of a soul, I have often found in them salt slime.

They have learned from the sea also its vanity: is not the sea the peacock of peacocks?

Even before the ugliest of all buffaloes doth it spread out its tail; never doth it tire of its lace-fan of silver and silk. Disdainfully doth the buffalo glance thereat, nigh to the sand with its soul, nigher still to the thicket, nighest, however, to the swamp.

What is beauty and sea and peacock-splendour to it! This parable I speak unto the poets.

Verily, their spirit itself is the peacock of peacocks, and a sea of vanity!

Spectators seeketh the spirit of the poet – should they even be buffaloes!

But of this spirit became I weary; and I see the time coming when it will become weary of itself.

Yea, changed have I seen the poets, and their glance turned towards themselves.

Penitents of the spirit have I seen appearing; they grew out of the poets.

Thus spake Zarathustra.

40 Great Events

There is an isle in the sea – not far from the Happy Isles of Zarathustra – on which a volcano ever smoketh; of which isle the people, and especially the old women amongst them, say that it is placed as a rock before the gate of the nether-world; but that through the volcano itself the narrow way leadeth downwards which conducteth to this gate.

Now about the time that Zarathustra sojourned on the Happy Isles, it happened that a ship anchored at the isle on which standeth the smoking mountain, and the crew went ashore to shoot rabbits. About the noontide hour, however, when the captain and his men were together again, they saw suddenly a man coming towards them through the air, and a voice said distinctly: It is time! It is the highest time! But when the figure was nearest to them (it flew past quickly, however, like a shadow, in the direction of the volcano), then did they recognise with the greatest surprise that it was Zarathustra; for they had all seen him before except the captain himself, and they loved him as the people love: in such wise that love and awe were combined in equal degree.

Behold! said the old helmsman, there goeth Zarathustra to hell!

About the same time that these sailors landed on the fire-isle, there was a rumour that Zarathustra had disappeared; and when his friends were asked about it, they said that he had gone on board a ship by night, without saying whither he was going.

Thus there arose some uneasiness. After three days, however, there came the story of the ship's crew in addition to this uneasiness – and then did all the people say that the devil had taken Zarathustra. His disciples laughed, sure enough, at this talk; and one of them said even: Sooner would I believe that Zarathustra hath taken the devil. But at the bottom of their hearts they were all full of anxiety and longing: so their joy was great when on the fifth day Zarathustra appeared amongst them.

And this is the account of Zarathustra's interview with the fire-dog:

The earth, said he, hath a skin; and this skin hath diseases. One of these diseases, for example, is called 'man'.

And another of these diseases is called 'the fire-dog'; concerning him men have greatly deceived themselves, and let themselves be deceived.

To fathom this mystery did I go o'er the sea; and I have seen the truth naked – verily, barefooted up to the neck!

Now do I know how it is concerning the fire-dog; and likewise concerning all the spouting and subversive devils, of which not only old women are afraid.

'Up with thee, fire-dog, out of thy depth,' cried I, 'and confess how deep that depth is! Whence cometh that which thou snortest up?

Thou drinkest copiously at the sea that doth thine embittered eloquence betray! In sooth, for a dog of the depths thou takest thy nourishment too much from the surface!

At the most, I regard thee as the ventriloquist of the earth; and ever, when I have heard subversive and spouting devils speak, I have found them like thee: embittered, mendacious and shallow.

Ye understand how to roar and obscure with ashes! Ye are the best braggarts, and have sufficiently learned the art of making dregs boil.

Where ye are, there must always be dregs at hand, and much that is spongy, hollow and compressed; it wanteth to have freedom.

"Freedom," ye all roar most eagerly; but I have unlearned the belief in "great events", when there is much roaring and smoke about them.

And believe me, friend Hollaballoo! The greatest events – are not our noisiest, but our stillest hours.

Not around the inventors of new noise, but around the inventors of new values, doth the world revolve; *inaudibly* it revolveth.

And just own to it! Little had ever taken place when thy noise and smoke passed away. What, if a city did become a mummy, and a statue lay in the mud!

And this do I say also to the o'erthrowers of statues: it is certainly the greatest folly to throw salt into the sea, and statues into the mud.

In the mud of your contempt lay the statue; but it is just its law that out of contempt, its life and living beauty grow again!

With diviner features doth it now arise, seducing by its suffering; and verily, it will yet thank you for o'erthrowing it, ye subverters!

This counsel, however, do I counsel to kings and churches and to all that is weak with age or virtue – let yourselves be o'erthrown! That ye may again come to life, and that virtue – may come to you!'

Thus spake I before the fire-dog; then did he interrupt me sullenly and asked: 'Church? What is that?'

'Church?' I answered. 'That is a kind of state, and indeed the most mendacious. But remain quiet, thou dissembling dog! Thou surely knowest thine own species best!

Like thyself the state is a dissembling dog; like thee doth it like to speak with smoke and roaring – to make believe, like thee, that it speaketh out of the heart of things.

For it seeketh by all means to be the most important creature on earth, the state; and people think it so.'

When I had said this, the fire-dog acted as if mad with envy. 'What,' cried he, 'the most important creature on earth? And people think it so?' And so much vapour and terrible voices came out of his throat that I thought he would choke with vexation and envy.

At last he became calmer and his panting subsided; as soon, however, as he was quiet, I said laughingly:

'Thou art angry, fire-dog: so I am in the right about thee!

And that I may also maintain the right, hear the story of another fire-dog; he speaketh actually out of the heart of the earth.

Gold doth his breath exhale, and golden rain: so doth his heart desire. What are ashes and smoke and hot dregs to him!

Laughter flitteth from him like a variegated cloud; adverse is he to thy gargling and spewing and grips in the bowels!

The gold, however, and the laughter – these doth he take out of the heart of the earth; for, that thou mayst know it, *the heart of the earth is of gold.*'

When the fire-dog heard this, he could no longer endure to listen to me. Abashed did he draw in his tail, said 'bow-wow!' in a cowed voice, and crept down into his cave.

Thus told Zarathustra. His disciples, however, hardly listened to him: so great was their eagerness to tell him about the sailors, the rabbits, and the flying man.

What am I to think of it! said Zarathustra. Am I indeed a ghost?

But it may have been my shadow. Ye have surely heard something of the Wanderer and his Shadow?

One thing, however, is certain: I must keep a tighter hold of it; otherwise it will spoil my reputation.

And once more Zarathustra shook his head and wondered. What am I to think of it! said he once more.

Why did the ghost cry: 'It is time! It is the highest time!'

For what is it then – the highest time?

Thus spake Zarathustra.

41 *The Soothsayer*

And I saw a great sadness come over mankind. The best turned weary of their works.

A doctrine appeared, a faith ran beside it: 'All is empty, all is alike, all hath been!'

And from all hills there re-echoed: 'All is empty, all is alike, all hath been!'

To be sure we have harvested; but why have all our fruits become rotten and brown? What was it fell last night from the evil moon?

In vain was all our labour, poison hath our wine become, the evil eye hath singed yellow our fields and hearts.

Arid have we all become; and fire falling upon us, then do we turn dust like ashes – yea, the fire itself have we made aweary.

All our fountains have dried up, even the sea hath receded. All the ground trieth to gape, but the depth will not swallow!

'Alas! where is there still a sea in which one could be drowned?' So soundeth our plaint – across shallow swamps.

Verily, even for dying have we become too weary; now do we keep awake and live on – in sepulchres.

Thus did Zarathustra hear a soothsayer speak; and the foreboding touched his heart and transformed him. Sorrowfully did he go about and wearily; and he became like unto those of whom the soothsayer had spoken.

Verily, said he unto his disciples, a little while, and there cometh the long twilight. Alas, how shall I preserve my light through it!

That it may not smother in this sorrowfulness! To remoter worlds shall it be a light, and also to remotest nights!

Thus did Zarathustra go about grieved in his heart, and for three days he did not take any meat or drink; he had no rest, and lost his speech. At last it came to pass that he fell into a deep sleep. His disciples, however, sat around him in long night-watches, and waited anxiously to see if he would awake, and speak again, and recover from his affliction.

And this is the discourse that Zarathustra spake when he awoke; his voice, however, came unto his disciples as from afar:

Hear, I pray you, the dream that I dreamed, my friends, and help me to divine its meaning!

A riddle is it still unto me, this dream; the meaning is hidden in it and encaged, and doth not yet fly above it on free pinions.

All life had I renounced, so I dreamed. Night-watchman and grave-guardian had I become, aloft, in the lone mountain-fortress of Death.

There did I guard his coffins; full stood the musty vaults of those trophies of victory. Out of glass coffins did vanquished life gaze upon me.

The odour of dust-covered eternities did I breathe; sultry and dust-covered lay my soul. And who could have aired his soul there!

Brightness of midnight was ever around me; lonesomeness cowered beside her; and as a third, death-rattle stillness, the worst of my female friends.

Keys did I carry, the rustiest of all keys; and I knew how to open with them the most creaking of all gates.

Like a bitterly angry croaking ran the sound through the long corridors when the leaves of the gate opened; ungraciously did this bird cry, unwillingly was it awakened.

But more frightful even, and more heart-strangling was it, when it again became silent and still all around, and I alone sat in that malignant silence.

Thus did time pass with me and slip by, if time there still was: what do I know thereof! But at last there happened that which awoke me.

Thrice did there peal peals at the gate like thunders, thrice did the vaults resound and howl again; then did I go to the gate.

Alpa! cried I. Who carrieth his ashes unto the mountain? Alpa! Alpa! Who carrieth his ashes unto the mountain?

And I pressed the key, and pulled at the gate, and exerted myself. But not a finger's-breadth was it yet open.

Then did a roaring wind tear the folds apart; whistling, whizzing, and piercing, it threw unto me a black coffin.

And in the roaring and whistling and whizzing the coffin burst up, and spouted out a thousand peals of laughter.

And a thousand caricatures of children, angels, owls, fools and child-sized butterflies laughed and mocked, and roared at me.

Fearfully was I terrified thereby; it prostrated me. And I cried with horror as I ne'er cried before.

But mine own crying awoke me – and I came to myself.

Thus did Zarathustra relate his dream, and then was silent; for as yet he knew not the interpretation thereof. But the disciple whom he loved most arose quickly, seized Zarathustra's hand, and said:

Thy life itself interpreteth unto us this dream, O Zarathustra!

Art thou not thyself the wind with shrill whistling, which bursteth open the gates of the fortress of Death?

Art thou not thyself the coffin full of many-hued malices and angel-caricatures of life?

Verily, like a thousand peals of children's laughter cometh Zarathustra into all sepulchres, laughing at those night-watchmen and grave-guardians, and whoever else rattleth with sinister keys.

With thy laughter wilt thou frighten and prostrate them; fainting and recovering will demonstrate thy power over them.

And when the long twilight cometh and the mortal weariness, even then wilt thou not disappear from our firmament, thou advocate of life!

New stars hast thou made us see, and new nocturnal glories; verily, laughter itself hast thou spread out over us like a many-hued canopy.

Now will children's laughter ever from coffins flow; now will a strong wind ever come victoriously unto all mortal weariness: of this thou art thyself the pledge and the prophet!

Verily, *they themselves didst thou dream*, thine enemies: that was thy sorest dream.

But as thou awokest from them and camest to thyself, so shall they awaken from themselves – and come unto thee!

Thus spake the disciple; and all the others then thronged around Zarathustra, grasped him by the hands, and tried to persuade him to leave his bed and his sadness, and return unto them. Zarathustra, however, sat upright on his couch, with an absent look. Like one returning from long foreign sojourn did he look on his disciples, and examined their features; but still he knew them not. When, however, they raised him, and set him upon his feet, behold, all on a sudden his eye changed; he understood everything that had happened, stroked his beard, and said with a strong voice:

Well, this hath just its time! But see to it, my disciples, that we have a good repast, and without delay! Thus do I mean to make amends for bad dreams!

The soothsayer, however, shall eat and drink at my side; and verily, I will yet show him a sea in which he can drown himself!

Thus spake Zarathustra. Then did he gaze long into the face of the disciple who had been the dream-interpreter, and shook his head.

42 Redemption

When Zarathustra went one day over the great bridge, then did the cripples and beggars surround him, and a hunchback spake thus unto him:

Behold, Zarathustra! Even the people learn from thee, and acquire faith in thy teaching; but for them to believe fully in thee, one thing is still needful – thou must first of all convince us cripples! Here hast thou now a fine selection, and verily, an opportunity with more than one forelock! The blind canst thou heal, and make the lame run; and from him who hath too much behind, couldst thou well, also, take away a little – that, I think, would be the right method to make the cripples believe in Zarathustra!

Zarathustra, however, answered thus unto him who so spake: When one taketh his hump from the hunchback, then doth one take from him his spirit – so do the people teach. And when one giveth the blind man eyes, then doth he see too many bad things on the earth, so that he curseth him who healed him. He, however, who maketh the lame man run, inflicteth upon him the greatest injury; for hardly can he run, when his vices run away with him – so do the people teach concerning cripples. And why should not Zarathustra also learn from the people, when the people learn from Zarathustra?

It is, however, the smallest thing unto me since I have been amongst men, to see one person lacking an eye, another an ear, and a third a leg, and that others have lost the tongue, or the nose, or the head.

I see and have seen worse things, and divers things so hideous that I should neither like to speak of all matters, nor even keep silent about some of them: namely, men who lack everything, except that they have too much of one thing – men who are nothing more than a big eye, or a big mouth, or a big belly, or something else big – reversed cripples, I call such men.

And when I came out of my solitude, and for the first time passed over this bridge, then I could not trust mine eyes, but looked again and again, and said at last: 'That is an ear! An ear as big as a man!' I looked still more attentively – and actually there did move under the ear something that was pitiably small and poor and slim. And in truth this immense ear was perched on a small thin stalk – the stalk, however, was a man! A person putting a glass to his eyes, could even recognise further a small envious countenance, and also that a bloated soullet dangled at the stalk. The people told me, however, that the big ear was not only a man, but a great man, a genius. But I never believed in the people when they spake of great men – and I hold to my belief that it was a reversed cripple who had too little of everything, and too much of one thing.

When Zarathustra had spoken thus unto the hunchback, and unto those of whom the hunchback was the mouthpiece and advocate, then did he turn to his disciples in profound dejection, and said:

Verily, my friends, I walk amongst men as amongst the fragments and limbs of human beings!

This is the terrible thing to mine eye, that I find man broken up, and scattered about as on a battle- and butcher-ground.

And when mine eye fleeth from the present to the bygone, it findeth ever the same: fragments and limbs and fearful chances – but no men!

The present and the bygone upon earth – ah, my friends, that is my most unbearable trouble; and I should not know how to live, if I were not a seer of what is to come.

A seer, a purposer, a creator, a future itself, and a bridge to the future – and alas, also, as it were a cripple on this bridge: all that is Zarathustra.

And ye also asked yourselves often: 'Who is Zarathustra to us? What shall he be called by us?' And like me did ye give yourselves questions for answers.

Is he a promiser? Or a fulfiller? A conqueror? Or an inheritor? A harvest? Or a ploughshare? A physician? Or a healed one?

Is he a poet? Or a genuine one? An emancipator? Or a subjugator? A good one? Or an evil one?

I walk amongst men as the fragments of the future: that future which I contemplate.

And it is all my poetisation and aspiration, to compose and

collect into unity what is fragment and riddle and fearful chance.

And how could I endure to be a man, if man were not also the composer, and riddle-reader, and redeemer of chance!

To redeem what is past, and to transform every 'It was' into 'Thus would I have it!' – that only do I call redemption!

Will – so is the emancipator and joy-bringer called: thus have I taught you, my friends! But now learn this likewise: the Will itself is still a prisoner.

Willing emancipateth; but what is that called which still putteth the emancipator in chains?

'It was': thus is the Will's teeth-gnashing and lonesomest tribulation called. Impotent towards what hath been done – it is a malicious spectator of all that is past.

Not backward can the Will will; that it cannot break time and time's desire – that is the Will's lonesomest tribulation.

Willing emancipateth: what doth Willing itself devise in order to get free from its tribulation and mock at its prison?

Ah, a fool becometh every prisoner! Foolishly delivereth itself also the imprisoned Will.

That time doth not run backward – that is its animosity. 'That which was': so is the stone which it cannot roll called.

And thus doth it roll stones out of animosity and ill-humour, and taketh revenge on whatever doth not, like it, feel rage and ill-humour.

Thus did the Will, the emancipator, become a torturer; and on all that is capable of suffering it taketh revenge, because it cannot go backward.

This, yea this alone is *revenge* itself: the Will's antipathy to time, and its 'It was'.

Verily, a great folly dwelleth in our Will; and it became a curse unto all humanity, that this folly acquired spirit!

The spirit of revenge, my friends, that hath hitherto been man's best contemplation; and where there was suffering, it was claimed there was always penalty.

'Penalty', so calleth itself revenge. With a lying word it feigneth a good conscience.

And because in the willer himself there is suffering, because he cannot will backwards, thus was Willing itself, and all life, claimed – to be penalty!

And then did cloud after cloud roll over the spirit, until at last madness preached: 'Everything perisheth, therefore everything deserveth to perish!'

'And this itself is justice, the law of time – that he must devour his children': thus did madness preach.

'Morally are things ordered according to justice and penalty. Oh, where is there deliverance from the flux of things and from the "existence" of penalty?' Thus did madness preach.

'Can there be deliverance when there is eternal justice? Alas, unrollable is the stone "It was"; eternal must also be all penalties!' Thus did madness preach.

'No deed can be annihilated; how could it be undone by the penalty! This, this is what is eternal in the "existence" of penalty, that existence also must be eternally recurring deed and guilt!

Unless the Will should at last deliver itself, and Willing become non-Willing.' But ye know, my brethren, this fabulous song of madness!

Away from those fabulous songs did I lead you when I taught you: 'The Will is a creator.'

All 'It was' is a fragment, a riddle, a fearful chance – until the creating Will saith thereto: 'But thus would I have it.'

Until the creating Will saith thereto: 'But thus do I will it! Thus shall I will it!'

But did it ever speak thus? And when doth this take place? Hath the Will been unharnessed from its own folly?

Hath the Will become its own deliverer and joy-bringer? Hath it unlearned the spirit of revenge and all teeth-gnashing?

And who hath taught it reconciliation with time, and something higher than all reconciliation?

Something higher than all reconciliation must the Will will which is the Will to Power; but how doth that take place? Who hath taught it also to will backwards?

– But at this point in his discourse it chanced that Zarathustra suddenly paused, and looked like a person in the greatest alarm. With terror in his eyes did he gaze on his disciples; his glances pierced as with arrows their thoughts and arrear-thoughts. But after a brief space he again laughed, and said soothedly:

It is difficult to live amongst men, because silence is so difficult – especially for a babbler.

Thus spake Zarathustra. The hunchback, however, had listened to the conversation and had covered his face during the time; but when he heard Zarathustra laugh, he looked up with curiosity, and said slowly:

But why doth Zarathustra speak otherwise unto us than unto his disciples?

Zarathustra answered: What is there to be wondered at! With hunchbacks one may well speak in a hunchbacked way!

Very good, said the hunchback, and with pupils one may well tell tales out of school.

But why doth Zarathustra speak otherwise unto his pupils – than unto himself?

43 *Manly Prudence*

Not the height, it is the declivity that is terrible!

The declivity, where the gaze shooteth *downwards*, and the hand graspeth *upwards*. There doth the heart become giddy through its double will.

Ah, friends, do ye divine also my heart's double will?

This, this is *my* declivity and my danger, that my gaze shooteth towards the summit, and my hand would fain clutch and lean – on the depth!

To man clingeth my will; with chains do I bind myself to man, because I am pulled upwards to the Superman; for thither doth mine other will tend.

And *therefore* do I live blindly among men, as if I knew them not, that my hand may not entirely lose belief in firmness.

I know not you men; this gloom and consolation is often spread around me.

I sit at the gateway for every rogue, and ask: Who wisheth to deceive me?

This is my first manly prudence, that I allow myself to be deceived, so as not to be on my guard against deceivers.

Ah, if I were on my guard against man, how could man be an anchor to my ball! Too easily would I be pulled upwards and away!

This providence is over my fate, that I have to be without foresight.

And he who would not languish amongst men must learn to drink out of all glasses; and he who would keep clean amongst men must know how to wash himself even with dirty water.

And thus spake I often to myself for consolation: 'Courage! Cheer up, old heart! An unhappiness hath failed to befall thee; enjoy that as thy – happiness!'

This, however, is mine other manly prudence: I am more forbearing to the *vain* than to the proud.

Is not wounded vanity the mother of all tragedies? Where, however, pride is wounded, there groweth up something better than pride.

That life may be fair to behold, its game must be well played; for that purpose, however, it needeth good actors.

Good actors have I found all the vain ones; they play, and wish people to be fond of beholding them – all their spirit is in this wish.

They represent themselves, they invent themselves; in their neighbourhood I like to look upon life – it cureth of melancholy.

Therefore am I forbearing to the vain, because they are the physicians of my melancholy, and keep me attached to man as to a drama.

And further, who conceiveth the full depth of the modesty of the vain man! I am favourable to him, and sympathetic on account of his modesty.

From you would he learn his belief in himself; he feedeth upon your glances, he eateth praise out of your hands.

Your lies doth he even believe when you lie favourably about him; for in its depths sigheth his heart: 'What am I?'

And if that be the true virtue which is unconscious of itself – well, the vain man is unconscious of his modesty!

This is, however, my third manly prudence: I am not put out of conceit with the *wicked* by your timorousness.

I am happy to see the marvels the warm sun hatcheth: tigers and palms and rattle-snakes.

Also amongst men there is a beautiful brood of the warm sun, and much that is marvellous in the wicked.

In truth, as your wisest did not seem to me so very wise, so found I also human wickedness below the fame of it.

And oft did I ask with a shake of the head: 'Why still rattle, ye rattle-snakes?'

Verily, there is still a future even for evil! And the warmest south is still undiscovered by man.

How many things are now called the worst wickedness, which are only twelve feet broad and three months long! Some day, however, will greater dragons come into the world.

For that the Superman may not lack his dragon, the superdragon that is worthy of him, there must still much warm sun glow on moist virgin forests!

Out of your wild cats must tigers have evolved, and out of your poison-toads, crocodiles; for the good hunter shall have a good hunt!

And verily, ye good and just! In you there is much to be laughed at, and especially your fear of what hath hitherto been called 'the devil'!

So alien are ye in your souls to what is great that to you the Superman would be *frightful* in his goodness!

And ye wise and knowing ones, ye would flee from the solar-glow of the wisdom in which the Superman joyfully batheth his nakedness!

Ye highest men who have come within my ken, this is my doubt of you, and my secret laughter: I suspect ye would call my Superman – a devil!

Ah, I became tired of those highest and best ones; from their 'height' did I long to be up, out, and away to the Superman!

A horror came over me when I saw those best ones naked; then there grew for me the pinions to soar away into distant futures.

Into more distant futures, into more southern souths than ever artist dreamed of: thither, where Gods are ashamed of all clothes!

But disguised do I want to see you, ye neighbours and fellow-men, and well-attired and vain and estimable, as 'the good and just' –

And disguised will I myself sit amongst you – that I may *mistake* you and myself; for that is my last manly prudence.

Thus spake Zarathustra.

44 The Stillest Hour

What hath happened unto me, my friends? Ye see me troubled, driven forth, unwillingly obedient, ready to go – alas, to go away from you!

Yea, once more must Zarathustra retire to his solitude; but unjoyously this time doth the bear go back to his cave!

What hath happened unto me? Who ordereth this? Ah, mine angry mistress wisheth it so; she spake unto me. Have I ever named her name to you?

Yesterday towards evening there spake unto me my *stillest hour*: that is the name of my terrible mistress.

And thus did it happen – for everything must I tell you, that your heart may not harden against the suddenly departing one!

Do ye know the terror of him who falleth asleep?

To the very toes he is terrified, because the ground giveth way under him, and the dream beginneth.

This do I speak unto you in parable. Yesterday at the stillest hour did the ground give way under me; the dream began.

The hour-hand moved on, the timepiece of my life drew breath – never did I hear such stillness around me, so that my heart was terrified.

Then was there spoken unto me without voice: *'Thou knowest it, Zarathustra?'* –

And I cried in terror at this whispering, and the blood left my face; but I was silent.

Then was there once more spoken unto me without voice: 'Thou knowest it, Zarathustra, but thou dost not speak it!'

And at last I answered, like one defiant: 'Yea, I know it, but I will not speak it!'

Then was there again spoken unto me without voice: 'Thou *wilt* not, Zarathustra? Is this true? Conceal thyself not behind thy defiance!'

And I wept and trembled like a child, and said: 'Ah, I would indeed, but how can I do it! Exempt me only from this! It is beyond my power!'

Then was there again spoken unto me without voice: 'What matter about thyself, Zarathustra! Speak thy word, and succumb!'

And I answered: 'Ah, is it *my* word? Who am *I*? I await the worthier one; I am not worthy even to succumb by it.'

Then was there again spoken unto me without voice: 'What matter about thyself? Thou art not yet humble enough for me. Humility hath the hardest skin.'

And I answered: 'What hath not the skin of my humility endured! At the foot of my height do I dwell; how high are my summits, no one hath yet told me. But well do I know my valleys.'

Then was there again spoken unto me without voice: 'O Zarathustra, he who hath to remove mountains removeth also valleys and plains.'

And I answered: 'As yet hath my word not removed mountains, and what I have spoken hath not reached man. I went, indeed, unto men, but not yet have I attained unto them.'

Then was there again spoken unto me without voice: 'What knowest thou *thereof*! The dew falleth on the grass when the night is most silent.'

And I answered: 'They mocked me when I found and walked in mine own path; and certainly did my foot then tremble.

And thus did they speak unto me: "Thou forgottest the path before, now dost thou also forget how to walk!" '

Then was there again spoken unto me without voice: 'What matter about their mockery! Thou art one who hast unlearned to obey; now shalt thou command!

Knowest thou not who is most needed by all? He who commandeth great things.

To execute great things is difficult: but the more difficult task is to command great things.

This is thy most unpardonable obstinacy: thou hast the power, and thou wilt not rule.'

And I answered: 'I lack the lion's voice for all commanding.'

Then was there again spoken unto me as a whispering: 'It is the stillest words which bring the storm. Thoughts that come with doves' footsteps guide the world.

O Zarathustra, thou shalt go as a shadow of that which is to come: thus wilt thou command, and in commanding go foremost.'

And I answered: 'I am ashamed.'

Then was there again spoken unto me without voice: 'Thou must yet become a child, and be without shame.

The pride of youth is still upon thee; late hast thou become young, but he who would become a child must surmount even his youth.'

And I considered a long while, and trembled. At last, however, did I say what I had said at first. 'I will not.'

Then did a laughing take place all around me. Alas, how that laughing lacerated my bowels and cut into my heart!

And there was spoken unto me for the last time: 'O Zarathustra, thy fruits are ripe, but thou art not ripe for thy fruits!

So must thou go again into solitude; for thou shalt yet become mellow.'

And again was there a laughing, and it fled: then did it become still around me, as with a double stillness. I lay, however, on the ground, and the sweat flowed from my limbs.

Now have ye heard all, and why I have to return into my solitude. Nothing have I kept hidden from you, my friends.

But even this have ye heard from me, who am still the most reserved of men – and will be so!

Ah, my friends! I should have something more to say unto you! I should have something more to give unto you! Why do I not give it? Am I then a niggard?

When, however, Zarathustra had spoken these words, the violence of his pain and a sense of the nearness of his departure from his friends came over him, so that he wept aloud; and no one knew how to console him. In the night, however, he went away alone and left his friends.

THUS SPAKE ZARATHUSTRA

THIRD PART

Ye look aloft when ye long for exaltation, and I look downward because I am exalted.

Who among you can at the same time laugh and be exalted?

He who climbeth on the highest mountains, laugheth at all tragic plays and tragic realities.

ZARATHUSTRA I, 7 *Reading and Writing*

45 The Wanderer

Then, when it was about midnight, Zarathustra went his way over the ridge of the isle, that he might arrive early in the morning at the other coast, because there he meant to embark. For there was a good roadstead there, in which foreign ships also liked to anchor; those ships took many people with them who wished to cross over from the Happy Isles. So when Zarathustra thus ascended the mountain, he thought on the way of his many solitary wanderings from youth onwards, and how many mountains and ridges and summits he had already climbed.

I am a wanderer and mountain-climber, said he to his heart. I love not the plains, and it seemeth I cannot long sit still.

And whatever may still overtake me as fate and experience – a wandering will be therein, and a mountain-climbing; in the end one experienceth only oneself.

The time is now past when accidents could befall me; and what *could* now fall to my lot which would not already be mine own!

It returneth only, it cometh home to me at last – mine own Self, and such of it as hath been long abroad, and scattered among things and accidents.

And one thing more do I know: I stand now before my last summit, and before that which hath been longest reserved for me. Ah, my hardest path must I ascend! Ah, I have begun my lonesomest wandering!

He, however, who is of my nature doth not avoid such an hour, the hour that saith unto him: 'Now only dost thou go the way to thy greatness! Summit and abyss – these are now comprised together!

Thou goest the way to thy greatness; now hath it become thy last refuge, what was hitherto thy last danger!

Thou goest the way to thy greatness; it must now be thy best courage that there is no longer any path behind thee!

Thou goest the way to thy greatness; here shall no one steal after thee! Thy foot itself hath effaced the path behind thee, and over it standeth written: Impossibility.

And if all ladders henceforth fail thee, then must thou learn to mount upon thine own head; how couldst thou mount upward otherwise?

Upon thine own head, and beyond thine own heart! Now must the gentlest in thee become the hardest.

He who hath always much indulged himself, sickeneth at last by his much-indulgence. Praises on what maketh hardy! I do not praise the land where butter and honey – flow!

To learn *to look away from* oneself, is necessary in order to see *many things* – this hardiness is needed by every mountain-climber.

He, however, who is obtrusive with his eyes as a discerner, how can he ever see more of anything than its foreground!

But thou, O Zarathustra, wouldst view the ground of everything, and its background: thus must thou mount even above thyself – up, upwards, until thou hast even thy stars *under* thee!'

Yea! To look down upon myself, and even upon my stars: that only would I call my *summit*, that hath remained for me as my *last* summit!

Thus spake Zarathustra to himself while ascending, comforting his heart with harsh maxims: for he was sore at heart as he had never been before. And when he had reached the top of the mountain-ridge, behold, there lay the other sea spread out before him; and he stood still and was long silent. The night, however, was cold at this height, and clear and starry.

I recognise my destiny, said he at last, sadly. Well, I am ready! Now hath my last lonesomeness begun.

Ah, this sombre, sad sea below me! Ah, this sombre nocturnal vexation! Ah, fate and sea! To you must I now *go down*!

Before my highest mountain do I stand, and before my longest wandering; therefore must I first go deeper down than I ever ascended –

Deeper down into pain than I ever ascended, even into its darkest flood! So willeth my fate. Well, I am ready!

Whence come the highest mountains? So did I once ask. Then did I learn that they come out of the sea.

That testimony is inscribed on their stones, and on the walls of their summits. Out of the deepest must the highest come to its height.

Thus spake Zarathustra on the ridge of the mountain where it was cold; when, however, he came into the vicinity of the sea, and at last stood alone amongst the cliffs, then had he become weary on his way, and more eager than ever before.

Everything as yet sleepeth, said he; even the sea sleepeth. Drowsily and strangely doth its eye gaze upon me.

But it breatheth warmly – I feel it. And I feel also that it dreameth. It tosseth about dreamily on hard pillows.

Hark! Hark! How it groaneth with evil recollections! Or evil expectations?

Ah, I am sad along with thee, thou dusky monster, and angry with myself even for thy sake.

Ah, that my hand hath not strength enough! Gladly, indeed, would I free thee from evil dreams!

And while Zarathustra thus spake, he laughed at himself with melancholy and bitterness. What, Zarathustra, said he. Wilt thou even sing consolation to the sea?

Ah, thou amiable fool, Zarathustra, thou too-blindly confiding one! But thus hast thou ever been; ever hast thou approached confidently all that is terrible.

Every monster wouldst thou caress. A whiff of warm breath, a little soft tuft on its paw – and immediately wert thou ready to love and lure it.

Love is the danger of the lonesomest one, love to anything, *if it only live*! Laughable, verily, is my folly and my modesty in love!

Thus spake Zarathustra, and laughed thereby a second time. Then, however, he thought of his abandoned friends – and as if he had done them a wrong with his thoughts, he upbraided himself because of his thoughts. And forthwith it came to pass that the laugher wept – with anger and longing wept Zarathustra bitterly.

46 *The Vision and the Enigma*

1

When it got abroad among the sailors that Zarathustra was on board the ship – for a man who came from the Happy Isles had gone on board along with him – there was great curiosity and expectation. But Zarathustra kept silent for two days, and was cold and deaf with sadness, so that he neither answered looks nor questions. On the evening of the second day, however, he again opened his ears, though he still kept silent; for there were many curious and dangerous things to be heard on board the ship, which came from afar, and was to go still further. Zarathustra, however, was fond of all those who make distant voyages and dislike to live without danger. And behold, when listening, his own tongue was at last loosened, and the ice of his heart broke! Then did he begin to speak thus:

To you, the daring venturers and adventurers, and whoever hath embarked with cunning sails upon frightful seas –

To you the enigma-intoxicated, the twilight-enjoyers, whose souls are allured by flutes to every treacherous gulf –

For ye dislike to grope at a thread with cowardly hand; and where ye can *divine*, there do ye hate to *calculate* –

To you only do I tell the enigma that I *saw* – the vision of the lonesomest one –

Gloomily walked I lately in corpse-coloured twilight – gloomily and sternly, with compressed lips. Not only one sun had set for me.

A path which ascended daringly among boulders, an evil, lonesome path, which neither herb nor shrub any longer cheered, a mountain-path, crunched under the daring of my foot.

Mutely marching over the scornful clinking of pebbles, trampling the stone that let it slip: thus did my foot force his way upwards.

Upwards – in spite of the spirit that drew it downwards, towards the abyss, the spirit of gravity, my devil and arch-enemy.

Upwards – although it sat upon me, half-dwarf, half-mole,

paralysed, paralysing, dripping lead in mine ear, and thoughts like drops of lead into my brain.

'O Zarathustra,' it whispered scornfully, syllable by syllable, 'thou stone of wisdom! Thou threwest thyself high, but every thrown stone must – fall!

O Zarathustra, thou stone of wisdom, thou sling-stone, thou star-destroyer! Thyself threwest thou so high, but every thrown stone – must fall!

Condemned of thyself, and to thine own stoning: O Zarathustra, far indeed threwest thou thy stone – but upon *thyself* will it recoil!'

Then was the dwarf silent; and it lasted long. The silence, however, oppressed me; and to be thus in pairs, one is verily lonesomer than when alone!

I ascended, I ascended, I dreamt, I thought – but everything oppressed me. A sick one did I resemble, whom bad torture wearieth, and a worse dream reawakeneth out of his first sleep.

But there is something in me which I call courage; it hath hitherto slain for me every dejection. This courage at last bade me stand still and say: 'Dwarf! Thou, or I!'

For courage is the best slayer – courage which *attacketh*; for in every attack there is sound of triumph.

Man, however, is the most courageous animal: thereby hath he overcome every animal. With sound of triumph hath he overcome every pain; human pain, however, is the sorest pain.

Courage slayeth also giddiness at abysses; and where doth man not stand at abysses! Is not seeing itself seeing abysses?

Courage is the best slayer; courage slayeth also fellow-suffering. Fellow-suffering, however, is the deepest abyss; as deeply as man looketh into life, so deeply also doth he look into suffering.

Courage, however, is the best slayer, courage which attacketh; it slayeth even death itself, for it saith: 'Was *that* life? Well! Once more!'

In such speech, however, there is much sound of triumph. He who hath ears to hear, let him hear.

2

'Halt, dwarf!' said I. 'Either I – or thou! I, however, am the stronger of the two – thou knowest not mine abysmal thought! *It* – couldst thou not endure!'

Then happened that which made me lighter: for the dwarf sprang from my shoulder, the prying sprite! And it squatted on a stone in front of me. There was however a gateway just where we halted.

'Look at this gateway, dwarf!' I continued. 'It hath two faces. Two roads come together here; these hath no one yet gone to the end of.

This long lane backwards, it continueth for an eternity. And that long lane forward – that is another eternity.

They are antithetical to one another, these roads; they directly abut on one another – and it is here, at this gateway, that they come together. The name of the gateway is inscribed above: "This Moment."

But should one follow them further – and ever further and further on – thinkest thou, dwarf, that these roads would be eternally antithetical?'

'Everything straight lieth,' murmured the dwarf, contemptuously. 'All truth is crooked; time itself is a circle.'

'Thou spirit of gravity,' said I wrathfully, 'do not take it too lightly! Or I shall let thee squat where thou squattest, Haltfoot – and I carried thee *high*!'

'Observe,' continued I, 'This Moment! From the gateway, This Moment, there runneth a long eternal lane *backwards*; behind us lieth an eternity.

Must not whatever *can* run its course of all things, have already run along that lane? Must not whatever *can* happen of all things have already happened, resulted, and gone by?

And if everything have already existed, what thinkest thou, dwarf, of This Moment? Must not this gateway also – have already existed?

And are not all things closely bound together in such wise that This Moment draweth all coming things after it? *Consequently* – itself also?

For whatever *can* run its course of all things, also in this long lane *outward – must* it once more run!

And this slow spider which creepeth in the moonlight, and this moonlight itself, and thou and I in this gateway whispering together, whispering of eternal things – must we not all have already existed?

– And must we not return and run in that other lane out before us, that long weird lane – must we not eternally return?'

Thus did I speak, and always more softly; for I was afraid of mine own thoughts, and arrear-thoughts. Then, suddenly did I hear a dog *howl* near me.

Had I ever heard a dog howl thus? My thoughts ran back. Yes! When I was a child, in my most distant childhood –

Then did I hear a dog howl thus. And saw it also, with hair bristling, its head upwards, trembling in the stillest midnight, when even dogs believe in ghosts –

So that it excited my commiseration. For just then went the full moon, silent as death, over the house; just then did it stand still, a glowing globe – at rest on the flat roof, as if on some one's property –

Thereby had the dog been terrified: for dogs believe in thieves and ghosts. And when I again heard such howling, then did it excite my commiseration once more.

Where was now the dwarf? And the gateway? And the spider? And all the whispering? Had I dreamt? Had I awakened? 'Twixt rugged rocks did I suddenly stand alone, dreary in the dreariest moonlight.

But there lay a man! And there! The dog leaping, bristling, whining – now did it see me coming – then did it howl again, then did it cry – had I ever heard a dog cry so for help?

And verily, what I saw, the like had I never seen. A young shepherd did I see, writhing, choking, quivering, with distorted countenance, and with a heavy black serpent hanging out of his mouth.

Had I ever seen so much loathing and pale horror on one countenance? He had perhaps gone to sleep? Then had the serpent crawled into his throat – there had it bitten itself fast.

My hand pulled at the serpent, and pulled – in vain! I failed to pull the serpent out of his throat. Then there cried out of me: 'Bite! Bite!

Its head off! Bite!' – so cried it out of me; my horror, my hatred, my loathing, my pity, all my good and my bad cried with one voice out of me.

Ye daring ones around me! Ye venturers and adventurers, and whoever of you have embarked with cunning sails on unexplored seas! Ye enigma-enjoyers!

Solve unto me the enigma that I then beheld, interpret unto me the vision of the lonesomest one!

For it was a vision and a foresight: *what* did I then behold in parable? And *who* is it that must come some day?

Who is the shepherd into whose throat the serpent thus crawled? *Who* is the man into whose throat all the heaviest and blackest will thus crawl?

The shepherd however bit as my cry had admonished him; he bit with a strong bite! Far away did he spit the head of the serpent, and sprang up –

No longer shepherd, no longer man – a transfigured being, a light-surrounded being that *laughed*! Never on earth laughed a man as *he* laughed!

O my brethren, I heard a laughter which was no human laughter – and now gnaweth a thirst at me, a longing that is never allayed.

My longing for that laughter gnaweth at me. Oh, how can I still endure to live! And how could I endure to die at present!

Thus spake Zarathustra.

47 *Involuntary Bliss*

With such enigmas and bitterness in his heart did Zarathustra sail o'er the sea. When, however, he was four day-journeys from the Happy Isles and from his friends, then had he surmounted all his pain; triumphantly and with firm foot did he again accept his fate. And then talked Zarathustra in this wise to his exulting conscience:

Alone am I again, and like to be so, alone with the pure heaven, and the open sea; and again is the afternoon around me.

On an afternoon did I find my friends for the first time; on an afternoon, also, did I find them a second time – at the hour when all light becometh stiller.

For whatever happiness is still on its way 'twixt heaven and earth, now seeketh for lodging a luminous soul; *with happiness* hath all light now become stiller.

O afternoon of my life! Once did my happiness also descend to the valley that it might seek a lodging; then did it find those open hospitable souls.

O afternoon of my life! What did I not surrender that I might have one thing: this living plantation of my thoughts, and this dawn of my highest hope!

Companions did the creating one once seek, and children of *his* hope; and lo, it turned out that he could not find them, except he himself should first create them.

Thus am I in the midst of my work, to my children going and from them returning; for the sake of his children must Zarathustra perfect himself.

For in one's heart one loveth only one's child and one's work; and where there is great love to oneself, then is it the sign of pregnancy: so have I found it.

Still are my children verdant in their first spring, standing nigh one another and shaken in common by the winds – the trees of my garden and of my best soil.

And verily, where such trees stand beside one another, there *are* Happy Isles!

But one day will I take them up, and put each by itself alone, that it may learn lonesomeness and defiance and prudence.

Gnarled and crooked and with flexible hardness shall it then stand by the sea, a living lighthouse of unconquerable life.

Yonder where the storms rush down into the sea, and the snout of the mountain drinketh water, shall each on a time have his day and night watches, for *his* testing and recognition.

Recognised and tested shall each be, to see if he be of my type and lineage: if he be master of a long will, silent even when he speaketh, and giving in such wise that he *taketh* in giving –

So that he may one day become my companion, a fellow-creator and fellow-enjoyer with Zarathustra: such a one as writeth my will on my tables, for the fuller perfection of all things.

And for his sake and for those like him, must I perfect *myself*: therefore do I now avoid my happiness, and present myself to every misfortune – for my final testing and recognition.

And verily, it were time that I went away; and the wanderer's shadow and the longest tedium and the stillest hour – have all said unto me: 'It is the highest time!'

The word blew to me through the keyhole and said 'Come!' The door sprang subtly open unto me, and said 'Go!'

But I lay enchained to my love for my children; desire spread this snare for me – the desire for love – that I should become the prey of my children, and lose myself in them.

Desiring – that is now for me to have lost myself. *I possess you, my children!* In this possessing shall everything be assurance and nothing desire.

But brooding lay the sun of my love upon me; in his own juice stewed Zarathustra – then did shadows and doubts fly past me.

For frost and winter I now longed: 'Oh, that frost and winter would again make me crack and crunch!' sighed I; then arose icy mist out of me.

My past burst its tomb, many pains buried alive woke up; fully slept had they merely, concealed in corpse-clothes.

So called everything unto me in signs: 'It is time!' But I – heard not, until at last mine abyss moved, and my thought bit me.

Ah, abysmal thought, which art my thought! When shall I find strength to hear thee burrowing, and no longer tremble?

To my very throat throbbeth my heart when I hear thee

burrowing! Thy muteness even is like to strangle me, thou abysmal mute one!

As yet have I never ventured to call thee up; it hath been enough that I – have carried thee about with me! As yet have I not been strong enough for my final lion-wantonness and playfulness.

Sufficiently formidable unto me hath thy weight ever been; but one day shall I yet find the strength and the lion's voice which will call thee up!

When I shall have surmounted myself therein, then will I surmount myself also in that which is greater; and a victory shall be the seal of my perfection!

Meanwhile do I sail along on uncertain seas; chance flattereth me, smooth-tongued chance; forward and backward do I gaze – still see I no end.

As yet hath the hour of my final struggle not come to me – or doth it come to me perhaps just now? Verily, with insidious beauty do sea and life gaze upon me round about.

O afternoon of my life! O happiness before eventide! O haven upon high seas! O peace in uncertainty! How I distrust all of you!

Verily, distrustful am I of your insidious beauty! Like the lover am I, who distrusteth too sleek smiling.

As he pusheth the best-beloved before him – tender even in severity, the jealous one – so do I push this blissful hour before me.

Away with thee, thou blissful hour! With thee hath there come to me an involuntary bliss! Ready for my severest pain do I here stand – at the wrong time hast thou come!

Away with thee, thou blissful hour! Rather harbour there – with my children! Hasten, and bless them before eventide with my happiness!

There! Already approacheth eventide; the sun sinketh. Away – my happiness!

Thus spake Zarathustra. And he waited for his misfortune the whole night; but he waited in vain. The night remained clear and calm, and happiness itself came nigher and nigher unto him. Towards morning, however, Zarathustra laughed to his heart, and said mockingly: 'Happiness runneth after me. That is because I do not run after women. Happiness, however, is a woman.'

48 Before Sunrise

O heaven above me, thou pure, thou deep heaven! Thou abyss of light! Gazing on thee, I tremble with divine desires.

Up to thy height to toss myself – that is my depth! In thy purity to hide myself – that is *mine* innocence!

The God veileth his beauty: thus hidest thou thy stars. Thou speakest not: *thus* proclaimest thou thy wisdom unto me.

Mute o'er the raging sea hast thou risen for me today; thy love and thy modesty make a revelation unto my raging soul.

In that thou camest unto me beautiful, veiled in thy beauty, in that thou spakest unto me mutely, obvious in thy wisdom:

Oh, how could I fail to divine all the modesty of thy soul! *Before* the sun didst thou come unto me – the lonesomest one.

We have been friends from the beginning: to us are grief, gruesomeness and ground common; even the sun is common to us.

We do not speak to each other, because we know too much – we keep silent to each other, we smile our knowledge to each other.

Art thou not the light of my fire? Hast thou not the sister-soul of mine insight?

Together did we learn everything; together did we learn to ascend beyond ourselves to ourselves, and to smile uncloudedly –

Uncloudedly to smile down out of luminous eyes and out of miles of distance, when under us constraint and purpose and guilt steam like rain.

And wandered I alone, for *what* did my soul hunger by night and in labyrinthine paths? And climbed I mountains, *whom* did I ever seek, if not thee, upon mountains?

And all my wandering and mountain-climbing: a necessity was it merely, and a makeshift of the unhappy one; to fly only, wanteth mine entire will, to fly into *thee*!

And what have I hated more than passing clouds, and whatever tainteth thee? And mine own hatred have I even hated, because it tainted thee!

The passing clouds I detest – those stealthy cats of prey; they take from thee and me what is common to us – the vast unbounded Yea- and Amen-saying.

These mediators and mixers we detest – the passing clouds: those half-and-half ones, that have neither learned to bless nor to curse from the heart.

Rather will I sit in a tub under a closed heaven, rather will I sit in the abyss without heaven, than see thee, thou luminous heaven, tainted with passing clouds!

And oft have I longed to pin them fast with the jagged gold-wires of lightning, that I might, like the thunder, beat the drum upon their kettle-bellies –

An angry drummer, because they rob me of thy Yea and Amen, thou heaven above me, thou pure, thou luminous heaven! Thou abyss of light, because they rob thee of my Yea and Amen!

For rather will I have noise and thunders and tempest-blasts than this discreet, doubting cat-repose; and also amongst men do I hate most of all the soft-treaders, and half-and-half ones, and the doubting, hesitating, passing clouds.

And 'he who cannot bless shall *learn* to curse!' – this clear teaching dropt unto me from the clear heaven; this star standeth in my heaven even in dark nights.

I, however, am a blesser and a Yea-sayer, if thou be but around me, thou pure, thou luminous heaven! Thou abyss of light, into all abysses do I then carry my beneficent Yea-saying!

A blesser have I become and a Yea-sayer, and therefore strove I long and was a striver, that I might one day get my hands free for blessing.

This, however, is my blessing: to stand above everything as its own heaven, its round roof, its azure bell and eternal security; and blessed is he who thus blesseth!

For all things are baptized at the font of eternity, and beyond good and evil; good and evil themselves, however, are but fugitive shadows and damp afflictions and passing clouds.

Verily, it is a blessing and not a blasphemy when I teach that 'above all things there standeth the heaven of chance, the heaven of innocence, the heaven of hazard, the heaven of wantonness'.

'Of Hazard' – that is the oldest nobility in the world; that gave I back to all things; I emancipated them from bondage under purpose.

This freedom and celestial serenity did I put like an azure bell above all things, when I taught that over them and through them, no 'eternal Will' – willeth.

This wantonness and folly did I put in place of that Will, when I taught that 'In everything there is one thing impossible – rationality!'

A *little* reason, to be sure, a germ of wisdom scattered from star to star – this leaven is mixed in all things; for the sake of folly, wisdom is mixed in all things!

A little wisdom is indeed possible; but this blessed security have I found in all things, that they prefer – *to dance* on the feet of chance.

O heaven above me! Thou pure, thou lofty heaven! This is now thy purity unto me, that there is no eternal reason-spider and reason-cobweb –

That thou art to me a dancing-floor for divine chances, that thou art to me a table of the Gods, for divine dice and dice-players!

But thou blushest? Have I spoken unspeakable things? Have I abused, when I meant to bless thee?

Or is it the shame of being two of us that maketh thee blush! Dost thou bid me go and be silent, because now – *day* cometh?

The world is deep – and deeper than e'er the day could read. Not everything may be uttered in presence of day. But day cometh; so let us part!

O heaven above me, thou modest one! Thou glowing one! O thou, my happiness before sunrise! The day cometh; so let us part!

Thus spake Zarathustra.

49 *The Bedwarfing Virtue*

1

When Zarathustra was again on the continent, he did not go straightway to his mountains and his cave, but made many wanderings and questionings, and ascertained this and that; so that he said of himself jestingly: Lo, a river that floweth back unto its source in many windings! For he wanted to learn what had taken place *among men* during the interval: whether they had become greater or smaller. And once, when he saw a row of new houses, he marvelled, and said:

What do these houses mean? Verily, no great soul put them up as its simile!

Did perhaps a silly child take them out of its toy-box? Would that another child put them again into the box!

And these rooms and chambers – can *men* go out and in there? They seem to be made for silk dolls; or for dainty-eaters, who perhaps let others eat with them.

And Zarathustra stood still and meditated. At last he said sorrowfully: There hath *everything* become smaller!

Everywhere do I see lower doorways; he who is of *my* type can still go through, but – he must stoop!

Oh, when shall I arrive again at my home, where I shall no longer have to stoop – shall no longer have to stoop *before the small ones*! And Zarathustra sighed, and gazed into the distance –

The same day, however, he gave his discourse on the bedwarfing virtue.

2

I pass through this people and keep mine eyes open; they do not forgive me for not envying their virtues.

They bite at me, because I say unto them that for small people, small virtues are necessary – and because it is hard for me to understand that small people are *necessary*!

Here am I still like a cock in a strange farm-yard, at which even the hens peck; but on that account I am not unfriendly to the hens.

I am courteous towards them, as towards all small annoyances; to be prickly towards what is small seemeth to me wisdom for hedgehogs.

They all speak of me when they sit around their fire in the evening; they speak of me, but no one thinketh – of me!

This is the new stillness which I have experienced: their noise around me spreadeth a mantle over my thoughts.

They shout to one another: 'What is this gloomy cloud about to do to us? Let us see that it doth not bring a plague upon us!'

And recently did a woman seize upon her child that was coming unto me: 'Take the children away,' cried she, 'such eyes scorch children's souls.'

They cough when I speak; they think coughing an objection to strong winds – they divine nothing of the boisterousness of my happiness!

'We have not yet time for Zarathustra' – so they object; but what matter about a time that 'hath no time' for Zarathustra?

And if they should altogether praise me, how could I go to sleep on *their* praise? A girdle of spines is their praise unto me: it scratcheth me even when I take it off.

And this also did I learn among them: the praiser doeth as if he gave back; in truth, however, he wanteth more to be given him!

Ask my foot if their lauding and luring strains please it! Verily, to such measure and ticktack it liketh neither to dance nor to stand still.

To small virtues would they fain lure and laud me; to the ticktack of small happiness would they fain persuade my foot.

I pass through this people and keep mine eyes open; they have become *smaller*, and ever become smaller – *the reason thereof is their doctrine of happiness and virtue.*

For they are moderate also in virtue – because they want comfort. With comfort, however, moderate virtue only is compatible.

To be sure, they also learn in their way to stride on and stride forward: that, I call their *hobbling*. Thereby they become a hindrance to all who are in haste.

And many of them go forward, and look backwards thereby,

with stiffened necks; those do I like to run up against.

Foot and eye shall not lie, nor give the lie to each other. But there is much lying among small people.

Some of them *will*, but most of them *are willed*. Some of them are genuine, but most of them are bad actors.

There are actors without knowing it amongst them, and actors without intending it; the genuine ones are always rare, especially the genuine actors.

Of man there is little here: therefore do their women masculinise themselves. For only he who is man enough, will – *save the woman* in woman.

And this hypocrisy found I worst amongst them, that even those who command feign the virtues of those who serve.

'I serve, thou servest, we serve' – so chanteth here even the hypocrisy of the rulers – and alas, if the first lord be *only* the first servant!

Ah, even upon their hypocrisy did mine eyes' curiosity alight; and well did I divine all their fly-happiness, and their buzzing around sunny window-panes.

So much kindness, so much weakness do I see. So much justice and pity, so much weakness.

Round, fair and considerate are they to one another, as grains of sand are round, fair and considerate to grains of sand.

Modestly to embrace a small happiness – that do they call 'submission'! And at the same time they peer modestly after a new small happiness.

In their hearts they want simply one thing most of all: that no one hurt them. Thus do they anticipate every one's wishes and do well unto every one.

That, however, is *cowardice*, though it be called 'virtue'.

And when they chance to speak harshly, those small people, then do I hear therein only their hoarseness – every draught of air maketh them hoarse.

Shrewd indeed are they, their virtues have shrewd fingers. But they lack fists; their fingers do not know how to creep behind fists.

Virtue for them is what maketh modest and tame: therewith have they made the wolf a dog, and man himself man's best domestic animal.

'We set our chair in the *midst*' – so saith their smirking unto me – 'and as far from dying gladiators as from satisfied swine.'

That, however, is – *mediocrity*, though it be called moderation.

3

I pass through this people and let fall many words; but they know neither how to take nor how to retain them.

They wonder why I came not to revile venery and vice; and verily, I came not to warn against pickpockets either!

They wonder why I am not ready to abet and whet their wisdom: as if they had not yet enough of wiseacres whose voices grate on mine ear like slate-pencils!

And when I call out: 'Curse all the cowardly devils in you, that would fain whimper and fold the hands and adore' – then do they shout: 'Zarathustra is godless.'

And especially do their teachers of submission shout this – but precisely in their ears do I love to cry: 'Yea! I am Zarathustra, the godless!'

Those teachers of submission! Wherever there is aught puny, or sickly, or scabby, there do they creep like lice; and only my disgust preventeth me from cracking them.

Well, this is my sermon for *their* ears: I am Zarathustra the godless, who saith: 'Who is more godless than I, that I may enjoy his teaching?'

I am Zarathustra the godless: where do I find mine equal? And all those are mine equals who give unto themselves their Will, and divest themselves of all submission.

I am Zarathustra the godless! I cook every chance in *my* pot. And only when it hath been quite cooked do I welcome it as *my* food.

And verily, many a chance came imperiously unto me; but still more imperiously did my *Will* speak unto it. Then did it lie imploringly upon its knees –

Imploring that it might find home and heart with me, and saying flatteringly: 'See, O Zarathustra, how friend only cometh unto friend!'

But why talk I, when no one hath *mine* ears! And so will I shout it out unto all the winds:

Ye ever become smaller, ye small people! Ye crumble away, ye comfortable ones! Ye will yet perish –

By your many small virtues, by your many small omissions, and by your many small submissions!

Too tender, too yielding: so is your soil! But for a tree to become *great*, it seeketh to twine hard roots around hard rocks!

Also what ye omit weaveth at the web of all the human future; even your naught is a cobweb, and a spider that liveth on the blood of the future.

And when ye take, then is it like stealing, ye small virtuous ones; but even among knaves *honour* saith that 'one shall only steal when one cannot rob'.

'It giveth itself' – that is also a doctrine of submission. But I say unto you, ye comfortable ones, that it *taketh to itself*, and will ever take more and more from *you*!

Ah, that ye would renounce all half-willing, and would decide for idleness as ye decide for action!

Ah, that ye understood my word: 'Do ever what ye will – but first be such as *can will*.

Love ever your neighbour as yourselves – but first be such as *love themselves* –

Such as love with great love, such as love with great contempt!' Thus speaketh Zarathustra the godless.

But why talk I, when no one hath *mine* ears! It is still an hour too early for me here.

Mine own forerunner am I among this people, mine own cockcrow in dark lanes.

But *their* hour cometh! And there cometh also mine! Hourly do they become smaller, poorer, unfruitfuller – poor herbs, poor earth!

And *soon* shall they stand before me like dry grass and prairie, and verily, weary of themselves – and panting for *fire*, more than for water!

O blessed hour of the lightning! O mystery before noontide! Running fires will I one day make of them, and heralds with flaming tongues –

Herald shall they one day with flaming tongues: 'It cometh, it is nigh, *the great noontide*!'

Thus spake Zarathustra.

50 On The Olive-mount

Winter, a bad guest, sitteth with me at home; blue are my hands with his friendly hand-shaking.

I honour him, that bad guest, but gladly leave him alone. Gladly do I run away from him; and when one runneth *well*, then one escapeth him!

With warm feet and warm thoughts do I run where the wind is calm – to the sunny corner of mine olive-mount.

There do I laugh at my stern guest, and am still fond of him, because he cleareth my house of flies, and quieteth many little noises.

For he suffereth it not if a gnat wanteth to buzz, or even two of them; also the lanes maketh he lonesome, so that the moonlight is afraid there at night.

A hard guest is he – but I honour him, and do not worship, like the tenderlings, the pot-bellied fire-idol.

Better even a little teeth-chattering than idol-adoration! So willeth my nature. And especially have I a grudge against all ardent, steaming, steamy fire-idols.

Him whom I love, I love better in winter than in summer; better do I now mock at mine enemies, and more heartily, when winter sitteth in my house.

Heartily, verily, even when I *creep* into bed – there still laugheth and wantoneth my hidden happiness; even my deceptive dream laugheth.

I, a – creeper? Never in my life did I creep before the powerful; and if ever I lied, then did I lie out of love. Therefore am I glad even in my winter-bed.

A poor bed warmeth me more than a rich one, for I am jealous of my poverty. And in winter she is most faithful unto me.

With a wickedness do I begin every day: I mock at the winter with a cold bath; on that account grumbleth my stern house-mate.

Also do I like to tickle him with a wax-taper, that he may finally let the heavens emerge from ashy-grey twilight.

For especially wicked am I in the morning: at the early hour when the pail rattleth at the well, and horses neigh warmly in grey lanes –

Impatiently do I then wait, that the clear sky may finally dawn for me, the snow-bearded winter-sky, the hoary one, the white-head –

The winter-sky, the silent winter-sky, which often stifleth even its sun!

Did I perhaps learn from it the long clear silence? Or did it learn it from me? Or hath each of us devised it himself?

Of all good things the origin is a thousandfold – all good roguish things spring into existence for joy; how could they always do so – for once only!

A good roguish thing is also the long silence, and to look, like the winter-sky, out of a clear, round-eyed countenance –

Like it, to stifle one's sun, and one's inflexible solar will: verily, this art and this winter-roguishness have I learnt *well*!

My best-loved wickedness and art is it, that my silence hath learned not to betray itself by silence.

Clattering with diction and dice, I outwit the solemn assistants; all those stern watchers shall my will and purpose elude.

That no one might see down into my depth and into mine ultimate will – for that purpose did I devise the long clear silence.

Many a shrewd one did I find: he veiled his countenance and made his water muddy, that no one might see therethrough and thereunder.

But precisely unto him came the shrewder distrusters and nut-crackers: precisely from him did they fish his best-concealed fish!

But the clear, the honest, the transparent – these are for me the wisest silent ones; in them, so *profound* is the depth that even the clearest water doth not – betray it.

Thou snow-bearded, silent winter-sky, thou round-eyed white-head above me! Oh, thou heavenly simile of my soul and its wantonness!

And *must* I not conceal myself like one who hath swallowed gold – lest my soul should be ripped up?

Must I not wear stilts, that they may *overlook* my long legs – all those enviers and injurers around me?

Those dingy, fire-warmed, used-up, green-tinted, ill-natured souls – how *could* their envy endure my happiness!

Thus do I show them only the ice and winter of my peaks – and *not* that my mountain windeth all the solar girdles around it!

They hear only the whistling of my winter-storms, and know *not* that I also travel over warm seas, like longing, heavy, hot south-winds.

They commiserate also my accidents and chances – but my word saith: 'Suffer the chance to come unto me; innocent is it as a little child!'

How *could* they endure my happiness, if I did not put around it accidents, and winter-privations, and bear-skin caps, and enmantling snowflakes –

If I did not myself commiserate their *pity*, the pity of those enviers and injurers –

– If I did not myself sigh before them, and chatter with cold, and patiently *let* myself be swathed in their pity!

This is the wise waggish-will and good-will of my soul that it *concealeth not* its winters and glacial storms; it concealeth not its chilblains either.

To one man, lonesomeness is the flight of the sick one; to another, it is the flight *from* the sick ones.

Let them *hear* me chattering and sighing with winter-cold, all those poor squinting knaves around me! With such sighing and chattering do I flee from their heated rooms.

Let them sympathise with me and sigh with me on account of my chilblains: 'At the ice of knowledge will he yet *freeze* to *death*!' So they mourn.

Meanwhile do I run with warm feet hither and thither on mine olive-mount; in the sunny corner of mine olive-mount do I sing, and mock at all pity.

Thus sang Zarathustra.

51 *On Passing-by*

Thus slowly wandering through many peoples and divers cities did Zarathustra return by round-about roads to his mountains and his cave. And behold, thereby came he unawares also to the gate of the *great city*. Here, however, a foaming fool, with extended hands, sprang forward to him and stood in his way. It was the same fool whom the people called 'the ape of Zarathustra'; for he had learned from him something of the expression and modulation of language, and perhaps liked also to borrow from the store of his wisdom. And the fool talked thus to Zarathustra:

O Zarathustra, here is the great city: here hast thou nothing to seek and everything to lose.

Why wouldst thou wade through this mire? Have pity upon thy foot! Spit rather on the gate of the city, and – turn back!

Here is the hell for anchorites' thoughts; here are great thoughts seethed alive and boiled small.

Here do all great sentiments decay; here may only rattleboned sensations rattle!

Smellest thou not already the shambles and cookshops of the spirit? Steameth not this city with the fumes of slaughtered spirit?

Seest thou not the souls hanging like limp dirty rags? And they make newspapers also out of these rags!

Hearest thou not how spirit hath here become a verbal game? Loathsome verbal swill doth it vomit forth! And they make newspapers also out of this verbal swill.

They hound one another, and know not whither! They inflame one another, and know not why! They tinkle with their pinchbeck, they jingle with their gold.

They are cold, and seek warmth from distilled waters; they are inflamed, and seek coolness from frozen spirits; they are all sick and sore through public opinion.

All lusts and vices are here at home; but here there are also the virtuous; there is much appointable appointed virtue –

Much appointable virtue with scribe-fingers and hardy sitting-flesh and waiting-flesh blessed with small breaststars, and padded, hauchless daughters.

There is here also much piety, and much faithful spittle-licking and spittle-backing, before the God of Hosts.

'From on high' drippeth the star, and the gracious spittle; for the high, longeth every starless bosom.

The moon hath its court, and the court hath its moon-calves; unto all, however, that cometh from the court do the mendicant people pray, and all appointable mendicant virtues.

'I serve, thou servest, we serve' – so prayeth all appointable virtue to the prince, that the merited star may at last stick on the slender breast!

But the moon still revolveth around all that is earthly: so revolveth also the prince around what is earthliest of all – that, however, is the gold of the shopman.

The God of the Hosts of war is not the God of the golden bar; the prince proposeth but the shopman – disposeth!

By all that is luminous and strong and good in thee, O Zarathustra, spit on this city of shopmen and return back!

Here floweth all blood putridly and tepidly and frothily through all veins; spit on the great city, which is the great slum where all the scum frotheth together!

Spit on the city of compressed souls and slender breasts, of pointed eyes and sticky fingers –

On the city of the obtrusive, the brazen-faced, the pen-demagogues and tongue-demagogues, the overheated ambitious –

Where everything maimed, ill-famed, lustful, untrustful, over-mellow, sickly-yellow and seditious, festereth pernicious –

Spit on the great city and turn back!

Here, however, did Zarathustra interrupt the foaming fool, and shut his mouth –

Stop this at once! called out Zarathustra. Long have thy speech and thy species disgusted me!

Why didst thou live so long by the swamp, that thou thyself hadst to become a frog and a toad?

Floweth there not a tainted, frothy swamp-blood in thine own veins, when thou hast thus learned to croak and revile?

Why wentest thou not into the forest? Or why didst thou not till the ground? Is the sea not full of green islands?

I despise thy contempt; and when thou warnedst me – why didst thou not warn thyself?

Out of love alone shall my contempt and my warning bird take wing; but not out of the swamp!

They call thee mine ape, thou foaming fool; but I call thee my grunting-pig – by thy grunting thou spoilest even my praise of folly.

What was it that first made thee grunt? Because no one sufficiently *flattered* thee: therefore didst thou seat thyself beside this filth, that thou mightest have cause for much grunting –

That thou mightest have cause for much *vengeance*! For vengeance, thou vain fool, is all thy foaming; I have divined thee well!

But thy fool's-word injureth *me*, even when thou art right! And even if Zarathustra's word *were* a hundred times justified, thou wouldst ever – *do* wrong with my word!

Thus spake Zarathustra. Then did he look on the great city and sighed, and was long silent. At last he spake thus:

I loathe also this great city, and not only this fool. Here and there – there is nothing to better, nothing to worsen.

Woe to this great city! And I would that I already saw the pillar of fire in which it will be consumed!

For such pillars of fire must precede the great noontide. But this hath its time and its own fate.

This precept, however, give I unto thee in parting, thou fool: Where one can no longer love, there should one – *pass by*!

Thus spake Zarathustra, and passed by the fool and the great city.

52 *The Apostates*

1

Ah, lieth everything already withered and grey which but lately stood green and many-hued on this meadow! And how much honey of hope did I carry hence into my beehives!

Those young hearts have already all become old – and not old even! Only weary, ordinary, comfortable. They declare it: 'We have again become pious.'

Of late did I see them run forth at early morn with valorous steps; but the feet of their knowledge became weary, and now do they malign even their morning valour!

Verily, many of them once lifted their legs like the dancer; to them winked the laughter of my wisdom – then did they bethink themselves. Just now have I seen them bent down – to creep to the cross.

Around light and liberty did they once flutter like gnats and young poets. A little older, a little colder: and already are they mystifiers, and mumblers and mollycoddles.

Did perhaps their hearts despond, because lonesomeness had swallowed me like a whale? Did their ear perhaps hearken yearningly-long for me *in vain*, and for my trumpet-notes and herald-calls?

Ah, ever are there but few of those whose hearts have persistent courage and exuberance; and in such remaineth also the spirit patient. The rest, however, are *cowardly*.

The rest: these are always the great majority, the commonplace, the superfluous, the far-too-many – those all are cowardly!

Him who is of my type, will also the experiences of my type meet on the way; so that his first companions must be corpses and buffoons.

His second companions, however – they will call themselves his *believers* – will be a living host, with much love, much folly, much unbearded veneration.

To those believers shall he who is of my type among men not

bind his heart; in those spring-times and many-hued meadows shall he not believe, who knoweth the fickle faint-hearted human species!

Could they do otherwise, then would they also *will* otherwise. The half-and-half spoil every whole. That leaves become withered – what is there to lament about that!

Let them go and fall away, O Zarathustra, and do not lament! Better even to blow amongst them with rustling winds –

Blow amongst those leaves, O Zarathustra, that everything *withered* may run away from thee the faster!

2

'We have again become pious' – so do those apostates confess; and some of them are still too pusillanimous thus to confess.

Unto them I look into the eye – before them I say it unto their face and unto the blush on their cheeks: Ye are those who again *pray*!

It is however a shame to pray! Not for all, but for thee, and me, and whoever hath his conscience in his head. For *thee* it is a shame to pray!

Thou knowest it well: the faint-hearted devil in thee, which would fain fold its arms and place its hands in its bosom, and take it easier – this faint-hearted devil persuadeth thee that 'there is a God'!

Thereby, however, dost thou belong to the light-dreading type, to whom light never permitteth repose; now must thou daily thrust thy head deeper into obscurity and vapour!

And verily, thou choosest the hour well: for just now do the nocturnal birds again fly abroad. The hour hath come for all light-dreading people, the vesper hour and leisure hour, when they do not – 'take leisure'.

I hear it and smell it: it hath come – their hour for hunt and procession, not indeed for a wild hunt, but for a tame, lame, snuffling, soft-treaders', soft-prayers' hunt –

For a hunt after susceptible simpletons: all mousetraps for the heart have again been set! And whenever I lift a curtain, a night-moth rusheth out of it.

Did it perhaps squat there along with another night-moth? For everywhere do I smell small concealed communities; and wherever there are closets there are new devotees therein, and the atmosphere of devotees.

They sit for long evenings beside one another, and say: 'Let us again become like little children and say, 'good God!' – ruined in mouths and stomachs by the pious confectioners.

Or they look for long evenings at a crafty, lurking cross-spider, that preacheth prudence to the spiders themselves, and teacheth that 'under crosses it is good for cobweb-spinning'!

Or they sit all day at swamps with angle-rods, and on that account think themselves *profound;* but whoever fisheth where there are no fish, I do not even call him superficial!

Or they learn in godly-gay style to play the harp with a hymn-poet, who would fain harp himself into the heart of young girls – for he hath tired of old girls and their praises.

Or they learn to shudder with a learned semi-madcap, who waiteth in darkened rooms for spirits to come to him – and the spirit runneth away entirely!

Or they listen to an old roving howl- and growl-piper who hath learnt from the sad winds the sadness of sounds; now pipeth he as the wind, and preacheth sadness in sad strains.

And some of them have even become night-watchmen: they know now how to blow horns, and go about at night and awaken old things which have long fallen asleep.

Five words about old things did I hear yesternight at the garden-wall: they came from such old, sorrowful, arid night-watchmen.

'For a father he careth not sufficiently for his children: human fathers do this better!'

'He is too old! He now careth no more for his children,' answered the other night-watchman.

'*Hath* he then children? No one can prove it unless he himself prove it! I have long wished that he would for once prove it thoroughly.'

'Prove? As if *he* had ever proved anything! Proving is difficult to him; he layeth great stress on one's *believing* him.'

'Ay! Ay! Belief saveth him: belief in him. That is the way with old people! So it is with us also!'

Thus spake to each other the two old night-watchmen and

light-scarers, and tooted thereupon sorrowfully on their horns; so did it happen yesternight at the garden wall.

To me, however, did the heart writhe with laughter, and was like to break; it knew not where to go, and sunk into the midriff.

Verily, it will be my death yet – to choke with laughter when I see asses drunken, and hear night-watchmen thus doubt about God.

Hath the time not *long* since passed for all such doubts? Who may nowadays awaken such old slumbering, light-shunning things!

With the old Deities hath it long since come to an end – and verily, a good joyful Deity-end had they!

They did not 'begloom' themselves to death – that do people fabricate! On the contrary, they – *laughed* themselves to death once on a time!

That took place when the ungodliest utterance came from a God himself – the utterance: 'There is but one God! Thou shalt have no other Gods before me!' –

An old grim-beard of a God, a jealous one, forgot himself in such wise –

And all the Gods then laughed, and shook upon their thrones, and exclaimed: 'Is it not just divinity that there are Gods, but no God?'

He that hath an ear let him hear.

Thus talked Zarathustra in the city he loved, which is surnamed 'The Pied Cow'. For from here he had but two days to travel to reach once more his cave and his animals; his soul, however, rejoiced unceasingly on account of the nighness of his return home.

53 The Return Home

O lonesomeness! My *home*, lonesomeness! Too long have I lived wildly in wild remoteness, to return to thee without tears!

Now threaten me with the finger as mothers threaten; now smile upon me as mothers smile; now say just: 'Who was it that like a whirlwind once rushed away from me?

Who when departing called out: 'Too long have I sat with lonesomeness; there have I unlearned silence!' *That* hast thou learned now – surely?

O Zarathustra, everything do I know; and that thou wert *more forsaken* amongst the many, thou unique one, than thou ever wert with me!

One thing is forsakenness, another matter is lonesomeness: *that* hast thou now learned! And that amongst men thou wilt ever be wild and strange –

Wild and strange even when they love thee; for above all they want to be *treated indulgently*!

Here, however, art thou at home and house with thyself; here canst thou utter everything, and unbosom all motives; nothing is here ashamed of concealed, congealed feelings.

Here do all things come caressingly to thy talk and flatter thee; for they want to ride upon thy back. On every simile dost thou here ride to every truth.

Uprightly and openly mayest thou here talk to all things; and verily, it soundeth as praise in their ears, for one to talk to all things – directly!

Another matter, however, is forsakenness. For, dost thou remember, O Zarathustra? When thy bird screamed overhead, when thou stoodest in the forest irresolute, ignorant where to go, beside a corpse –

When thou spakest: 'Let mine animals lead me! More dangerous have I found it among men than among animals' – *that* was forsakenness!

And dost thou remember, O Zarathustra? When thou sattest in thine isle, a well of wine-giving and granting amongst empty buckets, bestowing and distributing amongst the thirsty –

Until at last thou alone sattest thirsty amongst the drunken ones, and wailedst nightly: 'Is taking not more blessed than giving? And stealing yet more blessed than taking?' – *That* was forsakenness!

And dost thou remember, O Zarathustra? When thy stillest hour came and drove thee forth from thyself, when with wicked whispering it said: 'Speak and succumb!' –

When it disgusted thee with all thy waiting and silence, and discouraged thy humble courage: *that* was forsakenness!

O lonesomeness! My home, lonesomeness! How blessedly and tenderly speaketh thy voice unto me!

We do not question each other, we do not complain to each other; we go together openly through open doors.

For all is open with thee and clear; and even the hours run here on lighter feet. For in the dark time weigheth heavier upon one than in the light.

Here fly open unto me all being's words and word-cabinets; here all being wanteth to become words; here all becoming wanteth to learn of me how to talk.

Down there, however – all talking is in vain! There, forgetting and passing-by are the best wisdom: *that* have I learned now!

He who would understand everything in man must handle everything. But for that I have too clean hands.

I do not like even to inhale their breath; alas, that I have lived so long among their noise and bad breaths!

O blessed stillness around me! O pure odours around me! How from a deep breast this stillness fetcheth pure breath! How it hearkeneth, this blessed stillness!

But down there – there speaketh everything, there is everything misheard. If one announce one's wisdom with bells, the shopmen in the market-place will out-jingle it with pennies!

Everything among them talketh; no one knoweth any longer how to understand. Everything falleth into the water; nothing falleth any longer into deep wells.

Everything among them talketh, nothing succeedeth any longer and accomplisheth itself. Everything cackleth, but who will still sit quietly on the nest and hatch eggs?

Everything among them talketh, everything is out-talked. And that which yesterday was still too hard for time itself and its tooth, hangeth today, outchamped and outchewed, from the mouths of the men of today.

Everything among them talketh, everything is betrayed. And what was once called the secret and secrecy of profound souls, belongeth today to the street-trumpeters and other butterflies.

O human hubbub, thou wonderful thing! Thou noise in dark streets! Now art thou again behind me – my greatest danger lieth behind me!

In indulging and pitying lay ever my greatest danger; and all human hubbub wisheth to be indulged and tolerated.

With suppressed truths, with fool's hand and befooled heart, and rich in petty lies of pity – thus have I ever lived among men.

Disguised did I sit amongst them, ready to misjudge *myself* that I might endure *them*, and willingly saying to myself: 'Thou fool, thou dost not know men!'

One unlearneth men when one liveth amongst them: there is too much foreground in all men – what can farseeing, far-longing eyes do *there*!

And, fool that I was, when they misjudged me, I indulged them on that account more than myself, being habitually hard on myself, and often even taking revenge on myself for the indulgence.

Stung all over by poisonous flies, and hollowed like the stone by many drops of wickedness: thus did I sit among them, and still said to myself: 'Innocent is every thing petty of its pettiness!'

Especially did I find those who call themselves 'the good' the most poisonous flies; they sting in all innocence, they lie in all innocence; how *could* they – be just towards me!

He who liveth amongst the good – pity teacheth him to lie. Pity maketh stifling air for all free souls. For the stupidity of the good is unfathomable.

To conceal myself and my riches – *that* did I learn down there; for every one did I still find poor in spirit. It was the lie of my pity, that I knew in every one –

That I saw and scented in every one, what was *enough* of spirit for him and what was *too much*!

Their stiff wise men: I call them wise, not stiff – thus did I learn to slur over words.

The grave-diggers dig for themselves diseases. Beneath old

rubbish rest bad vapours. One should not stir up the marsh. One should live on mountains.

With blessed nostrils do I again breathe mountain freedom. Freed at last is my nose from the smell of all human hubbub!

With sharp breezes tickled, as with sparkling wine, *sneezeth* my soul – sneezeth, and shouteth self-congratulatingly: 'Health to thee!'

Thus spake Zarathustra.

54 The Three Evil Things

1

In my dream, in my last morning-dream, I stood today on a promontory – beyond the world; I held a pair of scales and *weighed* the world.

Alas, that the rosy dawn came too early to me; she glowed me awake, the jealous one! Jealous is she always of the glows of my morning-dream.

Measurable by him who hath time, weighable by a good weigher, attainable by strong pinions, divinable by divine nutcrackers: thus did my dream find the world –

My dream, a bold sailor, half-ship, half-hurricane, silent as the butterfly, impatient as the falcon; how had it the patience and leisure today for world-weighing!

Did my wisdom perhaps speak secretly to it, my laughing, wide-awake day-wisdom, which mocketh at all 'infinite worlds'? For it saith: 'Where force is, there becometh *number* the master: it hath more force.'

How confidently did my dream contemplate this finite world; not new-fangledly, not old-fangledly, not timidly, not entreatingly –

As if a big round apple presented itself to my hand, a ripe golden apple, with a coolly-soft, velvety skin: thus did the world present itself unto me –

As if a tree nodded unto me, a broad-branched, strong-willed tree, curved as a recline and a foot-stool for weary travellers: thus did the world stand on my promontory –

As if delicate hands carried a casket towards me – a casket open for the delectation of modest adoring eyes: thus did the world present itself before me today –

Not riddle enough to scare human love from it, not solution enough to put to sleep human wisdom: a humanly good thing was the world to me today, of which such bad things are said!

How I thank my morning-dream that I thus at today's dawn weighed the world! As a humanly good thing did it come unto me, this dream and heart-comforter!

And that I may do the like by day, and imitate and copy its best, now will I put the three worst things on the scales, and weigh them humanly well.

He who taught to bless taught also to curse: what are the three best-cursed things in the world? These will I put on the scales.

Voluptuousness, passion for power, and *selfishness:* these three things have hitherto been best cursed, and have been in worst and falsest repute – these three things will I weigh humanly well.

Well, here is my promontory, and there is the sea! It rolleth hither unto me, shaggily and fawningly, the old faithful, hundred-headed dog-monster that I love!

Well, here will I hold the scales over the weltering sea; and also a witness do I choose to look on – thee, the anchorite-tree, thee, the strong-odoured, broad-arched tree that I love!

On what bridge goeth the now to the hereafter? By what constraint doth the high stoop to the low? And what enjoineth even the highest still – to grow upwards?

Now stand the scales poised and at rest: three heavy questions have I thrown in; three heavy answers carrieth the other scale.

2

Voluptuousness: unto all hair-shirted despisers of the body, a sting and stake; and cursed as 'the world' by all backworldsmen: for it mocketh and befooleth all erring, misinferring teachers.

Voluptuousness: to the rabble, the slow fire at which it is burnt; to all wormy wood, to all stinking rags, the prepared heat and stew furnace.

Voluptuousness: to free hearts, a thing innocent and free, the garden-happiness of the earth, all the future's thanks-overflow to the present.

Voluptuousness: only to the withered a sweet poison; to the lion-willed, however, the great cordial, and the reverently saved wine of wines.

Voluptuousness: the great symbolic happiness of a higher happiness and highest hope. For to many is marriage promised, and more than marriage –

To many that are more unknown to each other than man and woman – and who hath fully understood *how unknown* to each other are man and woman!

Voluptuousness: but I will have hedges around my thoughts, and even around my words, lest swine and libertine should break into my gardens!

Passion for power: the glowing scourge of the hardest of the heart-hard; the cruel torture reserved for the cruellest themselves; the gloomy flame of living pyres.

Passion for power: the wicked gadfly which is mounted on the vainest peoples, the scorner of all uncertain virtue; which rideth on every horse and on every pride.

Passion for power: the earthquake which breaketh and upbreaketh all that is rotten and hollow; the rolling, rumbling, punitive demolisher of whited sepulchres; the flashing interrogative-sign beside premature answers.

Passion for power: before whose glance man creepeth and croucheth and drudgeth, and becometh lower than the serpent and the swine; until at last great contempt crieth out of him –

Passion for power: the terrible teacher of great contempt, which preacheth to their face to cities and empires: 'Away with thee!' – until a voice crieth out of themselves: 'Away with me!'

Passion for power: which, however, mounteth alluringly even to the pure and lonesome, and up to self-satisfied elevations, glowing like a love that painteth purple felicities alluringly on earthly heavens.

Passion for power: but who would call it *passion*, when the height longeth to stoop for power! Verily, nothing sick or diseased is there in such longing and descending!

That the lonesome height may not for ever remain lonesome and self-sufficing; that the mountains may come to the valleys and the winds of the heights to the plains –

Oh, who could find the right praenomen and honouring name for such longing! 'Bestowing virtue' – thus did Zarathustra once name the unnamable.

And then it happened also – and verily, it happened for the first time – that his word blessed *selfishness*, the wholesome, healthy selfishness that springeth from the powerful soul –

From the powerful soul, to which the high body appertaineth, the handsome, triumphing, refreshing body around which everything becometh a mirror –

The pliant, persuasive body, the dancer whose symbol and epitome is the self-enjoying soul. Of such bodies and souls the self-enjoyment calleth itself 'virtue'.

With its words of good and bad doth such self-enjoyment shelter itself as with sacred groves; with the names of its happiness doth it banish from itself everything contemptible.

Away from itself doth it banish everything cowardly; it saith: 'Bad – *that is* cowardly!' Contemptible seem to it the ever-solicitous, the sighing, the complaining, and whoever pick up the most trifling advantage.

It despiseth also all bitter-sweet wisdom; for verily there is also wisdom that bloometh in the dark, a nightshade wisdom, which ever sigheth: 'All is vain!'

Shy distrust is regarded by it as base, and every one who wanteth oaths instead of looks and hands; also all overdistrustful wisdom – for such is the mode of cowardly souls.

Baser still it regardeth the obsequious, doggish one, who immediately lieth on his back, the submissive one; and there is also wisdom that is submissive, and doggish, and pious, and obsequious.

Hateful to it altogether, and a loathing, is he who will never defend himself, he who swalloweth down poisonous spittle and bad looks, the all-too-patient one, the all-endurer, the all-satisfied one; for that is the mode of slaves.

Whether they be servile before Gods and divine spurnings, or before men and stupid human opinions, at *all* kinds of slaves doth it spit, this blessed selfishness!

Bad: thus doth it call all that is spirit-broken, and sordidly-servile – constrained, blinking eyes, depressed hearts, and the false submissive style, which kisseth with broad cowardly lips.

And spurious wisdom: so doth it call all the wit that slaves and hoary-headed and weary ones affect; and especially all the cunning, spurious-witted, curious-witted foolishness of priests!

The spurious wise, however – all the priests, the world-weary, and those whose souls are of feminine and servile nature – oh, how hath their game all along abused selfishness!

And precisely *that* was to be virtue and was to be called virtue – to abuse selfishness! And 'selfless' – so did they wish themselves with good reason, all those world-weary cowards and cross-spiders!

But to all those cometh now the day, the change, the sword of judgment, *the great noontide*: then shall many things be revealed!

And he who proclaimeth the *ego* wholesome and holy, and selfishness blessed, verily he, the prognosticator, speaketh also what he knoweth: '*Behold, it cometh, it is nigh, the great noontide*!'

Thus spake Zarathustra.

55 The Spirit of Gravity

1

My mouthpiece is of the people: too coarsely and cordially do I talk for Angora rabbits. And still stranger soundeth my word unto all ink-fish and pen-foxes.

My hand – is a fool's hand: woe unto all tables and walls and whatever hath room for fool's sketching, fool's scrawling!

My foot – is a horse-foot; therewith do I trample and trot over stick and stone, in the fields up and down, and am bedevilled with delight in all fast racing.

My stomach – is surely an eagle's stomach? For it preferreth lamb's flesh. Certainly it is a bird's stomach.

Nourished with innocent things, and with few, ready and impatient to fly away – that is now my nature; why should there not be something of bird-nature therein.

And especially that I am hostile to the spirit of gravity, that is bird-nature; verily, deadly hostile, supremely hostile, originally hostile! Oh, whither hath my hostility not flown and misflown!

Thereof could I sing a song – and *will* sing it, though I be alone in an empty house, and must sing it to mine own ears.

Other singers are there, to be sure, to whom only the full house maketh the voice soft, the hand eloquent, the eye expressive, the heart wakeful: those do I not resemble.

2

He who one day teacheth men to fly will have shifted all landmarks; to him will all landmarks themselves fly into the air; the earth will he christen anew – as 'the light body'.

The ostrich runneth faster than the fastest horse, but it also thrusteth its head heavily into the heavy earth; thus is it with the man who cannot yet fly.

Heavy unto him are earth and life, and so *willeth* the spirit of gravity! But he who would become light, and be a bird, must love himself – thus do *I* teach.

Not, to be sure, with the love of the sick and infected, for with them stinketh even self-love!

One must learn to love oneself – thus do I teach – with a wholesome and healthy love, that one may endure to be with oneself, and not go roving about.

Such roving about christeneth itself 'brotherly love'; with these words hath there hitherto been the best lying and dissembling, and especially by those who have been burdensome to every one.

And verily, it is no commandment for today and tomorrow to *learn* to love oneself. Rather is it of all arts the finest, subtlest, last and most patient.

For to its possessor is all possession well concealed, and of all treasure-pits one's own is last excavated – so causeth the spirit of gravity.

Almost in the cradle are we apportioned with heavy words and worths: 'good' and 'evil' – so calleth itself this dowry. For the sake of it we are forgiven for living.

And therefore suffereth one little children to come unto one, to forbid them betimes to love themselves – so causeth the spirit of gravity.

And we – we bear loyally what is apportioned unto us, on hard shoulders, over rugged mountains! And when we sweat, then do people say to us: 'Yea, life is hard to bear!'

But man himself only is hard to bear! The reason thereof is that he carrieth too many extraneous things on his shoulders. Like the camel kneeleth he down, and letteth himself be well laden.

Especially the strong load-bearing man in whom reverence resideth. Too many *extraneous* heavy words and worths loadeth he upon himself – then seemeth life to him a desert!

And verily! Many a thing also that is *our own* is hard to bear! And many internal things in man are like the oyster – repulsive and slippery and hard to grasp –

So that an elegant shell, with elegant adornment, must plead for them. But this art also must one learn: to *have* a shell, and a fine appearance, and sagacious blindness!

Again, it deceiveth about many things in man that many a shell is poor and pitiable and too much of a shell. Much concealed goodness and power is never dreamt of; the choicest dainties find no tasters!

Women know that, the choicest of them: a little fatter, a little leaner – oh, how much fate is in so little!

Man is difficult to discover, and unto himself most difficult of all; often lieth the spirit concerning the soul. So causeth the spirit of gravity.

He, however, hath discovered himself who saith: 'This is *my* good and evil.' Therewith hath he silenced the mole and the dwarf, who say: 'Good for all, evil for all.'

Verily, neither do I like those who call everything good, and this world the best of all. Those do I call the all-satisfied.

All-satisfiedness, which knoweth how to taste everything – that is not the best taste! I honour the refractory, fastidious tongues and stomachs which have learned to say 'I' and 'Yea' and 'Nay.'

To chew and digest everything, however – that is the genuine swine-nature! Ever to say YE-A – that hath only the ass learnt, and those like it!

Deep yellow and hot red – so wanteth my taste – it mixeth blood with all colours. He, however, who white-washeth his house, betrayeth unto me a whitewashed soul.

With mummies some fall in love, others with phantoms; both alike hostile to all flesh and blood – oh, how repugnant are both to my taste! For I love blood.

And there will I not reside and abide, where every one spitteth and speweth: that is now my taste – rather would I live amongst thieves and perjurers. Nobody carrieth gold in his mouth.

Still more repugnant unto me, however, are all lickspittles; and the most repugnant animal of man that I found did I christen 'parasite': it would not love, and would yet live by love.

Unhappy do I call all those who have only one choice: either to become evil beasts or evil beast-tamers. Amongst such would I not build my tabernacle.

Unhappy do I also call those who have ever to wait – they are repugnant to my taste: all the toll-gatherers and traders and kings and other landkeepers and shopkeepers.

Verily, I learned waiting also, and thoroughly so – but only waiting for *myself*. And above all did I learn standing and walking and running and leaping and climbing and dancing.

This however is my teaching: he who wisheth one day to fly, must first learn standing and walking and running and climbing and dancing – one doth not fly into flying!

With rope-ladders learned I to reach many a window, with nimble legs did I climb high masts; to sit on high masts of perception seemed to me no small bliss –

To flicker like small flames on high masts: a small light, certainly, but a great comfort to cast-away sailors and shipwrecked ones!

By divers ways and wendings did I arrive at my truth; not by one ladder did I mount to the height where mine eye roveth into my remoteness.

And unwillingly only did I ask my way – that was always counter to my taste! Rather did I question and test the ways themselves.

A testing and a questioning hath been all my travelling – and verily, one must also *learn* to answer such questioning! That, however, is my taste –

Neither a good nor a bad taste, but my taste, of which I have no longer either shame or secrecy.

'This – is now *my* way. Where is yours?' Thus did I answer those who asked me 'the way'. For *the* way – it doth not exist!

Thus spake Zarathustra.

56 Old and New Tables

1

Here do I sit and wait, old broken tables around me and also new half-written tables. When cometh mine hour?

The hour of my descent, of my down-going; for once more will I go unto men.

For that hour do I now wait; for first must the signs come unto me that it is *mine* hour – namely, the laughing lion with the flock of doves.

Meanwhile do I talk to myself as one who hath time. No one telleth me anything new, so I tell myself mine own story.

2

When I came unto men, then found I them resting on an old infatuation: all of them thought they had long known what was good and bad for men.

An old wearisome business seemed to them all discourse about virtue; and he who wished to sleep well spake of 'good' and 'bad' ere retiring to rest.

This somnolence did I disturb when I taught that *no one yet knoweth* what is good and bad – unless it be the creating one!

It is he, however, who createth man's goal, and giveth to the earth its meaning and its future: he only *effecteth* it *that* aught is good or bad.

And I bade them upset their old academic chairs, and wherever that old infatuation had sat, I bade them laugh at their great moralists, their saints, their poets, and their Saviours.

At their gloomy sages did I bid them laugh, and whoever had sat admonishing as a black scarecrow on the tree of life.

On their great grave-highway did I seat myself, and even beside the carrion and vultures – and I laughed at all their bygone and its mellow decaying glory.

Verily, like penitential preachers and fools did I cry wrath and shame on all their greatness and smallness. Oh, that their best is so very small! Oh, that their worst is so very small! Thus did I laugh.

Thus did my wise longing, born in the mountains, cry and laugh in me; a wild wisdom, verily – my great pinion-rustling longing!

And oft did it carry me off and up and away and in the midst of laughter; then flew I quivering like an arrow with sun-intoxicated rapture –

Out into distant futures, which no dream hath yet seen into warmer souths than ever sculptor conceived – where gods in their dancing are ashamed of all clothes:

(That I may speak in parables and halt and stammer like the poets; and verily I am ashamed that I have still to be a poet!)

Where all becoming seemed to me dancing of Gods, and wantoning of Gods, and the world unloosed and unbridled and fleeing back to itself –

As an eternal self-fleeing and re-seeking of one another of many Gods, as the blessed self-contradicting, recommuning, and refraternising with one another of many Gods –

Where all time seemed to me a blessed mockery of moments, where necessity was freedom itself, which played happily with the goad of freedom –

Where I also found again mine old devil and arch-enemy, the spirit of gravity, and all that it created: constraint, law, necessity and consequence and purpose and will and good and evil –

For must there not be that which is danced *over*, danced beyond? Must there not, for the sake of the nimble, the nimblest – be moles and clumsy dwarfs?

3

There was it also where I picked up from the path the word 'Superman', and that man is something that must be surpassed –

That man is a bridge and not a goal – rejoicing over his noontides and evenings, as advances to new rosy dawns –

The Zarathustra word of the great noontide, and whatever else I have hung up over men like purple evening-afterglows.

Verily, also new stars did I make them see, along with new

nights; and over cloud and day and night did I spread out laughter like a gay-colour canopy.

I taught them all my poetisation and aspiration: to compose and collect into unity what is fragment in man, and riddle and fearful chance –

As composer, riddle-reader, and redeemer of chance did I teach them to create the future, and all that *hath been* – to redeem by creating.

The past of man to redeem, and every 'It was' to transform, until the Will saith: 'But so did I will it! So shall I will it' –

This did I call redemption; this alone taught I them to call redemption –

Now do I await my redemption – that I may go unto them for the last time.

For once more will I go unto men: *amongst* them will my sun set; in dying will I give them my choicest gift!

From the sun did I learn this, when it goeth down, the exuberant one; gold doth it then pour into the sea, out of inexhaustible riches –

So that the poorest fisherman roweth even with *golden* oars! For this did I once see, and did not tire of weeping in beholding it –

Like the sun will also Zarathustra go down; now sitteth he here and waiteth, old broken tables around him, and also new tables – half-written.

4

Behold, here is a new table; but where are my brethren who will carry it with me to the valley and into hearts of flesh?

Thus demandeth my great love to the remotest ones: *be not considerate of thy neighbour.* Man is something that must be surpassed.

There are many divers ways and modes of surpassing: see *thou* thereto! But only a buffoon thinketh: 'man can also be *overleapt*'.

Surpass thyself even in thy neighbour; and a right which thou canst seize upon, shalt thou not allow to be given thee!

What thou doest can no one do to thee again. Lo, there is no requital.

He who cannot command himself shall obey. And many a one *can* command himself, but still sorely lacketh self-obedience!

5

Thus wisheth the type of noble souls: they desire to have nothing *gratuitously*, least of all life.

He who is of the populace wisheth to live gratuitously; we others, however, to whom life hath given itself – we are ever considering *what* we can best give *in return*!

And verily, it is a noble dictum which saith: 'What life promiseth us, that promise will *we* keep – to life!'

One should not wish to enjoy where one doth not contribute to the enjoyment. And one should not *wish* to enjoy!

For enjoyment and innocence are the most bashful things. Neither likes to be sought for. One should *have* them – but one should rather *seek* for guilt and pain!

6

O my brethren, he who is a firstling is ever sacrificed. Now, however, are we firstlings!

We all bleed on secret sacrificial altars; we all burn and broil in honour of ancient idols.

Our best is still young; this exciteth old palates. Our flesh is tender, our skin is only lambs' skin – how could we not excite old idol-priests!

In ourselves dwelleth he still, the old idol-priest who broileth our best for his banquet. Ah, my brethren, how could firstlings fail to be sacrifices!

But so wisheth our type, and I love those who do not wish to preserve themselves; the down-going ones do I love with mine entire love, for they go beyond.

7

To be true – that *can* few be! And he who can, will not! Least of all, however, can the good be true.

Oh, those good ones! *Good men never speak the truth.* For the spirit thus to be good is a malady.

They yield, those good ones, they submit themselves; their heart repeateth, their soul obeyeth; *he*, however, who obeyeth, *doth not listen to himself!*

All that is called evil by the good must come together in order that one truth may be born. O my brethren, are ye also evil enough for *this* truth?

The daring venture, the prolonged distrust, the cruel Nay, the tedium, the cutting-into-the-quick – how seldom do *these* come together! Out of such seed, however – is truth produced!

Beside the bad conscience hath hitherto grown all *knowledge!* Break up, break up, ye discerning ones, the old tables!

8

When the water hath planks, when gangways and railings o'erspan the stream, verily, he is not believed who then saith: 'All is in flux.'

But even the simpletons contradict him. 'What,' say the simpletons, 'all in flux? Planks and railings are still *over* the stream!'

'*Over* the stream all is stable, all the values of things, the bridges and bearings, all "good" and "evil": these are all *stable*!'

Cometh, however, the hard winter, the stream-tamer, then learn even the wittiest distrust, and verily, not only the simpletons then say: 'Should not everything – *stand still*?'

'Fundamentally standeth everything still' – that is an appropriate winter doctrine, good cheer for an unproductive period, a great comfort for winter-sleepers and fireside-loungers.

'Fundamentally standeth everything still' – but *contrary* thereto preacheth the thawing wind!

The thawing wind, a bullock which is no ploughing bullock – a furious bullock, a destroyer, which with angry horns breaketh the ice! The ice however – *breaketh gangways*!

O my brethren, is not everything *at present in flux*? Have not all railings and gangways fallen into the water? Who would still *hold on* to 'good' and 'evil'?

'Woe to us! Hail to us! The thawing wind bloweth!' Thus preach, my brethren, through all the streets.'

9

There is an old illusion – it is called good and evil. Around soothsayers and astrologers hath hitherto revolved the orbit of this illusion.

Once did one *believe* in soothsayers and astrologers; and *therefore* did one believe: 'Everything is fate; thou shalt, for thou must!'

Then again did one distrust all soothsayers and astrologers; and *therefore* did one believe: 'Everything is freedom; thou canst, for thou willest!'

O my brethren, concerning the stars and the future there hath hitherto been only illusion, and not knowledge; and *therefore* concerning good and evil there hath hitherto been only illusion and not knowledge!

10

'Thou shalt not rob! Thou shalt not slay!' – such precepts were once called holy; before them did one bow the knee and the head, and took off one's shoes.

But I ask you: Where have there ever been better robbers and slayers in the world than such holy precepts?

Is there not even in all life – robbing and slaying? And for such precepts to be called holy, was not *truth* itself thereby – slain?

Or was it a sermon of death that called holy what contradicted and dissuaded from life? O my brethren, break up, break up for me the old tables!

11

It is my sympathy with all the past that I see it is abandoned –

Abandoned to the favour, the spirit and the madness of every generation that cometh, and reinterpreteth all that hath been as its bridge!

A great potentate might arise, an artful prodigy, who with approval and disapproval could strain and constrain all the past, until it became for him a bridge, a harbinger, a herald, and a cock-crowing.

This however is the other danger, and mine other sympathy: he who is of the populace, his thoughts go back to his grandfather – with his grandfather, however, doth time cease.

Thus is all the past abandoned; for it might some day happen for the populace to become master, and drown all time in shallow waters.

Therefore, O my brethren, a *new nobility* is needed, which shall be the adversary of all populace and potentate rule, and shall inscribe anew the word 'noble' on new tables.

For many noble ones are needed, and many kinds of noble ones, *for a new nobility*! Or, as I once said in parable: 'That is just divinity, that there are Gods, but no God!'

12

O my brethren, I consecrate you and point you to a new nobility: ye shall become procreators and cultivators and sowers of the future –

Verily, not to a nobility which ye could purchase like traders with traders' gold; for little worth is all that hath its price.

Let it not be your honour henceforth whence ye come, but whither ye go! Your Will and your feet which seek to surpass you – let these be your new honour!

Verily, not that ye have served a prince – of what account are princes now! Nor that ye have become a bulwark to that which standeth, that it may stand more firmly.

Not that your family have become courtly at courts, and that ye have learned – gay-coloured, like the flamingo – to stand long hours in shallow pools:

(For ability-to-stand is a merit in courtiers; and all courtiers believe that unto blessedness after death pertaineth – permission-to-sit!)

Nor even that a Spirit called 'Holy' led your forefather into promised lands, which I do not praise: for where the worst of all trees grew – the cross – in that land there is nothing to praise!

And verily, wherever this 'Holy Spirit' led its knights, always in such campaigns did – goats and geese, and wry-heads and guy-heads, run *foremost*!

O my brethren, not backward shall your nobility gaze, but *outward*! Exiles shall ye be from all fatherlands and forefather-lands!

Your *children's land* shall ye love; let this love be your new nobility – the undiscovered in the remotest seas! For it do I bid your sails search and search!

Unto your children shall ye *make amends* for being the children of your fathers: all the past shall ye *thus* redeem! This new table do I place over you!

13

'Why should one live? All is vain! To live – that is to thrash straw; to live – that is to burn oneself and yet not get warm.'

Such ancient babbling still passeth for 'wisdom'; because it is old, however, and smelleth mustily, *therefore* is it the more honoured. Even mould ennobleth –

Children might thus speak; they *shun* the fire because it hath burnt them! There is much childishness in the old books of wisdom.

And he who ever 'thrasheth straw', why should he be allowed to rail at thrashing! Such a fool one would have to muzzle!

Such persons sit down to the table and bring nothing with them, not even good hunger – and then do they rail: 'All is vain!'

But to eat and drink well, my brethren, is verily no vain art! Break up, break up for me the tables of the never-joyous ones!

14

'To the clean are all things clean' – thus say the people. I, however, say unto you: 'To the swine all things become swinish!'

Therefore preach the visionaries and bowed-heads (whose hearts are also bowed down): 'The world itself is a filthy monster.'

For these are all unclean spirits; especially those, however, who have no peace or rest unless they see the world *from the backside* – the backworldsmen!

To those do I say it to the face, although it sound unpleasantly: the world resembleth man, in that it hath a backside – *so much* is true!

There is in the world much filth: *so much* is true! But the world itself is not therefore a filthy monster!

There is wisdom in the fact that much in the world smelleth badly; loathing itself createth wings, and fountain-divining powers!

In the best there is still something to loathe; and the best is still something that must be surpassed –

O my brethren, there is much wisdom in the fact that much filth is in the world!

15

Such sayings did I hear pious backworldsmen speak to their consciences, and verily without wickedness or guile – although there is nothing more guileful in the world, or more wicked.

'Let the world be as it is! Raise not a finger against it!'

'Let whoever will choke and stab and skin and scrape the people; raise not a finger against it! Thereby will they learn to renounce the world.'

'And thine own reason – this shalt thou thyself stifle and choke, for it is a reason of this world; thereby wilt thou learn thyself to renounce the world.'

Shatter, shatter, O my brethren, those old tables of the pious! Tatter the maxims of the world-maligners!

16

'He who learneth much unlearneth all violent cravings' – that do people now whisper to one another in all the dark lanes.

'Wisdom wearieth, nothing is worth while; thou shalt not crave!' This new table found I hanging even in the public markets.

Break up for me, O my brethren, break up also that new table! The weary-o'-the-world put it up, and the preachers of death and the jailer; for lo, it is also a sermon for slavery –

Because they learned badly and not the best, and everything too early and everything too fast; because they ate badly: from thence hath resulted their ruined stomach –

For a ruined stomach, is their spirit; it persuadeth to death! For verily, my brethren, the spirit is a stomach!

Life is a well of delight, but to him in whom the ruined stomach speaketh, the father of affliction, all fountains are poisoned.

To discern: that is *delight* to the lion-willed! But he who hath become weary is himself merely 'willed'; with him play all the waves.

And such is always the nature of weak men: they lose themselves on their way. And at last asketh their weariness: 'Why did we ever go on the way? All is indifferent!'

To them soundeth it pleasant to have preached in their ears: 'Nothing is worth while! Ye shall not will!' That, however, is a sermon for slavery.

O my brethren, a fresh blustering wind cometh Zarathustra unto all way-weary ones; many noses will he yet make sneeze!

Even through walls bloweth my free breath, and in into prisons and imprisoned spirits!

Willing emancipateth; for willing is creating: so do I teach. And *only* for creating shall ye learn!

And also the learning shall ye *learn* only from me, the learning well! He who hath ears let him hear!

17

There standeth the boat; thither goeth it over, perhaps into vast nothingness – but who willeth to enter into this 'Perhaps'?

None of you want to enter into the death-boat! How should ye then be *world-weary* ones!

World-weary ones! And have not even withdrawn from the earth! Eager did I ever find you for the earth, amorous still of your own earth-weariness!

Not in vain doth your lip hang down: a small worldly wish still sitteth thereon! And in your eye – floateth there not a cloudlet of unforgotten earthly bliss?

There are on the earth many good inventions, some useful, some pleasant: for their sake is the earth to be loved.

And many such good inventions are there, that they are like woman's breasts: useful at the same time, and pleasant

Ye world-weary ones, however! Ye earth-idlers! You shall one beat with stripes! With stripes shall one again make you sprightly limbs.

For if ye be not invalids, or decrepit creatures, of whom the earth is weary, then are ye sly sloths, or dainty, sneaking pleasure-cats. And if ye will not again run gaily, then shall ye – pass away!

To the incurable shall one not seek to be a physician: thus teacheth Zarathustra – so shall ye pass away!

But more *courage is* needed to make an end than to make a new verse: that do all physicians and poets know well.

18

O my brethren, there are tables which weariness framed, and tables which slothtulness framed, corrupt slothfulness; although they speak similarly, they want to be heard differently –

See this languishing one! Only a span-breadth is he from his goal; but from weariness hath he lain down obstinately in the dust, this brave one!

From weariness yawneth he at the path, at the earth, at the goal, and at himself; not a step further will he go – this brave one!

Now gloweth the sun upon him, and the dogs lick at his sweat; but he lieth there in his obstinacy and preferreth to languish –

A span-breadth from his goal, to languish! Verily, ye will have to drag him into his heaven by the hair of his head – this hero!

Better still that ye let him lie where he hath lain down, that sleep may come unto him, the comforter, with cooling patter-rain.

Let him lie, until of his own accord he awakeneth – until of his own accord he repudiateth all weariness, and what weariness hath taught through him!

Only, my brethren, see that ye scare the dogs away from him, the idle skulkers, and all the swarming vermin –

All the swarming vermin of the 'cultured', that – feast on the sweat of every hero!

19

I form circles around me and holy boundaries; ever fewer ascend with me ever higher mountains; I build a mountain-range out of ever holier mountains –

But wherever ye would ascend with me, O my brethren, take care lest a *parasite* ascend with you!

A parasite: that is a reptile, a creeping, cringing reptile that trieth to fatten on your infirm and sore places.

And *this* is its art: it divineth where ascending souls are weary; in your trouble and dejection, in your sensitive modesty, doth it build its loathsome nest.

Where the strong are weak, where the noble are all-too-gentle – there buildeth it its loathsome nest; the parasite liveth where the great have small sore-places.

What is the highest of all species of being, and what is the lowest? The parasite is the lowest species; he, however, who is of the highest species feedeth most parasites.

For the soul which hath the longest ladder, and can go deepest down: how could there fail to be most parasites upon it?

The most comprehensive soul, which can run and stray and rove furthest in itself; the most necessary soul, which out of joy flingeth itself into chance –

The soul in Being, which plungeth into Becoming; the possessing soul, which *seeketh* to attain desire and longing –

The soul fleeing from itself, which overtaketh itself in the widest circuit; the wisest soul, unto which folly speaketh most sweetly –

The soul most self-loving, in which all things have their current and counter-current, their ebb and their flow – oh, how could *the loftiest soul* fail to have the worst parasites?

20

O my brethren, am I then cruel? But I say: 'What falleth, that shall one also push!'

Everything of today – it falleth, it decayeth; who would preserve it! But I – I wish also to push it!

Know ye the delight which rolleth stones into precipitous depths? Those men of today, see just how they roll into my depths!

A prelude am I to better players, O my brethren! An example! *Do* according to mine example!

And him whom ye do not teach to fly, teach I pray you – *to fall faster*!

21

I love the brave; but it is not enough to be a swordsman – one must also know *whereon* to use swordsmanship!

And often is it greater bravery to keep quiet and pass by, that *thereby* one may reserve oneself for a worthier foe!

Ye shall only have foes to be hated, but not foes to be despised; ye must be proud of your foes. Thus have I already taught.

For the worthier foe, O my brethren, shall ye reserve yourselves: therefore must ye pass by many a one –

Especially many of the rabble, who din your ears with noise about people and peoples.

Keep your eye clear of their For and Against! There is there much right, much wrong; he who looketh on becometh wroth.

Therein viewing, therein hewing – they are the same thing: therefore depart into the forests and lay your sword to sleep!

Go *your* ways! and let the people and peoples go theirs! Gloomy ways, verily, on which not a single hope glinteth any more!

Let there the trader rule, where all that still glittereth is – traders' gold. It is the time of kings no longer; that which now calleth itself the people is unworthy of kings.

See how these peoples themselves now do just like the traders: they pick up the smallest advantage out of all kinds of rubbish!

They lay lures for one another, they lure things out of one another – that they call 'good neighbourliness'. O blessed remote period when a people said to itself: 'I will be – *master* over peoples!'

For, my brethren, the best shall rule, the best also *willeth* to rule! And where the teaching is different, there – the best is *lacking*.

22

If *they* had – bread for nothing, alas, for what would *they* cry! Their maintainment – that is their true entertainment; and they shall have it hard!

Beasts of prey are they; in their 'working' – there is even plundering, in their 'earning' – there is even overreaching! Therefore shall they have it hard!

Better beasts of prey shall they thus become, subtler, cleverer, *more man-like*; for man is the best beast of prey.

All the animals hath man already robbed of their virtues: that is why of all animals it hath been hardest for man.

Only the birds are still beyond him, and if man should yet learn to fly, alas, *to what height* – would his rapacity fly?

23

Thus would I have man and woman: fit for war, the one; fit for maternity, the other. Both, however, fit for dancing with head and legs.

And lost be the day to us in which a measure hath not been danced. And false be every truth which hath not had laughter along with it!

24

Your marriage-arranging: see that it be not a bad *arranging*! Ye have arranged too hastily; so there *followeth* therefrom – marriage-breaking!

And better marriage-breaking than marriage-bending, marriage-lying! Thus spake a woman unto me: 'Indeed, I broke the marriage, but first did the marriage break – me!'

The badly paired found I ever the most revengeful: they make every one suffer for it that they no longer run singly.

On that account want I the honest ones to say to one another: 'We love each other: let us *see to it* that we maintain our love! Or shall our pledging be blundering?'

'Give us a set term and a small marriage, that we may see if we are fit for the great marriage! It is a great matter always to be twain.'

Thus do I counsel all honest ones; and what would be my love to the Superman, and to all that is to come, if I should counsel and speak otherwise!

Not only to propagate yourselves onwards but *upwards* – thereto, O my brethren, may the garden of marriage help you!

25

He who hath grown wise concerning old origins, lo, he will at last seek after the fountains of the future and new origins.

O my brethren, not long will it be until *new peoples* shall arise and new fountains shall rush down into new depths.

For the earthquake – it choketh up many wells, it causeth much languishing; but it bringeth also to light inner powers and secrets.

The earthquake discloseth new fountains. In the earthquake of old peoples new fountains burst forth.

And whoever calleth out: 'Lo, here is a well for many thirsty ones, one heart for many longing ones, one will for many instruments' – around him collecteth a *people*, that is to say, many attempting ones.

Who can command, who must obey – *that is there attempted*! Ah, with what long seeking and solving and failing and learning and re-attempting!

Human society: it is an attempt – so I teach – a long seeking; it seeketh however the ruler –

An attempt, my brethren! And *no* 'contract'! Destroy, I pray you, destroy that word of the soft-hearted and half-and-half!

26

O my brethren! With whom lieth the greatest danger to the whole human future? Is it not with the good and just?

As those who say and feel in their hearts: 'We already know what is good and just, we possess it also; woe to those who still seek thereafter!'

And whatever harm the wicked may do, the harm of the good is the harmfulest harm!

And whatever harm the world-maligners may do, the harm of the good is the harmfulest harm!

O my brethren, into the hearts of the good and just looked some one once on a time, who said: 'They are the Pharisees.' But people did not understand him.

The good and just themselves were not free to understand him; their spirit was imprisoned in their good conscience. The stupidity of the good is unfathomably wise.

It is the truth, however, that the good *must* be Pharisees – they have no choice!

The good must crucify him who deviseth his own virtue! That is the truth!

The second one, however, who discovered their country – the country, heart and soil of the good and just – it was he who asked: 'Whom do they hate most?'

The *creator* hate they most, him who breaketh the tables and old values, the breaker – him they call the law-breaker.

For the good – they *cannot* create; they are always the beginning of the end –

They crucify him who writeth new values on new tables, they sacrifice *unto themselves* the future – they crucify the whole human future!

The good – they have always been the beginning of the end.

27

O my brethren, have ye also understood this word? And what I once said of the 'last man'?

With whom lieth the greatest danger to the whole human future? Is it not with the good and just?

Break up, break up, I pray you, the good and just! – O my brethren, have ye understood also this word?

28

Ye flee from me? Ye are frightened? Ye tremble at this word?

O my brethren, when I enjoined on you to break up the good, and the tables of the good, then only did I embark man on his high seas.

And now only cometh unto him the great terror, the great outlook, the great sickness, the great nausea, the great sea-sickness.

False shores and false securities did the good teach you; in the lies of the good were ye born and bred. Everything hath been radically contorted and distorted by the good.

But he who discovered the country of 'man', discovered also the country of 'man's future'. Now shall ye be sailors for me, brave, patient!

Keep yourselves up betimes, my brethren, learn to keep yourselves up! The sea stormeth; many seek to raise themselves again by you.

The sea stormeth; all is in the sea. Well! Cheer up, ye old seaman-hearts!

What of fatherland! *Thither* striveth our helm where our *children's land* is! Thitherwards, stormier than the sea, stormeth our great longing!

29

'Why so hard!' – said to the diamond one day the charcoal; 'are we then not near relatives?'

Why so soft, O my brethren? Thus do I ask you: are ye then not – my brethren?

Why so soft, so submissive and yielding? Why is there so much negation and abnegation in your hearts? Why is there so little fate in your looks?

And if ye will not be fates and inexorable ones, how can ye one day – conquer with me?

And if your hardness will not glance and cut and chip to pieces, how can ye one day – create with me?

For the creators are hard. And blessedness must it seem to you to press your hand upon millenniums as upon wax –

Blessedness to write upon the will of millenniums as upon brass – harder than brass, nobler than brass. Entirely hard is only the noblest.

This new table, O my brethren, put I up over you: *Become hard!*

30

O thou, my Will! Thou change of every need, my needfulness! Preserve me from all small victories!

Thou fatedness of my soul, which I call fate! Thou In-me! Over-me! Preserve and spare me for one great fate!

And thy last greatness, my Will, spare it for thy last – that thou mayest be inexorable in thy victory! Ah, who hath not succumbed to his victory!

Ah, whose eye hath not bedimmed in this intoxicated twilight! Ah, whose foot hath not faltered and forgotten in victory – how to stand!

That I may one day be ready and ripe in the great noontide; ready and ripe like the glowing ore, the lightning-bearing cloud, and the swelling milk-udder –

Ready for myself and for my most hidden Will: a bow eager for its arrow, an arrow eager for its star –

A star, ready and ripe in its noontide, glowing, pierced, blessed, by annihilating sun-arrows –

A sun itself, and an inexorable sun-will, ready for annihilation in victory!

O Will, thou change of every need, my needfulness! Spare me for one great victory!

Thus spake Zarathustra.

57 *The Convalescent*

1

One morning, not long after his return to his cave, Zarathustra sprang up from his couch like a madman, crying with a frightful voice, and acting as if some one still lay on the couch who did not wish to rise. Zarathustra's voice also resounded in such a manner that his animals came to him frightened, and out of all the neighbouring caves and lurking-places all the creatures slipped away – flying, fluttering, creeping or leaping, according to their variety of foot or wing. Zarathustra, however, spake these words:

Up, abysmal thought out of my depth! I am thy cock and morning dawn, thou overslept reptile. Up! Up! My voice shall soon crow thee awake!

Unbind the fetters of thine ears: listen! For I wish to hear thee! Up! Up! There is thunder enough to make the very graves listen!

And rub the sleep and all the dimness and blindness out of thine eyes! Hear me also with thine eyes; my voice is a medicine even for those born blind.

And once thou art awake, then shalt thou ever remain awake. It is not my custom to awake great-grandmothers out of their sleep that I may bid them – sleep on!

Thou stirrest, stretchest thyself, wheezest? Up! Up! Not wheeze, shalt thou – but speak unto me! Zarathustra calleth thee! Zarathustra the godless!

I, Zarathustra, the advocate of living, the advocate of suffering, the advocate of the circuit – thee do I call, my most abysmal thought!

Joy to me! Thou comest – I hear thee! Mine abyss *speaketh*, my lowest depth have I turned over into the light!

Joy to me! Come hither! Give me thy hand – ha! let be! aha! – Disgust, disgust, disgust – alas to me!

2

Hardly, however, had Zarathustra spoken these words when he fell down as one dead, and remained long as one dead. When however he again came to himself, then was he pale and trembling, and remained lying; and for long he would neither eat nor drink. This condition continued for seven days; his animals, however, did not leave him day nor night, except that the eagle flew forth to fetch food. And what it fetched and foraged, it laid on Zarathustra's touch; so that Zarathustra at last lay among yellow and red berries, grapes, rosy apples, sweet-smelling herbage, and pine-cones. At his feet, however, two lambs were stretched, which the eagle had with difficulty carried off from their shepherds.

At last, after seven days, Zarathustra raised himself upon his couch, took a rosy apple in his hand, smelt it and found its smell pleasant. Then did his animals think the time had come to speak unto him.

O Zarathustra, said they, now hast thou lain thus for seven days with heavy eyes: wilt thou not set thyself again upon thy feet?

Step out of thy cave: the world waiteth for thee as a garden. The wind playeth with heavy fragrance which seeketh for thee; and all brooks would like to run after thee.

All things long for thee, since thou hast remained alone for seven days – step forth out of thy cave! All things want to be thy physicians!

Did perhaps a new knowledge come to thee, a bitter, grievous knowledge? Like leavened dough layest thou; thy soul arose and swelled beyond all its bounds.

O mine animals, answered Zarathustra, talk on thus and let me listen! It refresheth me so to hear your talk; where there is talk, there is the world as a garden unto me.

How charming it is that there are words and tones; are not words and tones rainbows and seeming bridges 'twixt the eternally separated?

To each soul belongeth another world; to each soul is every other soul a back-world.

Among the most alike doth semblance deceive most delightfully;

for the smallest gap is most difficult to bridge over.

For me – how could there be an outside-of-me? There is no outside! But this we forget on hearing tones; how delightful it is that we forget!

Have not names and tones been given unto things that man may refresh himself with them? It is a beautiful folly, speaking; therewith danceth man over everything.

How lovely is all speech and all falsehoods of tones! With tones danceth our love on variegated rainbows.

O Zarathustra, said then his animals, to those who think like us, things all dance themselves: they come and hold out the hand and laugh and flee – and return.

Everything goeth, everything returneth; eternally rolleth the wheel of existence. Everything dieth, everything blossometh forth again; eternally runneth on the year of existence.

Everything breaketh, everything is integrated anew; eternally buildeth itself the same house of existence. All things separate, all things again greet one another; eternally true to itself remaineth the ring of existence.

Every moment beginneth existence, around every 'Here' rolleth the ball 'There'. The middle is everywhere. Crooked is the path of eternity.'

O ye wags and barrel-organs, answered Zarathustra, and smiled once more. How well do ye know what had to be fulfilled in seven days –

And how that monster crept into my throat and choked me! But I bit off its head and spat it away from me.

And ye – ye have made a lyre-lay out of it? Now, however, do I lie here, still exhausted with that biting and spitting-away, still sick with mine own salvation.

And ye looked on at it all? O mine animals, are ye also cruel? Did ye like to look at my great pain as men do? For man is the cruellest animal.

At tragedies, bull-fights and crucifixions hath he hitherto been happiest on earth; and when he invented his hell, behold, that was his heaven on earth.

When the great man crieth – immediately runneth the little man thither, and his tongue hangeth out of his mouth for very lusting. He, however, calleth it his 'pity'.

The little man, especially the poet – how passionately doth he accuse life in words! Hearken to him, but do not fail to hear the delight which is in all accusation!

Such accusers of life – them life overcometh with a glance of the eye. 'Thou lovest me?' saith the insolent one. 'Wait a little, as yet have I no time for thee.'

Towards himself man is the cruellest animal; and in all who call themselves 'sinners' and 'bearers of the cross' and 'penitents', do not overlook the voluptuousness in their plaints and accusations!

And I myself – do I thereby want to be man's accuser? Ah, mine animals, this only have I learned hitherto, that for man his baddest is necessary for his best –

That all that is baddest is the best *power*, and the hardest stone for the highest creator; and that man must become better *and* badder –

Not to *this* torture-stake was I tied, that I know man is bad – but I cried, as no one hath yet cried:

'Ah, that his baddest is so very small! Ah, that his best is so very small!'

The great disgust at man – it strangled me and had crept into my throat; and what the soothsayer had presaged: 'All is alike, nothing is worth while, knowledge strangleth.'

A long twilight limped on before me, a fatally weary, fatally intoxicated sadness, which spake with yawning mouth.

'Eternally he returneth, the man of whom thou art weary, the small man' – so yawned my sadness, and dragged its foot and could not go to sleep.

A cavern became the human earth to me; its breast caved in, everything living became to me human dust and bones and mouldering past.

My sighing sat on all human graves, and could no longer arise; my sighing and questioning croaked and choked, and gnawed and nagged day and night:

'Ah, man returneth eternally! The small man returneth eternally!'

Naked had I once seen both of them, the greatest man and the smallest man: all too like one another – all too human, even the greatest man!

All too small, even the greatest man – that was my disgust at man! And the eternal return also of the smallest man – that was my disgust at all existence!

Ah! Disgust! Disgust! Disgust! Thus spake Zarathustra, and sighed and shuddered; for he remembered his sickness. Then did his animals prevent him from speaking further.

Do not speak further, thou convalescent! So answered his animals. But go out where the world waiteth for thee like a garden.

Go out unto the roses, the bees and the flocks of doves! Especially, however, unto the singing-birds, to learn *singing* from them!

For singing is for the convalescent; the sound ones may talk. And when the sound also want songs, then want they other songs than the convalescent.

O ye wags and barrel-organs, do be silent, answered Zarathustra, and smiled at his animals. How well ye know what consolation I devised for myself in seven days!

That I have to sing once more – *that* consolation did I devise for myself, and *this* convalescence; would ye also make another lyre-lay thereof?

Do not talk further, answered his animals once more. Rather, thou convalescent, prepare for thyself first a lyre, a new lyre!

For behold, O Zarathustra! For thy new lays there are needed new lyres.

Sing and bubble over, O Zarathustra, heal thy soul with new lays; that thou mayest bear thy great fate, which hath not yet been any one's fate!

For thine animals know it well, O Zarathustra, who thou art and must become: behold, *thou art the teacher of the eternal return* – that is now *thy* fate.

That thou must be the first to teach this teaching – how could this great fate not be thy greatest danger and infirmity!

Behold, we know what thou teachest: that all things eternally return, and ourselves with them, and that we have already existed times without number, and all things with us.

Thou teachest that there is a great year of Becoming, a prodigy of a great year; it must, like a sand-glass, ever turn up anew, that it may anew run down and run out –

So that all those years are like one another in the greatest and also in the smallest, so that we ourselves, in every great year, are like ourselves in the greatest and also in the smallest.

And if thou wouldst now die, O Zarathustra, behold, we know

also how thou wouldst then speak to thyself – but thine animals beseech thee not to die yet!

Thou wouldst speak, and without trembling, buoyant rather with bliss, for a great weight and worry would be taken from thee, thou patientest one!

'Now do I die and disappear,' wouldst thou say, 'and in a moment I am nothing. Souls are as mortal as bodies.

But the plexus of causes returneth in which I am intertwined – it will again create me! I myself pertain to the causes of the eternal return.

I come again with this sun, with this earth, with this eagle, with this serpent – *not* to a new life, or a better life, or a similar life:

I come again eternally to this identical and selfsame life, in its greatest and its smallest, to teach again the eternal return of all things –

To speak again the word of the great noontide of earth and man, to announce again to man the Superman.

I have spoken my word. I break down by my word: so willeth mine eternal fate – as announcer do I succumb!

The hour hath now come for the down-goer to bless himself. Thus – *endeth* Zarathustra's down-going.'

When the animals had spoken these words they were silent and waited, so that Zarathustra might say something to them; but Zarathustra did not hear that they were silent. On the contrary, he lay quietly with closed eyes like a person sleeping, although he did not sleep; for he communed just then with his soul. The serpent, however, and the eagle, when they found him silent in such wise, respected the great stillness around him, and prudently retired.

58 The Great Longing

O my soul, I have taught thee to say 'today' as 'once on a time' and 'formerly', and to dance thy measure over every Here and There and Yonder.

O my soul, I delivered thee from all by-places, I brushed down from thee dust and spiders and twilight.

O my soul, I washed the petty shame and the by-place virtue from thee, and persuaded thee to stand naked before the eyes of the sun.

With the storm that is called 'spirit' did I blow over thy surging sea; all clouds did I blow away from it; I strangled even the strangler called 'sin'.

O my soul, I gave thee the right to say Nay like the storm, and to say Yea as the open heaven saith Yea; calm as the light remainest thou, and now walkest through denying storms.

O my soul, I restored to thee liberty over the created and the uncreated; and who knoweth, as thou knowest, the voluptuousness of the future?

O my soul, I taught thee the contempt which doth not come like worm-eating; the great, the loving contempt, which loveth most where it contemneth most.

O my soul, I taught thee so to persuade that thou persuadest even the grounds themselves to thee; like the sun, which persuadeth even the sea to its height.

O my soul, I have taken from thee all obeying and knee-bending and homage-paying; I have myself given thee the names, 'Change of need' and 'Fate'.

O my soul, I have given thee new names and gay-coloured playthings, I have called thee 'Fate' and 'the Circuit of circuits' and 'the Navel-string of time' and 'the Azure bell'.

O my soul, to thy domain gave I all wisdom to drink, all new wines, and also all immemorially old strong wines of wisdom.

O my soul, every sun shed I upon thee, and every night and every silence and every longing – then grewest thou up for me as a vine.

O my soul, exuberant and heavy dost thou now stand forth, a vine with swelling udders and full clusters of brown golden grapes –

Filled and weighted by thy happiness, waiting from superabundance, and yet ashamed of thy waiting.

O my soul, there is nowhere a soul which could be more loving and more comprehensive and more extensive! Where could future and past be closer together than with thee?

O my soul, I have given thee everything, and all my hands have become empty by thee – and now! Now sayest thou to me, smiling and full of melancholy: 'Which of us oweth thanks?

Doth the giver not owe thanks because the receiver received? Is bestowing not a necessity? Is receiving not – pitying?'

O my soul, I understand the smiling of thy melancholy; thine over-abundance itself now stretcheth out longing hands!

Thy fulness looketh forth over raging seas, and seeketh and waiteth; the longing of over-fulness looketh forth from the smiling heaven of thine eyes!

And verily, O my soul! Who could see thy smiling and not melt into tears? The angels themselves melt into tears through the over-graciousness of thy smiling.

Thy graciousness and over-graciousness is it which will not complain and weep; and yet, O my soul, longeth thy smiling for tears, and thy trembling mouth for sobs.

'Is not all weeping complaining? And all complaining accusing?' Thus speakest thou to thyself; and therefore, O my soul, wilt thou rather smile than pour forth thy grief –

Than in gushing tears pour forth all thy grief concerning thy fulness, and concerning the craving of the vine for the vintager and vintage-knife!

But wilt thou not weep, wilt thou not weep forth thy purple melancholy, then wilt thou have to *sing*, O my soul! Behold, I smile myself, who foretell thee this:

Thou wilt have to sing with passionate song, until all seas turn calm to hearken unto thy longing –

Until over calm longing seas the bark glideth, the golden marvel, around the gold of which all good, bad and marvellous things frisk –

Also many large and small animals, and everything that hath light marvellous feet, so that it can run on violet-blue paths –

Towards the golden marvel, the spontaneous bark, and its master: he however, is the vintager who waiteth with the diamond vintage-knife –

Thy great deliverer, O my soul, the nameless one – for whom future songs only will find names! And verily, already hath thy breath the fragrance of future songs –

Already glowest thou and dreamest, already drinkest thou thirstily at all deep echoing wells of consolation, already reposeth thy melancholy in the bliss *of* future songs!

O my soul, now have I given thee all, and even my last possession, and all my hands have become empty by thee: *that I bade thee sing*, behold, that was my last thing to give!

That I bade thee sing; say now, say: *which of us* now – oweth thanks? Better still, however: sing unto me, sing, O my soul! And let me thank thee!

Thus spake Zarathustra.

59 The Second Dance-song

1

Into thine eyes gazed I lately, O Life: gold saw I gleam in thy night-eyes, my heart stood still with delight –

A golden bark saw I gleam on darkened waters, a sinking, drinking, reblinking, golden swing-bark!

At my dance-frantic foot dost thou cast a glance, a laughing, questioning, melting, thrown glance:

Twice only movedst thou thy rattle with thy little hand; then did my feet swing with dance-fury –

My heels reared aloft, my toes they hearkened – thee they would know: hath not the dancer his ear – in his toe!

Unto thee did I spring; then fledst thou back from my bound, and towards me waved thy fleeing, flying tresses round!

Away from thee did I spring, and from thy snaky tresses; then stoodst thou there half-turned, and in thine eye caresses.

With crooked glances – dost thou teach me crooked courses; on crooked courses learn my feet crafty fancies!

I fear thee near, I love thee far; thy flight allureth me, thy seeking secureth me – I suffer, but for thee what would I not gladly bear!

For thee, whose coldness inflameth, whose hatred misleadeth, whose flight enchaineth, whose mockery – pleadeth.

Who would not hate thee, thou great bindress, inwindress, temptress, seekress, findress! Who would not love thee, thou innocent, impatient, wind-swift, child-eyed sinner!

Whither pullest thou me now, thou paragon and tomboy? And now foolest thou me fleeing; thou sweet romp dost annoy!

I dance after thee, I follow even faint traces lonely. Where art thou? Give me thy hand! Or thy finger only!

Here are caves and thickets: we shall go astray! Halt! Stand still! Seest thou not owls and bats in fluttering fray?

Thou bat! Thou owl! Thou wouldst play me foul? Where are we? From the dogs hast thou learned thus to bark and howl.

Thou gnashest on me sweetly with little white teeth; thine evil eyes shoot out upon me, thy curly little mane from underneath!

This is a dance over stock and stone: I am the hunter – wilt thou be my hound, or my chamois anon?

Now beside me! And quickly, wickedly springing! Now up! And over! Alas! I have fallen myself overswinging!

Oh, see me lying, thou arrogant one, and imploring grace. Gladly would I walk with thee – in some lovelier place!

– In the paths of love, through bushes variegated, quiet, trim! Or there along the lake, where gold-fishes dance and swim!

Thou art now a-weary? There above are sheep and sunset stripes; is it not sweet to sleep – the shepherd pipes?

Thou art so very weary? I carry thee thither; let just thine arm sink! And art thou thirsty – I should have something, but thy mouth would not like it to drink!

Oh, that cursed, nimble, supple serpent and lurking-witch! Where art thou gone? But in my face do I feel through thy hand, two spots and red blotches itch!

I am verily weary of it, ever thy sheepish shepherd to be. Thou witch, if I have hitherto sung unto thee, now shalt *thou* – cry unto me!

To the rhythm of my whip shalt thou dance and cry! I forget not my whip? Not I!

2

Then did Life answer me thus, and kept thereby her fine ears closed:

O Zarathustra! Crack not so terribly with thy whip! Thou knowest surely that noise killeth thought – and just now there came to me such delicate thoughts.

We are both of us genuine ne'er-do-wells and ne'er-do-ills. Beyond good and evil found we our island and our green meadow – we two alone! Therefore must we be friendly to each other!

And even should we not love each other from the bottom of our hearts – must we then have a grudge against each other if we do not love each other perfectly?

And that I am friendly to thee, and often too friendly, that knowest thou: and the reason is that I am envious of thy Wisdom. Ah, this mad old fool, Wisdom!

If thy Wisdom should one day run away from thee – ah, then would also my love run away from thee quickly.

Thereupon did Life look thoughtfully behind and around and said softly: O Zarathustra, thou are not faithful enough to me!

Thou lovest me not nearly so much as thou sayest; I know thou thinkest of soon leaving me.

There is an old heavy, heavy booming-clock: it boometh by night up to thy cave –

When thou hearest this clock strike the hours at midnight, then thinkest thou between one and twelve thereon –

Thou thinkest thereon, O Zarathustra, I know it – of soon leaving me!

Yea, answered I, hesitatingly, but thou knowest it also – And I said something into her ear, in amongst her confused, yellow, foolish tresses.

Thou *knowest* that, O Zarathustra? That knoweth no one –

And we gazed at each other, and looked at the green meadow o'er which the cool evening was just passing, and we wept together. Then, however, was Life dearer unto me than all my Wisdom had ever been.

Thus spake Zarathustra.

3

One!
O man! Take heed!

Two!
What saith deep midnight's voice indeed?

Three!
'I slept my sleep –

Four!
'From deepest dream I've woke and plead –

Five!
'The world is deep,

Six!
'And deeper than the day could read.

Seven!
'Deep is its woe –

Eight!
'Joy – deeper still than grief can be:

Nine!
'Woe saith: Hence! Go!

Ten!
'But joys all want eternity –

Eleven!
'Want deep profound eternity!'

Twelve!

60 *The Seven Seals*

(*Or the Yea and Amen Lay*)

1

If I be a diviner and full of the divining spirit which wandereth on high mountain-ridges, 'twixt two seas –

Wandereth 'twixt the past and the future as a heavy cloud – hostile to sultry plains, and to all that is weary and can neither die nor live:

Ready for lightning in its dark bosom, and for the redeeming flash of light, charged with lightnings which say Yea, which laugh Yea, ready for divining flashes of lightning –

Blessed, however, is he who is thus charged! And verily, long must he hang like a heavy tempest on the mountain, who shall one day kindle the light of the future!

Oh, how could I not be ardent for Eternity and for the marriage-ring of rings – the ring of the return?

Never yet have I found the woman by whom I should like to have children, unless it be this woman whom I love; for I love thee, O Eternity!

For I love thee, O Eternity!

2

If ever my wrath hath burst graves, shifted landmarks, or rolled old shattered tables into precipitous depths –

If ever my scorn hath scattered mouldered words to the winds, and if I have come like a besom to cross-spiders, and as a cleansing wind to old charnel-houses –

If ever I have sat rejoicing where old Gods lie buried, world-blessing, world-loving, beside the monuments of old world-maligners –

For even churches and Gods'-graves do I love, if only heaven looketh through their ruined roofs with pure eyes; gladly do I sit like grass and red poppies on ruined churches –

Oh, how could I not be ardent for Eternity, and for the marriage-ring of rings – the ring of the return?

Never yet have I found the woman by whom I should like to have children, unless it be this woman whom I love; for I love thee, O Eternity!

For I love thee, O Eternity!

3

If ever a breath hath come to me of the creative breath, and of the heavenly necessity which compelleth even chances to dance star-dances –

If ever I have laughed with the laughter of the creative lightning, to which the long thunder of the deed followeth, grumblingly but obediently –

If ever I have played dice with the Gods at the divine table of the earth, so that the earth quaked and ruptured, and snorted forth fire-streams –

For a divine table is the earth, and trembling with new creative dictums and dice-casts of the Gods –

Oh, how could I not be ardent for Eternity, and for the marriage-ring of rings – the ring of the return?

Never yet have I found the woman by whom I should like to have children, unless it be this woman whom I love; for I love thee, O Eternity!

For I love thee, O Eternity!

4

If ever I have drunk a full draught of the foaming spice and confection-bowl in which all things are well mixed –

If ever my hand hath mingled the furthest with the nearest, fire with spirit, joy with sorrow, and the harshest with the kindest –

If I myself am a grain of the saving salt which maketh everything in the confection-bowl mix well –

For there is a salt which uniteth good with evil; and even the most evil is worthy, as spicing and as final overfoaming –

Oh, how could I not be ardent for Eternity, and for the marriage-ring of rings – the ring of the return?

Never yet have I found the woman by whom I should like to have children, unless it be this woman whom I love; for I love thee, O Eternity!

For I love thee, O Eternity!

5

If I be fond of the sea, and all that is sealike, and fondest of it when it angrily contradicteth me –

If the exploring delight be in me, which impelleth sails to the undiscovered, if the seafarer's delight be in my delight –

If ever my rejoicing hath called out: 'The shore hath vanished, now hath fallen from me the last chain –

The boundless roareth around me, far away sparkle for me space and time; well! Cheer up, old heart!' –

Oh, how could I not be ardent for Eternity, and for the marriage-ring of rings – the ring of the returns?

Never yet have I found the woman by whom I should like to have children, unless it be this woman whom I love; for I love thee, O Eternity!

For I love thee, O Eternity!

6

If my virtue be a dancer's virtue, and if I have often sprung with both feet into golden-emerald rapture –

If my wickedness be a laughing wickedness, at home among rose-banks and hedges of lilies –

For in laughter is all evil present, but it is sanctified and absolved by its own bliss –

And if it be my Alpha and Omega that everything heavy shall become light, every body a dancer, and every spirit a bird; and verily, that is my Alpha and Omega –

Oh, how could I not be ardent for Eternity, and for the marriage-ring of rings – the ring of the return?

Never yet have I found the woman by whom I should like to have children, unless it be this woman whom I love; for I love thee, O Eternity!

For I love thee, O Eternity!

7

If ever I have spread out a tranquil heaven above me, and have flown into mine own heaven with mine own pinions –

If I have swum playfully in profound luminous distances, and if my freedom's avian wisdom hath come to me –

Thus however speaketh avian wisdom: 'Lo, there is no above and no below! Throw thyself about – outward, backward, thou light one! Sing! speak no more!

Are not all words made for the heavy? Do not all words lie to the light ones? Sing! speak no more!'

Oh, how could I not be ardent for Eternity, and for the marriage-ring of rings – the ring of the return?

Never yet have I found the woman by whom I should like to have children, unless it be this woman whom I love; for I love thee, O Eternity!

For I love thee, O Eternity!

THUS SPAKE ZARATHUSTRA

FOURTH AND LAST PART

Ah, where in the world have there been greater follies than with the pitiful? And what in the world hath caused more suffering than the follies of the pitiful?

Woe unto all loving ones who have not an elevation which is above their pity!

Thus spake the devil unto me, once on a time: 'Even God hath his hell: it is his love for man.'

And lately, did I hear him say these words: 'God is dead: of his pity for man hath God died.'

ZARATHUSTRA II, *25 The Pitiful*

61 *The Honey Sacrifice*

And again passed moons and years over Zarathustra's soul, and he heeded it not; his hair, however, became white. One day when he sat on a stone in front of his cave, and gazed calmly into the distance – one there gazeth out on the sea, and away beyond sinuous abysses – then went his animals thoughtfully round about him, and at last set themselves in front of him.

O Zarathustra, said they, gazest thou out perhaps for thy happiness? Of what account is my happiness! answered he, I have long ceased to strive any more for happiness, I strive for my work. O Zarathustra, said the animals once more, that sayest thou as one who hath overmuch of good things. Liest thou not in a sky-blue lake of happiness? Ye wags, answered Zarathustra, and smiled. How well did ye choose the simile! But ye know also that my happiness is heavy, and not like a fluid wave of water; it presseth me and will not leave me, and is like molten pitch.

Then went his animals again thoughtfully around him, and placed themselves once more in front of him. O Zarathustra, said they, it is consequently *for that reason* that thou thyself always becometh yellower and darker, although thy hair looketh white and flaxen? Lo, thou sittest in thy pitch! What do ye say, mine animals? said Zarathustra, laughing. Verily I reviled when I spake of pitch. As it happeneth with me, so is it with all fruits that turn ripe. It is the *honey* in my veins that maketh my blood thicker, and also my soul stiller. So will it be, O Zarathustra, answered his animals, and pressed up to him; but wilt thou not today ascend a high mountain? The air is pure, and today one seeth more of the world than ever. Yea, mine animals, answered he, ye counsel admirably and according to my heart: I will today ascend a high mountain! But see that honey is there ready to hand: yellow, white, good, ice-cool, golden-comb-honey. For know that when aloft I will make the honey sacrifice.

When Zarathustra, however, was aloft on the summit, he sent his animals home that had accompanied him, and found that he was now alone; then he laughed from the bottom of his heart, looked around him, and spake thus:

That I spake of sacrifices and honey sacrifices, it was merely a ruse in talking and verily, a useful folly! Here aloft can I now speak freer than in front of mountain-caves and anchorites' domestic animals.

What to sacrifice! I squander what is given me, a squanderer with a thousand hands: how could I call that sacrificing!

And when I desired honey I only desired bait, and sweet mucus and mucilage, for which even the mouths of growling bears, and strange, sulky, evil birds, water –

The best bait, as huntsmen and fishermen require it. For if the world be as a gloomy forest of animals, and a pleasure-ground for all wild huntsmen, it seemeth to me rather – and preferably – a fathomless, rich sea –

A sea full of many-hued fishes and crabs, for which even the Gods might long, and might be tempted to become fishers in it, and casters of nets – so rich is the world in wonderful things, great and small!

Especially the human world, the human sea – towards it do I now throw out my golden angle-rod and say: Open up, thou human abyss!

Open up, and throw unto me thy fish and shining crabs! With my best bait shall I allure to myself today the strangest human fish!

My happiness itself do I throw out into all places far and wide 'twixt orient, noontide and occident, to see if many human fish will not learn to hug and tug at my happiness –

Until, biting at my sharp hidden hooks, they have to come up unto my height, the motleyest abyss-groundlings, to the wickedest of all fishers of men.

For *this* am I from the heart and from the beginning – drawing, hither-drawing, upward-drawing, upbringing; a drawer, a trainer, a training-master, who not in vain counselled himself once on a time: 'Become what thou art!'

Thus may men now come up to me, for as yet do I await the signs that it is time for my down-going; as yet do I not myself go down, as I must do, amongst men.

Therefore do I here wait, crafty and scornful upon high mountains, no impatient one, no patient one; rather one who hath even unlearnt patience – because he no longer 'suffereth'.

For my fate giveth me time; it hath forgotten me perhaps? Or doth it sit behind a big stone and catch flies?

And verily, I am well-disposed to mine eternal fate, because it doth not hound and hurry me, but leaveth me time for merriment and mischief; so that I have today ascended this high mountain to catch fish.

Did ever any one catch fish upon high mountains? And though it be a folly what I here seek and do, it is better so than that down below I should become solemn with waiting, and green and yellow –

A posturing wrath-snorter with waiting, a holy howl-storm from the mountains, an impatient one that shouteth down into the valleys: 'Hearken, else I will scourge you with the scourge of God!'

Not that I would have a grudge against such wrathful ones on that account: they are well enough for laughter to me! Impatient must they now be, those big alarm-drums, which find a voice now or never!

Myself, however, and my fate – we do not talk to the Present, neither do we talk to the Never; for talking we have patience and time and more than time. For one day must it yet come, and may not pass by.

What must one day come and may not pass by? Our great Hazar: that is to say, our great, remote human-kingdom, the Zarathustra-kingdom of a thousand years –

How remote may such 'remoteness' be? What doth it concern me? But on that account it is none the less sure unto me; with both feet stand I secure on this ground –

On an eternal ground, on hard primary rock, on this highest, hardest, primary mountain-ridge unto which all winds come, as unto the storm-parting, asking 'Where?' and 'Whence?' and 'Whither?'

Here laugh, laugh, my hearty, healthy wickedness! From high mountains cast down thy glittering scorn-laughter! Allure for me with thy glittering the finest human fish!

And whatever belongeth unto *me* in all seas, my in-and-for-me in all things – fish *that* out for me, bring *that* up to me: for that do I wait, the wickedest of all fish-catchers.

Out, out, my fishing-hook! In and down, thou bait of my happiness! Drip thy sweetest dew, thou honey of my heart! Bite, my fishing-hook, into the belly of all black affliction!

Look out, look out, mine eye! Oh, how many seas round about me, what dawning human futures! And above me – what rosy red stillness! What unclouded silence!

62 The Cry of Distress

The next day sat Zarathustra again on the stone in front of his cave, whilst his animals roved about in the world outside to bring home new food – also new honey; for Zarathustra had spent and wasted the old honey to the very last particle. When he thus sat, however, with a stick in his hand, tracing the shadow of his figure on the earth and reflecting – verily, not upon himself and his shadow – all at once he started and shrank back; for he saw another shadow beside his own. And when he hastily looked around and stood up, behold, there stood the soothsayer beside him, the same whom he had once given to eat and drink at his table, the proclaimer of the great weariness, who taught: 'All is alike, nothing is worthwhile, the world is without meaning, knowledge strangleth.' But his face had changed since then; and when Zarathustra looked into his eyes, his heart was startled once more: so much evil announcement and ashy-grey lightnings passed over that countenance.

The soothsayer, who had perceived what went on in Zarathustra's soul, wiped his face with his hand as if he would wipe out the impression; the same did also Zarathustra. And when both of them had thus silently composed and strengthened themselves, they gave each other the hand, as a token that they wanted once more to recognise each other.

Welcome hither, said Zarathustra, thou soothsayer of the great weariness, not in vain shalt thou once have been my messmate and guest. Eat and drink also with me today, and forgive it that a cheerful old man sitteth with thee at table! A cheerful old man? answered the soothsayer, shaking his head, but whoever thou art, or wouldst be, O Zarathustra, thou hast been here aloft the longest time – in a little while thy bark shall no longer rest on dry land! Do I then rest on dry land? asked Zarathustra laughing. The waves around thy mountain, answered the soothsayer, rise and rise, the waves of great distress and affliction; they will soon raise thy bark also and carry thee away. Thereupon was Zarathustra silent and wondered. Dost thou still hear nothing? continued the soothsayer; doth it not rush and roar out of the depth? Zarathustra was silent once more and listened; then heard he a long, long cry, which the abysses threw to one another and passed on: for none of them wished to retain it, so evil did it sound.

Thou ill announcer, said Zarathustra at last, that is a cry of distress, and the cry of a man; it may come perhaps out of a black sea. But what doth human distress matter to me! My last sin which hath been reserved for me – knowest thou what it is called?

Pity! answered the soothsayer from an overflowing heart, and raised both his hands aloft – O Zarathustra, I have come that I may seduce thee to thy last sin!

And hardly had those words been uttered when there sounded the cry once more, and longer and more alarming than before – also much nearer. Hearest thou? Hearest thou, O Zarathustra? called out the soothsayer. The cry concerneth thee, it calleth thee: 'Come, come, come: it is time, it is the highest time!'

Zarathustra was silent thereupon, confused and staggered; at last he asked, like one who hesitateth in himself: And who is it that there calleth me?

But thou knowest it, certainly, answered the soothsayer warmly. Why dost thou conceal thyself? It is *the higher man* that crieth for thee!

The higher man? cried Zarathustra, horror-stricken. What wanteth *he*? What wanteth *he*? The higher man! What wanteth he here? And his skin covered with perspiration.

The soothsayer, however, did not heed Zarathustra's alarm, but listened and listened in the downward direction. When, however, it had been still there for a long while, he looked behind, and saw Zarathustra standing trembling.

O Zarathustra, he began, with sorrowful voice, thou dost not stand there like one whose happiness maketh him giddy; thou wilt have to dance lest thou tumble down!

But although thou shouldst dance before me, and leap all thy side-leaps, no one may say unto me: Behold, here danceth the last joyous man!

In vain would any one come to this height who sought him here; caves would he find, indeed, and back-caves, hiding-places for hidden ones, but not lucky mines, nor treasure-chambers, nor new gold-veins of happiness.

Happiness – how indeed could one find happiness among such

buried-alive and solitary ones! Must I yet seek the last happiness on the Happy Isles, and far away among forgotten seas?

But all is alike, nothing is worth while, no seeking is of service, there are no longer any Happy Isles!

Thus sighed the soothsayer; with his last sigh, however, Zarathustra again became serene and assured, like one who hath come out of a deep chasm into the light. Nay! Nay! Three times Nay! exclaimed he with a strong voice, and stroked his beard. That do I know better! There are still Happy Isles! Silence *thereon*, thou sighing sorrow-sack!

Cease to splash *thereon*, thou rain-cloud of the forenoon! Do I not already stand here wet with thy misery, and drenched like a dog?

Now do I shake myself and run away from thee, that I may again become dry: thereat mayest thou not wonder! Do I seem to thee discourteous? Here however is *my* court.

But as regards the higher man: well, I shall seek him at once in those forests: *from thence* came his cry. Perhaps he is there hard beset by an evil beast.

He is in *my* domain; therein shall he receive no scath! And verily, there are many evil beasts about me.

With those words Zarathustra turned around to depart. Then said the soothsayer: O Zarathustra, thou art a rogue!

I know it well: thou wouldst fain be rid of me! Rather wouldst thou run into the forest and lay snares for evil beasts!

But what good will it do thee? In the evening wilt thou have me again; in thine own cave will I sit, patient and heavy like a block – and wait for thee!

So be it! shouted back Zarathustra, as he went away. And what is mine in my cave belongeth also unto thee, my guest!

Shouldst thou however find honey therein – well, just lick it up, thou growling bear, and sweeten thy soul! For in the evening we want both to be in good spirits –

In good spirits and joyful, because this day hath come to an end! And thou thyself shalt dance to my lays, as my dancing-bear.

Thou dost not believe this? Thou shakest thy head? Well! Cheer up, old bear! But I also – am a soothsayer.

Thus spake Zarathustra.

63 *The Talk with Kings*

1

Ere Zarathustra had been an hour on his way in the mountains and forests, he saw all at once a strange procession. Right on the path which he was about to descend came two kings walking, bedecked with crowns and purple girdles, and variegated like flamingoes; they drove before them a laden ass. What do these kings want in my domain? said Zarathustra in astonishment to his heart, and hid himself hastily behind a thicket. When however the kings approached to him, he said half-aloud, like one speaking only to himself: Strange! Strange! How doth this harmonise? Two kings do I see – and only one ass!

Thereupon the two kings made a halt; they smiled and looked towards the spot whence the voice proceeded, and afterwards looked into each other's faces. Such things do we also think among ourselves, said the king on the right. But we do not utter them.

The king on the left, however, shrugged his shoulders and answered: That may perhaps be a goat-herd. Or an anchorite who hath lived too long among rocks and trees. For no society at all spoileth also good manners.

Good manners? replied angrily and bitterly the other king. What then do we run out of the way of? Is it not 'good manners'? Or 'good society'?

Better, verily, to live among anchorites and goat-herds, than with our gilded, false, over-rouged populace – though it call itself 'good society'.

Though it call itself 'nobility'. But there all is false and foul, above all the blood – thanks to old evil diseases and worse curers.

The best and dearest to me at present is still a sound peasant, coarse, artful, obstinate and enduring: that is at present the noblest type.

The peasant is at present the best; and the peasant type should be master! But it is the kingdom of the populace – I no longer allow anything to be imposed upon me. The populace, however – that meaneth, hodgepodge.

Populace-hodgepodge: therein is everything mixed with everything, saint and swindler, gentleman and Jew, and every beast out of Noah's ark.

Good manners! Everything is false and foul with us. No one knoweth any longer how to reverence: it is *that* precisely that we run away from. They are fulsome obtrusive dogs; they gild palm-leaves.

This loathing choketh me, that we kings ourselves have become false, draped and disguised with the old faded pomp of our ancestors, show-pieces for the stupidest, the craftiest, and whosoever at present trafficketh for power.

We *are not* the first men – and have nevertheless to *stand for* them: of this imposture have we at last become weary and disgusted.

From the rabble have we gone out of the way, from all those bawlers and scribe-blowflies, from the trader-stench, the ambition-fidgeting, the bad breath; fie, to live among the rabble –

Fie, to stand for the first men among the rabble! Ah, loathing! Loathing! Loathing! What doth it now matter about us kings!

Thine old sickness seizeth thee, said here the king on the left. Thy loathing seizeth thee, my poor brother. Thou knowest, however, that some one heareth us.

Immediately thereupon, Zarathustra, who had opened ears and eyes to this talk, rose from his hiding-place, advanced towards the kings, and thus began:

He who hearkeneth unto you, he who gladly hearkeneth unto you, is called Zarathustra.

I am Zarathustra who once said: 'What doth it now matter about kings!' Forgive me; I rejoiced when ye said to each other: 'What doth it matter about us kings!'

Here, however, is *my* domain and jurisdiction; what may ye be seeking in my domain? Perhaps, however, ye have *found* on your way what *I* seek: namely, the higher man.

When the kings heard this, they beat upon their breasts and said with one voice: We are recognised!

With the sword of thine utterance severest thou the thickest darkness of our hearts. Thou hast discovered our distress; for lo, we are on our way to find the higher man –

The man that is higher than we, although we are kings. To him do we convey this ass. For the highest man shall also be the highest lord on earth.

There is no sorer misfortune in all human destiny than when the mighty of the earth are not also the first men. Then everything becometh false and distorted and monstrous.

And when they are even the last men, and more beast than man, then riseth and riseth the populace in honour, and at last saith even the populace-virtue: 'Lo, I alone am virtue!'

What have I just heard? answered Zarathustra. What wisdom in kings! I am enchanted, and verily, I have already promptings to make a rhyme thereon –

Even if it should happen to be a rhyme not suited for every one's ears. I unlearned long ago to have consideration for long ears. Well then! Well now!

(Here, however, it happened that the ass also found utterance: it said distinctly and with malevolence, YE-A.)

'Twas once – methinks year one of our blessed Lord –
Drunk without wine, the Sybil thus deplored:
'How ill things go!
Decline! Decline! Ne'er sank the world so low!
Rome now hath turned harlot and harlot-stew,
Rome's Caesar a beast, and God – hath turned Jew!'

2

With those rhymes of Zarathustra the kings were delighted; the king on the right, however, said: O Zarathustra, how well it was that we set out to see thee!

For thine enemies showed us thy likeness in their mirror; there lookedst thou with the grimace of a devil, and sneeringly, so that we were afraid of thee.

But what good did it do! Always didst thou prick us anew in heart and ear with thy sayings. Then did we say at last: What doth it matter how he look!

We must *hear* him, him who teacheth: 'Ye shall love peace as a means to new wars, and the short peace more than the long!'

No one ever spake such warlike words: 'What is good? To be brave is good. It is the good war that halloweth every cause.'

O Zarathustra, our fathers' blood stirred in our veins at such words: it was like the voice of spring to old winecasks.

When the swords ran among one another like red-spotted serpents, then did our fathers become fond of life; the sun of every peace seemed to them languid and lukewarm; the long peace, however, made them ashamed.

How they sighed, our fathers, when they saw on the wall brightly furbished, dried-up swords! Like those they thirsted for war. For a sword thirsteth to drink blood, and sparkleth with desire.'

When the kings thus discoursed and talked eagerly of the happiness of their fathers, there came upon Zarathustra no little desire to mock at their eagerness; for evidently they were very peaceable kings whom he saw before him, kings with old and refined features. But he restrained himself. Well, said he, thither leadeth the way, there lieth the cave of Zarathustra; and this day is to have a long evening! At present, however, a cry of distress calleth me hastily away from you.

It will honour my cave if kings want to sit and wait in it; but, to be sure, ye will have to wait long!

Well, what of that! Where doth one at present learn better to wait than at courts? And the whole virtue of kings that hath remained unto them – is it not called today: *ability* to wait?'

Thus spake Zarathustra.

64 *The Leech*

And Zarathustra went thoughtfully on, further and lower down, through forests and past moory bottoms; as it happeneth, however, to every one who meditateth upon hard matters, he trod thereby unawares upon a man. And lo, there spurted into his face all at once a cry of pain, and two curses and twenty bad invectives, so that in his fright he raised his stick and also struck the trodden one. Immediately afterwards, however, he regained his composure, and his heart laughed at the folly he had just committed.

Pardon me, said he to the trodden one, who had got up enraged, and had seated himself. Pardon me, and hear first of all a parable.

As a wanderer who dreameth of remote things on a lonesome highway runneth unawares against a sleeping dog, a dog which lieth in the sun –

As both of them then start up and snap at each other like deadly enemies, those two beings mortally frightened – so did it happen unto us.

And yet! And yet – how little was lacking for them to caress each other, that dog and that lonesome one! Are they not both – lonesome ones!

Whoever thou art, said the trodden one, still enraged, thou treadest also too nigh me with thy parable, and not only with thy foot!

Lo! am I then a dog? And thereupon the sitting one got up, and pulled his naked arm out of the swamp. For at first he had lain outstretched on the ground, hidden and indiscernible, like those who lie in wait for swamp-game.

But whatever art thou about! called out Zarathustra in alarm, for he saw a deal of blood streaming over the naked arm. What hath hurt thee? Hath an evil beast bit thee, thou unfortunate one?

The bleeding one laughed, still angry. What matter is it to thee! said he, and was about to go on. Here am I at home and in my province. Let him question me whoever will; to a dolt, however, I shall hardly answer.

Thou art mistaken, said Zarathustra sympathetically, and held him fast. Thou art mistaken. Here thou art not at home, but in my domain, and therein shall no one receive any hurt.

Call me however what thou wilt – I am who I must be. I call myself Zarathustra.

Well! Up thither is the way to Zarathustra's cave: it is not far – wilt thou not attend to thy wounds at my home?

It hath gone badly with thee, thou unfortunate one, in this life; first a beast bit thee, and then – a man trod upon thee!

When however the trodden one had heard the name of Zarathustra he was transformed. What happeneth unto me! he exclaimed. *Who* preoccupieth me so much in this life as this one man, namely Zarathustra, and that one animal that liveth on blood, the leech?

For the sake of the leech did I lie here by this swamp, like a fisher, and already had mine outstretched arm been bitten ten times, when there biteth a still finer leech at my blood, Zarathustra himself!

O happiness! O miracle! Praised be this day which enticed me into the swamp! Praised be the best, the livest cupping-glass, that at present liveth; praised be the great conscience-leech Zarathustra!

Thus spake the trodden one; and Zarathustra rejoiced at his words and their refined reverential style. Who art thou? asked he, and gave him his hand. There is much to clear up and elucidate between us, but already methinketh pure clear day is dawning.

I am *the spiritually conscientious one*, answered he who was asked, and in matters of the spirit it is difficult for any one to take it more rigorously, more restrictedly, and more severely than I, except him from whom I learnt it, Zarathustra himself.

Better know nothing than half-know many things! Better be a fool on one's own account than a sage on other people's approbation! I – go to the basis:

What matter if it be great or small? If it be called swamp or sky? A handbreadth of basis is enough for me, if it be actually basis and ground –

A handbreadth of basis: thereon can one stand. In the true knowing-knowledge there is nothing great and nothing small.

Then thou art perhaps an expert on the leech? asked Zarathustra. And thou investigatest the leech to its ultimate basis, thou conscientious one?

O Zarathustra, answered the trodden one, that would be something immense; how could I presume to do so!

That, however, of which I am master and knower, is the *brain* of the leech: that is my world!

And it is also a world! Forgive it, however, that my pride here findeth expression, for here I have not mine equal. Therefore said I: 'here am I at home.'

How long have I investigated this one thing, the brain of the leech, so that here the slippery truth might no longer slip from me! Here is my domain!

For the sake of this did I cast everything else aside; for the sake of this did everything else become indifferent to me; and close beside my knowledge lieth my black ignorance.

My spiritual conscience requireth from me that it should be so – that I should know one thing, and not know all else; they are a loathing unto me, all the semi-spiritual, all the hazy, hovering and visionary.

Where mine honesty ceaseth, there am I blind, and want also to be blind. Where I want to know, however, there want I also to be honest – namely, severe, rigorous, restricted, cruel and inexorable.

Because *thou* once saidest, O Zarathustra: 'Spirit is life which itself cutteth into life' – that led and allured me to thy doctrine. And verily, with mine own blood have I increased mine own knowledge!

As the evidence indicateth, broke in Zarathustra; for still was the blood flowing down on the naked arm of the conscientious one. For there had ten leeches bitten into it.

O thou strange fellow, how much doth this very evidence teach me – namely, thou thyself! And not all, perhaps, might I pour into thy rigorous ear!

Well then! We part here! But I would fain find thee again. Up thither is the way to my cave; tonight shalt thou there be my welcome guest!

Fain would I also make amends to thy body for Zarathustra treading upon thee with his feet: I think about that. Just now, however, a cry of distress calleth me hastily away from thee.

Thus spake Zarathustra.

65 The Magician

1

When however Zarathustra had gone round a rock, then saw he on the same path, not far below him, a man who threw his limbs about like a maniac, and at last tumbled to the ground on his belly. Halt! said then Zarathustra to his heart. He there must surely be the higher man; from him came that dreadful cry of distress – I will see if I can help him. When, however, he ran to the spot where the man lay on the ground, he found a trembling old man with fixed eyes; and in spite of all Zarathustra's efforts to lift him and set him again on his feet, it was all in vain. The unfortunate one, also, did not seem to notice that some one was beside him; on the contrary, he continually looked around with moving gestures, like one forsaken and isolated from all the world. At last, however, after much trembling and convulsion, and curling-himself-up, he began to lament thus:

Who warm'th me, who lov'th me still?
Give ardent fingers!
Give heartening charcoal-warmers!
Prone, outstretched, trembling,
Like him, half dead and cold, whose feet one warm'th –
And shaken, ah! by unfamiliar fevers,
Shivering with sharpened, icy-cold frost-arrows,
By thee pursued, my fancy! Ineffable! Recondite! Sore-frightening!
Thou huntsman 'hind the cloud-banks!
Now lightning-struck by thee,
Thou mocking eye that me in darkness watcheth –
Thus do I lie,
Bend myself, twist myself, convulsed
With all eternal torture,
And smitten
By thee, cruellest huntsman,
Thou unfamiliar – *God* . . .

Smite deeper!
Smite yet once more!
Pierce through and rend my heart!
What mean'th this torture
With dull, indented arrows?
Why look'st thou hither,
Of human pain not weary,
With mischief-loving, godly flash-glances?
Not murder wilt thou,
But torture, torture?
For why – *me* torture,
Thou mischief-loving, unfamiliar God?

Ha! Ha!
Thou stealest nigh
In midnight's gloomy hour?
What wilt thou?
Speak!
Thou crowdst me, pressest –
Ha! now far too closely!
Thou hear'st me breathing,
Thou o'erhear'st my heart,
Thou ever jealous one –
Of what, pray, ever jealous?
Off! Off!
For why the ladder?
Wouldst thou *get in*?
To heart in-clamber?
To mine own secretest
Conceptions in-clamber?
Shameless one! Thou unknown one! Thief!
What seekst thou by thy stealing?
What seekst thou by thy hearkening?
What seekst thou by thy torturing?
Thou torturer! Thou – hangman-God!
Or shall I, as the mastiffs do,
Roll me before thee?
And cringing, enraptured, frantical,
My tail friendly – waggle!

In vain!
Goad further!
Cruellest goader!
No dog – thy game just am I,
Cruellest huntsman!
Thy proudest of captives,
Thou robber 'hind the cloud-banks . . .
Speak finally!
Thou lightning-veiled one! Thou unknown one!
Speak.
What wilt thou, highway-ambusher. From – *me*?
What *wilt* thou, unfamiliar – God?
What?
Ransom-gold?
How much of ransom-gold?

Solicit much – that bid'th my pride!
And be concise – that bid'th mine other pride!

Ha! Ha!
Me – want'st thou? Me?
Entire? . . .

Ha! Ha!
And torturest me, fool that thou art,
Dead-torturest quite my pride?
Give *love* to me – who warm'th me still?
Who lov'th me still?
Give ardent fingers
Give heartening charcoal-warmers,
Give me, the lonesomest,
The ice (ah! seven-fold frozen ice
For very enemies,
For foes, doth make one thirst)
Give, yield to me,
Cruellest foe –
Thyself!

Away!
There fled he surely,
My final, only comrade.
My greatest foe,
Mine unfamiliar –
My hangman-God! . . .

Nay!
Come thou back!
With all of thy great tortures!
To me the last of lonesome ones,
Oh, come thou back!
All my hot tears in streamlets trickle
Their course to thee!
And all my final hearty fervour –
Up-glow'th to *thee*!
Oh, come thou back,
Mine unfamiliar God! My *pain*!
My final bliss!

2

Here, however, Zarathustra could no longer restrain himself; he took his staff and struck the wailer with all his might. Stop this, cried he to him with wrathful laughter. Stop this, thou stage-player! Thou false coiner! Thou liar from the very heart! I know thee well!

I will soon make warm legs to thee, thou evil magician: I know well how – to make it hot for such as thou!

Leave off, said the old man, and sprang up from the ground. Strike me no more, O Zarathustra! I did it only for amusement!

That kind of thing belongeth to mine art. Thee thyself I wanted to put to the proof when I gave this performance. And verily, thou hast well detected me!

But thou thyself – hast given me no small proof of thyself: thou art *hard*, thou wise Zarathustra! Hard strikest thou with thy 'truths', thy cudgel forceth from me – *this* truth!

Flatter not, answered Zarathustra, still excited and frowning, thou stage-player from the heart! Thou art false: why speakest thou – of truth!

Thou peacock of peacocks, thou sea of vanity; *what* didst thou represent before me, thou evil magician? *Whom* was I meant to believe in when thou wailedst in such wise?

The penitent in spirit, said the old man. It was him – I represented; thou thyself once devisedst this expression –

The poet and magician who at last turneth his spirit against himself, the transformed one who freezeth to death by his bad science and conscience.

And just acknowledge it: it was long, O Zarathustra, before thou discoveredst my trick and lie! Thou *believedst* in my distress when thou heldest my head with both thy hands –

I heard thee lament: 'We have loved him too little, loved him too little!' Because I so far deceived thee, my wickedness rejoiced in me.

Thou mayest have deceived subtler ones than I, said Zarathustra sternly. I am not on my guard against deceivers; I *have to be* without precaution: so willeth my lot.

Thou, however – must deceive: so far do I know thee! Thou must ever be equivocal, trivocal, quadrivocal, and quinquivocal! Even what thou hast now confessed is not nearly true enough nor false enough for me!

Thou bad false coiner, how couldst thou do otherwise! Thy very malady wouldst thou whitewash if thou showed thyself naked to thy physician.

Thus didst thou whitewash thy lie before me when thou saidst: 'I did so *only* for amusement!' There was also *seriousness* therein, thou *art* something of a penitent-in-spirit!

I divine thee well: thou hast become the enchanter of all the world; but for thyself thou hast no lie or artifice left – thou art disenchanted to thyself!

Thou hast reaped disgust as thy one truth. No word in thee is any longer genuine, but thy mouth is so: that is to say, the disgust that cleaveth unto thy mouth.

Who art thou at all, cried here the old magician with defiant voice, who dareth to speak thus unto *me*, the greatest man now living? And a green flash shot from his eye at Zarathustra. But immediately after he changed and said sadly:

O Zarathustra, I am weary of it. I am disgusted with mine arts, I am not *great*, why do I dissemble! But thou knowest it well – I sought for greatness!

A great man I wanted to appear, and persuaded many; but the lie hath been beyond my power. On it do I collapse.

O Zarathustra, everything is a lie in me; but that I collapse – this my collapsing is *genuine*!

It honoureth thee, said Zarathustra gloomily, looking down with sidelong glance. It honoureth thee that thou soughtest for greatness, but it betrayeth thee also. Thou art not great.

Thou bad old magician, that is the best and the honestest thing I honour in thee, that thou hast become weary of thyself, and hast expressed it: 'I am not great.'

Therein do I honour thee as a penitent-in-spirit, and although only for the twinkling of an eye, in that one moment wast thou – genuine.

But tell me, what seekest thou here in *my* forests and rocks? And if thou hast put thyself in *my* way, what proof of me wouldst thou have –

Wherein didst thou put *me* to the test?

Thus spake Zarathustra, and his eyes sparkled. But the old magician kept silence for a while; then said he: Did I put thee to the test? I – seek only.

O Zarathustra, I seek a genuine one, a right one, a simple one, an unequivocal one, a man of perfect honesty, a vessel of wisdom, a saint of knowledge, a great man!

Knowest thou it not, O Zarathustra? *I seek Zarathustra.*

And here there arose a long silence between them. Zarathustra, however, became profoundly absorbed in thought, so that he shut his eyes. But afterwards coming back to the situation, he grasped the hand of the magician, and said, full of politeness and policy:

Well! Up thither leadeth the way; there is the cave of Zarathustra. In it mayest thou seek him whom thou wouldst fain find.

And ask counsel of mine animals, mine eagle and my serpent: they shall help thee to seek. My cave however is large.

I myself, to be sure – I have as yet seen no great man. That which is great, the acutest eye is at present insensible to it. It is the kingdom of the populace.

Many a one have I found who stretched and inflated himself,

and the people cried: 'Behold, a great man!' But what good do all bellows do! The wind cometh out at last.

At last bursteth the frog which hath inflated itself too long: then cometh out the wind. To prick a swollen one in the belly, I call good pastime. Hear that, ye boys!

Our today is of the popular: who still *knoweth* what is great and what is small! Who could there seek successfully for greatness! A fool only: it succeedeth with fools.

Thou seekest for great men, thou strange fool? Who *taught* that *to* thee? Is today the time for it? Oh, thou bad seeker, why dost thou – tempt me?

Thus spake Zarathustra, comforted in his heart, and went laughing on his way.

66 Out of Service

Not long, however, after Zarathustra had freed himself from the magician, he again saw a person sitting beside the path which he followed, namely a tall, black man, with a haggard, pale countenance: *this man* grieved him exceedingly. Alas, said he to his heart, there sitteth disguised affliction; methinketh he is of the type of the priests: what do *they* want in my domain?

What! Hardly have I escaped from that magician, and must another necromancer again run across my path –

Some sorcerer with laying-on-of-hands, some sombre wonder-worker by the grace of God, some anointed world-maligner, whom may the devil take!

But the devil is never at the place which would be his right place; he always cometh too late, that cursed dwarf and club-foot!

Thus cursed Zarathustra impatiently in his heart, and considered how with averted look he might slip past the black man. But behold, it came about otherwise. For at the same moment had the sitting one already perceived him; and not unlike one whom an unexpected happiness overtaketh, he sprang to his feet, and went straight towards Zarathustra.

Whoever thou art, thou traveller, said he, help a strayed one, a seeker, an old man, who may here easily come to grief!

The world here is strange to me, and remote; wild beasts also did I hear howling; and he who could have given me protection – he is himself no more.

I was seeking the last pious man, a saint and an anchorite, who, alone in his forest, had not yet heard of what all the world knoweth at present.

What doth all the world know at present? asked Zarathustra. Perhaps that the old God no longer liveth, in whom all the world once believed?

Thou sayest it, answered the old man sorrowfully. And I served that old God until his last hour.

Now, however, am I out of service, without master, and yet not free; likewise am I no longer merry even for an hour, except it be in recollections.

Therefore did I ascend into these mountains, that I might finally have a festival for myself once more, as becometh an old pope and church-father: for know it, that I am the last pope! A festival of pious recollections and divine services.

Now, however, is he himself dead, the most pious of men, the saint in the forest, who praised his God constantly with singing and mumbling.

He himself found I no longer when I found his cot – but two wolves found I therein, which howled on account of his death, for all animals loved him. Then did I haste away.

Had I thus come in vain into these forests and mountains? Then did my heart determine that I should seek another, the most pious of all those who believe not in God – my heart determined that I should seek Zarathustra!

Thus spake the hoary man, and gazed with keen eyes at him who stood before him. Zarathustra however seized the hand of the old pope and regarded it a long while with admiration.

Lo! Thou venerable one, said he then. What a fine and long hand! That is the hand of one who hath ever dispensed blessings. Now, however, doth it hold fast him whom thou seekest, me Zarathustra.

It is I, the ungodly Zarathustra, who saith: 'Who is ungodlier than I, that I may enjoy his teaching?'

Thus spake Zarathustra, and penetrated with his glances the thoughts and arrear-thoughts of the old pope. At last the latter began:

He who most loved and possessed him hath now also lost him most –

Lo, I myself am surely the most godless of us at present! But who could rejoice at that?

Thou servedst him to the last? asked Zarathustra thoughtfully, after a deep silence. Thou knowest *how* he died? Is it true what they say, that sympathy choked him –

That he saw how *man* hung on the cross, and could not endure it – that his love to man became his hell, and at last his death?

The old pope however did not answer, but looked aside timidly, with a painful and gloomy expression.

Let him go, said Zarathustra, after prolonged meditation, still looking the old man straight in the eye.

Let him go, he is gone. And though it honoureth thee that thou speakest only in praise of this dead one, yet thou knowest as well as I *who* he was, and that he went curious ways.

To speak before three eyes, said the old pope cheerfully (he was blind of one eye), in divine matters I am more enlightened than Zarathustra himself – and may well be so.

My love served him long years, my will followed all his will. A good servant, however, knoweth everything, and many a thing even which a master hideth from himself.

He was a hidden God, full of secrecy. Verily, he did not come by his son otherwise than by secret ways. At the door of his faith standeth adultery.

Whoever extolleth him as a God of love, doth not think highly enough of love itself. Did not that God want also to be judge? But the loving one loveth irrespective of reward and requital.

When he was young, that God out of the Orient, then was he harsh and revengeful, and built himself a hell for the delight of his favourites.

At last however, he became old and soft and mellow and pitiful, more like a grandfather than a father, but most like a tottering old grandmother.

There did he sit shrivelled in his chimney-corner, fretting on account of his weak legs, world-weary, will-weary, and one day he suffocated of his all-too-great pity.

Thou old pope, said here Zarathustra interposing, hast thou seen *that* with thine eyes? It could well have happened in that way: in that way, *and* also otherwise. When Gods die they always die many kinds of death.

Well! At all events, one way or other – he is gone! He was counter to the taste of mine ears and eyes; worse than that I should not like to say against him.

I love everything that looketh bright and speaketh honestly. But he – thou knowest it, forsooth, thou old priest, there was something of thy type in him, the priest-type – he was equivocal.

He was also indistinct. How he raged at us, this wrath-snorter, because we understood him badly! But why did he not speak more clearly?

And if the fault lay in our ears, why did he give us ears that heard him badly? If there was dirt in our ears, well, who put it in them?

Too much miscarried with him, this potter who had not learned thoroughly! That he took revenge on his pots and creations, however, because they turned out badly – that was a sin against *good taste.*

There is also good taste in piety; *this* at last said: Away with *such* a God! Better to have no God, better to set up destiny on one's own account, better to be a fool, better to be God oneself!

What do I hear! said then the old pope, with intent ears; O Zarathustra, thou art more pious than thou believest, with such an unbelief! Some God in thee hath converted thee to thine ungodliness.

Is it not thy piety itself which no longer letteth thee believe in a God? And thine over-great honesty will yet lead thee even beyond good and evil!

Behold, what hath been reserved for thee? Thou hast eyes and hands and mouth which have been predestined for blessing from eternity. One doth not bless with the hand alone.

Nigh unto thee, though thou professest to be the ungodliest one, I feel a hale and holy odour of long benedictions; I feel glad and grieved thereby!

Let me be thy guest, O Zarathustra, for a single night! Nowhere on earth shall I now feel better than with thee!

Amen! So shall it be! said Zarathustra with great astonishment. Up thither leadeth the way, there lieth the cave of Zarathustra.

Gladly, forsooth, would I conduct thee thither myself, thou venerable one; for I love all pious men. But now a cry of distress calleth me hastily away from thee.

In my domain shall no one come to grief; my cave is a good haven. And best of all would I like to put every sorrowful one again on firm land and firm legs.

Who, however, could take thy melancholy off thy shoulders? For that I am too weak. Long, verily, should we have to wait until some one re-awoke thy God for thee.

For that old God liveth no more: he is indeed dead.

Thus spake Zarathustra.

67 The Ugliest Man

And again did Zarathustra's feet run through mountains and forests, and his eyes sought and sought, but nowhere was he to be seen whom they wanted to see – the sorely distressed sufferer and crier. On the whole way, however, he rejoiced in his heart and was full of gratitudes. What good things, said he, hath this day given me, as amends for its bad beginning! What strange interlocutors have I found!

At their words will I now chew a long while as at good corn; small shall my teeth grind and crush them, until they flow like milk into my soul!

When, however, the path again curved round a rock, all at once the landscape changed, and Zarathustra entered into a realm of death. Here bristled aloft black and red cliffs, without any grass, tree, or bird's voice. For it was a valley which all animals avoided, even the beasts of prey, except that a species of ugly, thick, green serpent came here to die when they became old. Therefore the shepherds called this valley 'Serpent-death'.

Zarathustra, however, became absorbed in dark recollections, for it seemed to him as if he had once before stood in this valley. And much heaviness settled on his mind, so that he walked slowly and always more slowly, and at last stood still. Then, however, when he opened his eyes, he saw something sitting by the wayside shaped like a man, and hardly like a man, something nondescript. And all at once there came over Zarathustra a great shame, because he had gazed on such a thing. Blushing up to the very roots of his white hair, he turned aside his glance, and raised his foot that he might leave this ill-starred place. Then, however, became the dead wilderness vocal: for from the ground a noise welled up, gurgling and rattling, as water gurgleth and rattleth at night through stopped-up waterpipes and at last it turned into human voice and human speech; it sounded thus:

Zarathustra! Zarathustra! Read my riddle! Say, *What is the revenge on the witness?*

I entice thee back; here is smooth ice! See to it, see to it, that thy pride do not here break its legs!

Thou thinkest thyself wise, thou proud Zarathustra! Read then the riddle, thou hard nut-cracker – the riddle that I am! Say then: who am I!

When however Zarathustra had heard these words, what think ye then took place in his soul? *Pity overcame him*, and he sank down all at once, like an oak that hath long withstood many tree-fellers – heavily, suddenly, to the terror even of those who meant to fell it. But immediately he got up again from the ground, and his countenance became stern.

I know thee well, said he, with a brazen voice. *Thou art the murderer of God*! Let me go.

Thou couldst not *endure* him who beheld *thee* – who ever beheld thee through and through, thou ugliest man. Thou tookest revenge on this witness!

Thus spake Zarathustra and was about to go; but the nondescript grasped at a corner of his garment and began anew to gurgle and seek for words. Stay, said he at last –

Stay! Do not pass by! I have divined what axe it was that struck thee to the ground: hail to thee, O Zarathustra, that thou art again upon thy feet!

Thou hast divined, I know it well, how the man feeleth who killed him – the murderer of God. Stay! Sit down here beside me; it is not to no purpose.

To whom would I go but unto thee? Stay, sit down! Do not however look at me! Honour thus – mine ugliness!

They persecute me: now art *thou* my last refuge. *Not* with their hatred, *not* with their bailiffs – Oh, such persecution would I mock at, and be proud and cheerful!

Hath not all success hitherto been with the well-persecuted ones? And he who persecuteth well learneth readily to be *obsequent*, when once he is – put behind! But it is their *pity* –

Their pity is it from which I flee away and flee to thee. O Zarathustra, protect me, thou my last refuge, thou sole one who divinedst me –

Thou hast divined how the man feeleth who killed him. Stay! And if thou wilt go, thou impatient one, go not the way that I came. *That* way is bad.

Art thou angry with me because I have already racked language too long? Because I have already counselled thee? But know that it is I, the ugliest man –

Who have also the largest, heaviest feet. Where I have gone, the way is bad. I tread all paths to death and destruction.

But that thou passedst me by in silence, that thou blushedst – I saw it well: thereby did I know thee as Zarathustra.

Every one else would have thrown to me his alms, his pity, in look and speech. But for that – I am not beggar enough: that didst thou divine.

For that I am too *rich*, rich in what is great, frightful, ugliest, most unutterable! Thy shame, O Zarathustra, *honoured* me!

With difficulty did I get out of the crowd of the pitiful, that I might find the only one who at present teacheth that 'pity is obtrusive' – thyself, O Zarathustra!

Whether it be the pity of a God, or whether it be human pity, it is offensive to modesty. And unwillingness to help may be nobler than the virtue that rusheth to do so.

That however – namely, pity – is called virtue itself at present by all petty people; they have no reverence for great misfortune, great ugliness, great failure.

Beyond all these do I look, as a dog looketh over the backs of thronging flocks of sheep. They are petty, good-wooled, good-willed, grey people.

As the heron looketh contemptuously at shallow pools, with backward-bent head, so do I look at the throng of grey little waves and wills and souls.

Too long have we acknowledged them to be right, those petty people: *so* we have at last given them power as well – and now do they teach that 'good is only what petty people call good'.

And 'truth' is at present what the preacher spake who himself sprang from them, that singular saint and advocate of the petty people, who testified of himself: 'I – am the truth.'

That immodest one hath long made the petty people greatly puffed up, he who taught no small error when he taught: 'I – am the truth.'

Hath an immodest one ever been answered more courteously? Thou, however, O Zarathustra, passedst him by, and saidst: 'Nay! Nay! Three times Nay!'

Thou warnedst against his error; thou warnedst – the first to do so – against pity: not every one, not none, but thyself and thy type.

Thou art ashamed of the shame of the great sufferer; and verily when thou sayest: 'From pity there cometh a heavy cloud; take heed, ye men!'

When thou teachest: 'All creators are hard, all great love is beyond their pity,' O Zarathustra, how well versed dost thou seem to me in weather-signs!

Thou thyself, however – warn thyself also against *thy* pity! For many are on their way to thee, many suffering, doubting, despairing, drowning, freezing ones –

I warn thee also against myself. Thou hast read my best, my worst riddle, myself, and what I have done. I know the axe that felleth thee.

But he – *had to* die; he looked with eyes which beheld *everything* – he beheld men's depths and dregs, all his hidden ignominy and ugliness.

His pity knew no modesty; he crept into my dirtiest corners. This most prying, over-intrusive, over-pitiful one had to die.

He ever beheld *me*: on such a witness I would have revenge – or not live myself.

The God who beheld everything, *and also man*: that God had to die! Man cannot *endure* it that such a witness should live.

Thus spake the ugliest man. Zarathustra however got up, and prepared to go on: for he felt frozen to the very bowels.

Thou nondescript, said he, thou warnedst me against thy path. As thanks for it I praise mine to thee. Behold, up thither is the cave of Zarathustra.

My cave is large and deep and hath many corners; there findeth he that is most hidden his hiding-place. And close beside it there are a hundred lurking-places and by-places for creeping, fluttering and hopping creatures.

Thou outcast, who hast cast thyself out, thou wilt not live amongst men and men's pity? Well then, do like me! Thus wilt thou learn also from me; only the doer learneth.

And talk first and foremost to mine animals! The proudest animal and the wisest animal – they might well be the right counsellors for us both!

Thus spake Zarathustra and went his way, more thoughtfully and slowly even than before; for he asked himself many things, and hardly knew what to answer.

How poor indeed is man, thought he in his heart, how ugly, how wheezy, how full of hidden shame!

They tell me that man loveth himself. Ah, how great must that self-love be! How much contempt is opposed to it!

Even this man hath loved himself, as he hath despised himself – a great lover methinketh he is, and a great despiser.

No one have I yet found who more thoroughly despised himself: even *that* is elevation. Alas, was *this* perhaps the higher man whose cry I heard?

I love the great despisers. Man is something that hath to be surpassed.

68 *The Voluntary Beggar*

When Zarathustra had left the ugliest man, he was chilled and felt lonesome; for much coldness and lonesomeness came over his spirit, so that even his limbs became colder thereby. When, however, he wandered on and on, uphill and down, at times past green meadows, though also sometimes over wild stony couches where formerly perhaps an impatient brook had made its bed, then he turned all at once warmer and heartier again.

What hath happened unto me? he asked himself. Something warm and living quickeneth me; it must be in the neighbourhood.

Already am I less alone; unconscious companions and brethren rove around me; their warm breath toucheth my soul.

When, however, he spied about and sought for the comforters of his lonesomeness, behold, there were kine there standing together on an eminence, whose proximity and smell had warmed his heart. The kine, however, seemed to listen eagerly to a speaker, and took no heed of him who approached. When, however, Zarathustra was quite nigh unto them, then did he hear plainly that a human voice spake in the midst of the kine; and apparently all of them had turned their heads towards the speaker.

Then ran Zarathustra up speedily and drove the animals aside; for he feared that some one had here met with harms which the pity of the kine would hardly be able to relieve. But in this he was deceived; for behold, there sat a man on the ground who seemed to be persuading the animals to have no fear of him, a peaceable man and Preacher-on-the-Mount, out of whose eyes kindness itself preached. What dost thou seek here? called out Zarathustra in astonishment.

What do I here seek? answered he: the same that thou seekest, thou mischief-maker; that is to say, happiness upon earth.

To that end, however, I would fain learn of these kine. For I tell thee that I have already talked half a morning unto them, and just now were they about to give me their answer. Why dost thou disturb them?

Except we be converted and become as kine, we shall in no wise enter into the kingdom of heaven. For we ought to learn from them one thing: ruminating.

And verily, although a man should gain the whole world, and yet not learn one thing, ruminating, what would it profit him! He would not be rid of his affliction –

His great affliction: that, however, is at present called *disgust.* Who hath not at present his heart, his mouth and his eyes full of disgust? Thou also! Thou also! But behold these kine!

Thus spake the Preacher-on-the-Mount, and turned then his own look towards Zarathustra – for hitherto it had rested lovingly on the kine; then, however, he put on a different expression. Who is this with whom I talk? he exclaimed, frightened, and sprang up from the ground.

This is the man without disgust, this is Zarathustra himself, the surmounter of the great disgust; this is the eye, this is the mouth, this is the heart of Zarathustra himself.

And whilst he thus spake he kissed with o'erflowing eyes the hands of him with whom he spake, and behaved altogether like one to whom a precious gift and jewel hath fallen unawares from heaven. The kine, however, gazed at it all and wondered.

Speak not of me, thou strange one; thou amiable one, said Zarathustra, and restrained his affection. Speak to me firstly of thyself! Art thou not the voluntary beggar who once cast away great riches –

Who was ashamed of his riches and of the rich, and fled to the poorest to bestow upon them his abundance and his heart? But they received him not.

But they received me not, said the voluntary beggar. Thou knowest it, forsooth. So I went at last to the animals and to those kine.

Then learnedst thou, interrupted Zarathustra, how much harder it is to give properly than to take properly, and that bestowing well is an art – the last, subtlest master-art of kindness.

Especially nowadays, answered the voluntary beggar. At present, that is to say, when everything low hath become rebellious and exclusive and haughty in its manner – in the manner of the populace.

For the hour hath come – thou knowest it forsooth – for the great, evil, long, slow mob-and-slave-insurrection: it extendeth and extendeth!

Now doth it provoke the lower classes, all benevolence and petty giving; and the overrich may be on their guard!

Whoever at present drip, like bulgy bottles out of all-too-small necks – of such bottles at present one willingly breaketh the necks.

Wanton avidity, bilious envy, careworn revenge, populace-pride: all these struck mine eye. It is no longer true that the poor are blessed. The kingdom of heaven, however, is with the kine.

And why is it not with the rich? asked Zarathustra temptingly, while he kept back the kine which sniffed familiarly at the peaceful one.

Why dost thou tempt me? answered the other. Thou knowest it thyself better even than I. What was it drove me to the poorest, O Zarathustra? Was it not my disgust at the richest?

At the culprits of riches, with cold eyes and rank thoughts, who pick up profit out of all kinds of rubbish – at this rabble that stinketh to heaven –

At this gilded, falsified populace, whose fathers were pickpockets, or carrion-crows, or rag-pickers, with wives compliant, lewd and forgetful; for they are all of them not far different from harlots –

Populace above, populace below! What are 'poor' and 'rich' at present! That distinction did I unlearn – then did I flee away further and ever further, until I came to those kine.

Thus spake the peaceful one, and puffed himself and perspired with his words, so that the kine wondered anew. Zarathustra, however, kept looking into his face with a smile all the time the man talked so severely – and shook silently his head.

Thou doest violence to thyself, thou Preacher-on-the-Mount, when thou usest such severe words. For such severity neither thy mouth nor thine eye have been given thee.

Nor, methinketh, hath thy stomach either: unto it all such rage and hatred and foaming-over is repugnant. Thy stomach wanteth softer things; thou art not a butcher.

Rather seemest thou to me a plant-eater and a root-man. Perhaps thou grindest corn. Certainly, however, thou art averse to fleshly joys, and thou lovest honey.

Thou hast divined me well, answered the voluntary beggar, with lightened heart. I love honey, I also grind corn; for I have sought out what tasteth sweetly and maketh pure breath –

Also what requireth a long time, a day's-work and a mouth's-work for gentle idlers and sluggards.

Furthest, to be sure, have those kine carried it; they have devised ruminating and lying in the sun. They also abstain from all heavy thoughts which inflate the heart.

Well, said Zarathustra, thou shouldst also see mine animals, mine eagle and my serpent – their like do not at present exist on earth.

Behold, thither leadeth the way to my cave: be tonight its guest. And talk to mine animals of the happiness of animals –

Until I myself come home. For now a cry of distress calleth me hastily away from thee. Also, shouldst thou find new honey with me – ice-cold, golden-comb-honey – eat it!

Now, however, take leave at once of thy kine, thou strange one, thou amiable one, though it be hard for thee! For they are thy warmest friends and preceptors –

One excepted, whom I hold still dearer, answered the voluntary beggar. Thou thyself art good, O Zarathustra, and better even than a cow!

Away, away with thee, thou evil flatterer! cried Zarathustra mischievously. Why dost thou spoil me with such praise and flattery-honey?

Away, away from me, cried he once more, and heaved his stick at the fond beggar, who, however, ran nimbly away.

69 *The Shadow*

Scarcely however was the voluntary beggar gone in haste and Zarathustra again alone, when he heard behind him a new voice which called out: Stay! Zarathustra! Do wait! It is myself, forsooth, O Zarathustra, myself, thy shadow! But Zarathustra did not wait; for a sudden irritation came over him on account of the crowd and the crowding in his mountains. Whither hath my lonesomeness gone? spake he.

It is verily becoming too much for me; these mountains swarm; my kingdom is no longer of *this* world; I require new mountains.

My shadow calleth me? What matter about my shadow! Let it run after me! I – run away from it.

Thus spake Zarathustra to his heart and ran away. But the one behind followed after him, so that immediately there were three runners, one after the other – namely, foremost the voluntary beggar, then Zarathustra, and thirdly, and hindmost, his shadow. But not long had they run thus when Zarathustra became conscious of his folly, and shook off with one jerk all his irritation and detestation

What, said he, have not the most ludicrous things always happened to us old anchorites and saints?

Verily, my folly hath grown big in the mountains! Now do I hear six old fools' legs rattling behind one another!

But doth Zarathustra need to be frightened by his shadow? Also, methinketh that after all it hath longer legs than mine.

Thus spake Zarathustra, and laughing with eyes and entrails he stood still and turned round quickly – and behold, he almost thereby threw his shadow and follower to the ground, so closely had the latter followed at his heels, and so weak was he. For when Zarathustra scrutinised him with his glance he was frightened as by a sudden apparition, so slender, swarthy, hollow and worn-out did this follower appear.

Who art thou? asked Zarathustra vehemently. What doest thou here? And why callest thou thyself my shadow? Thou art not pleasing unto me.

Forgive me, answered the shadow, that it is I; and if I please thee not – well, O Zarathustra, therein do I admire thee and thy good taste!

A wanderer am I, who have walked long at thy heels; always on the way, but without a goal, also without a home: so that verily, I lack little of being the eternally Wandering Jew, except that I am not eternal and not a Jew.

What? Must I ever be on the way? Whirled by every wind, unsettled, driven about? O earth, thou hast become too round for me!

On every surface have I already sat; like tired dust have I fallen asleep on mirrors and window-panes. Everything taketh from me, nothing giveth; I become thin – I am almost equal to a shadow.

After thee, however, O Zarathustra, did I fly and hie longest; and though I hid myself from thee, I was nevertheless thy best shadow: wherever thou hast sat, there sat I also.

With thee have I wandered about in the remotest, coldest worlds, like a phantom that voluntarily haunteth winter roofs and snows.

With thee have I pushed into all the forbidden, all the worst and the furthest: and if there be anything of virtue in me, it is that I have had no fear of any prohibition.

With thee have I broken up whatever my heart revered; all boundary-stones and statues have I o'erthrown, the most dangerous wishes did I pursue – verily, beyond every crime did I once go.

With thee did I unlearn the belief in words and worths and in great names. When the devil casteth his skin doth not his name also fall away? It is also skin. The devil himself is perhaps – skin.

Nothing is true, all is permitted: so said I to myself. Into the coldest water did I plunge with head and heart. Ah, how oft did I stand there naked on that account, like a red crab!

Ah, where have gone all my goodness and all my shame and all my belief in the good! Ah, where is the lying innocence which I once possessed, the innocence of the good and of their noble lies!

Too oft, verily, did I follow close to the heels of truth; then did it kick me on the face. Sometimes I meant to lie and behold! Then only did I hit – the truth.

Too much hath become clear unto me; now it doth not concern me any more. Nothing liveth any longer that I love – how should I still love myself?

To live as I incline, or not to live at all: so do I wish; so wisheth also the holiest. But alas! how have I still – inclination?

Have I – still a goal? A haven towards which my sail is set?

A good wind? Ah, he only who knoweth *whither* he saileth, knoweth what wind is good, and a fair wind for him.

What still remaineth to me? A heart weary and flippant; an unstable will; fluttering wings; a broken backbone.

This seeking for my home: O Zarathustra, dost thou know that this seeking hath been my home-sickening; it eateth me up.

Where is – my home? For it do I ask and seek, and have sought, but have not found it. O eternal everywhere, O eternal nowhere, O eternal – in-vain!

Thus spake the shadow, and Zarathustra's countenance lengthened at his words. Thou art my shadow! said he at last sadly.

Thy danger is not small, thou free spirit and wanderer! Thou hast had a bad day: see that a still worse evening doth not overtake thee!

To such unsettled ones as thou seemeth at last even a prisoner blessed. Didst thou ever see how captured criminals sleep? They sleep quietly, they enjoy their new security.

Beware lest in the end a narrow faith capture thee, a hard, rigorous delusion! For now everything that is narrow and fixed seduceth and tempteth thee.

Thou hast lost thy goal. Alas, how wilt thou forego and forget that loss? Thereby – hast thou also lost thy way!

Thou poor rover and rambler, thou tired butterfly! Wilt thou have a rest and a home this evening? Then go up to my cave!

Thither leadeth the way to my cave. And now will I run quickly away from thee again. Already lieth as it were a shadow upon me.

I will run alone, so that it may again become bright around me. Therefore must I still be a long time merrily upon my legs. In the evening, however, there will be – dancing with me!

Thus spake Zarathustra.

70 Noontide

And Zarathustra ran and ran, but he found no one else, and was alone and ever found himself again; he enjoyed and quaffed his solitude, and thought of good things – for hours. About the hour of noontide, however, when the sun stood exactly over Zarathustra's head, he passed an old, bent and gnarled tree, which was encircled round by the ardent love of a vine, and hidden from itself; from this there hung yellow grapes in abundance, confronting the wanderer. Then he felt inclined to quench a little thirst, and to break off for himself a cluster of grapes. When, however, he had already his arm outstretched for that purpose, he felt still more inclined for something else – namely, to lie down beside the tree at the hour of perfect noontide and sleep.

This Zarathustra did; and no sooner had he laid himself on the ground in the stillness and secrecy of the variegated grass, than he had forgotten his little thirst, and fell asleep. For as the proverb of Zarathustra saith – 'One thing is more necessary than the other.' Only that his eyes remained open – for they never grew weary of viewing and admiring the tree and the love of the vine. In falling asleep, however, Zarathustra spake thus to his heart:

Hush! Hush! Hath not the world now become perfect? What hath happened unto me?

As a delicate wind danceth invisibly upon parqueted seas, tight, feather-light, so – danceth sleep upon me.

No eye doth it close to me; it leaveth my soul awake. Light is it, verily, feather-light.

It persuadeth me, I know not how; it toucheth me inwardly with a caressing hand, it constraineth me. Yea, it constraineth me, so that my soul stretcheth itself out –

How long and weary it becometh, my strange soul! Hath a seventh-day evening come to it precisely at noontide? Hath it already wandered too long, blissfully, among good and ripe things?

It stretcheth itself out, long – longer! It lieth still, my strange soul. Too many good things hath it already tasted; this golden sadness oppresseth it, it distorteth its mouth –

As a ship that putteth into the calmest cove: it now draweth up to the land, weary of long voyages and uncertain seas. Is not the land more faithful?

As such a ship huggeth the shore, tuggeth the shore – then it sufficeth for a spider to spin its thread from the ship to the land. No stronger ropes are required there.

As such a weary ship in the calmest cove, so do I also now repose, nigh to the earth, faithful, trusting, waiting, bound to it with the lightest threads.

O happiness! O happiness! Wilt thou perhaps sing, O my soul? Thou liest in the grass. But this is the secret, solemn hour, when no shepherd playeth his pipe.

Take care! Hot noontide sleepeth on the fields. Do not sing! Hush! The world is perfect.

Do not sing, thou prairie-bird my soul! Do not even whisper! Lo, hush! The old noontide sleepeth, it moveth its mouth; doth it not just now drink a drop of happiness –

An old brown drop of golden happiness, golden wine? Something whisketh over it, its happiness laugheth. Thus – laugheth a God. Hush!

'For happiness, how little sufficeth for happiness!' Thus spake I once and thought myself wise. But it was a blasphemy: *that* have I now learned. Wise fools speak better.

The least thing precisely, the gentlest thing, the lightest thing, a lizard's rustling, a breath, a whisk, an eye-glance – *little* maketh up the *best* happiness. Hush!

What hath befallen me? Hark! Hath time flown away? Do I not fall? Have I not fallen – hark, into the well of eternity?

What happeneth to me? Hush! It stingeth me – alas – to the heart? To the heart! Oh, break up, break up, my heart, after such happiness, after such a sting!

What? Hath not the world just now become perfect? Round and ripe? Oh, for the golden round ring – whither doth it fly? Let me run after it! Quick!

Hush – (and here Zarathustra stretched himself, and felt that he was asleep.)

Up! said he to himself, thou sleeper! Thou noontide sleeper! Well then, up, ye old legs! It is time and more than time; many a good stretch of road is still awaiting you –

Now have ye slept your fill, for how long a time? A half-eternity! Well then, up now, mine old heart! For how long after such a sleep mayest thou – remain awake?

(But then did he fall asleep anew, and his soul spake against him and defended itself, and lay down again) – Leave me alone! Hush! Hath not the world just now become perfect? Oh, for the golden round ball!

Get up, said Zarathustra, thou little thief, thou sluggard! What! Still stretching thyself, yawning, sighing, falling into deep wells?

Who art thou then, O my soul! (And here he became frightened, for a sunbeam shot down from heaven upon his face.)

O heaven above me, said he sighing, and sat upright. Thou gazest at me? Thou hearkenest unto my strange soul?

When wilt thou drink this drop of dew that fell down upon all earthly things? When wilt thou drink this strange soul –

When, thou well of eternity! Thou joyous, awful, noontide abyss! When wilt thou drink my soul back into thee?

Thus spake Zarathustra, and rose from his couch beside the tree, as if awakening from a strange drunkenness: and behold, there stood the sun still exactly above his head! One might, however, rightly infer therefrom that Zarathustra had not then slept long.

71 The Greeting

It was late in the afternoon only when Zarathustra, after long useless searching and strolling about, again came home to his cave. When, however, he stood over against it, not more than twenty paces therefrom, the thing happened which he now least of all expected: he heard anew the great *cry of distress*. And extraordinary! This time the cry came out of his own cave. It was a long, manifold, peculiar cry, and Zarathustra plainly distinguished that it was composed of many voices, although heard at a distance it might sound like the cry out of a single mouth.

Thereupon Zarathustra rushed forward to his cave, and behold, what a spectacle awaited him after that concert! For there did they all sit together whom he had passed during the day: the king on the right and the king on the left, the old magician the pope, the voluntary beggar, the shadow, the intellectually conscientious one, the sorrowful soothsayer, and the ass; the ugliest man, however, had set a crown on his head, and had put round him two purple girdles – for he liked, like all ugly ones, to disguise himself and play the handsome person. In the midst, however, of that sorrowful company stood Zarathustra's eagle, ruffled and disquieted, for it had been called upon to answer too much for which its pride had not any answer; the wise serpent however hung round its neck.

All this did Zarathustra behold with great astonishment; then however he scrutinised each individual guest with courteous curiosity, read their souls and wondered anew. In the meantime the assembled ones had risen from their seats, and waited with reverence for Zarathustra to speak. Zarathustra however spake thus:

Ye despairing ones! Ye strange ones! So it was your cry of distress that I heard? And now do I know also where he is to be sought, whom I have sought for in vain today: *the higher man* –

In mine own cave sitteth he, the higher man! But why do I wonder! Have not I myself allured him to me by honey-offerings and artful lure-calls of my happiness?

But it seemeth to me that ye are badly adapted for company: ye make one another's hearts fretful, ye that cry for help, when ye sit here together. There is one that must first come –

One who will make you laugh once more, a good jovial buffoon, a dancer, a wind, a wild romp, some old fool – what think ye?

Forgive me, however, ye despairing ones, for speaking such trivial words before you: unworthy, verily, of such guests! But ye do not divine *what* maketh my heart wanton –

Ye yourselves do it, and your aspect, forgive it me! For every one becometh courageous who beholdeth a despairing one. To encourage a despairing one – every one thinketh himself strong enough to do so.

To myself have ye given this power – a good gift, mine honourable guests! An excellent guest's-present! Well, do not then upbraid when I also offer you something of mine.

This is mine empire and my dominion: that which is mine, however, shall this evening and tonight be yours. Mine animals shall serve you; let my cave be your resting-place!

At house and home with me shall no one despair; in my purlieus do I protect every one from his wild beasts. And that is the first thing which I offer you: security!

The second thing, however, is my little finger. And when ye have *that*, then take the whole hand also, yea and the heart with it! Welcome here, welcome to you my guests!'

Thus spake Zarathustra, and laughed with love and mischief. After this greeting his guests bowed once more and were reverentially silent; the king on the right, however, answered him in their name.

O Zarathustra, by the way in which thou hast given us thy hand and thy greeting, we recognise thee as Zarathustra. Thou hast humbled thyself before us; almost hast thou hurt our reverence –

Who however could have humbled himself as thou hast done, with such pride? *That* uplifteth us ourselves; a refreshment is it, to our eyes and hearts.

To behold this merely, gladly would we ascend higher mountains than this. For as eager beholders have we come; we wanted to see what brighteneth dim eyes.

And lo, now is it all over with our cries of distress! Now are our minds and hearts open and enraptured. Little is lacking for our spirits to become wanton.

There is nothing, O Zarathustra, that groweth more pleasingly on earth than a lofty, strong will; it is the finest growth. An entire landscape refresheth itself at one such tree.

To the pine do I compare him, O Zarathustra, which groweth up like thee – tall, silent, hardy, solitary, of the best, supplest wood, stately –

In the end, however, grasping out for *its* dominion with strong, green branches, asking weighty questions of the wind, the storm, and whatever is at home on high places –

Answering more weightily, a commander, a victor! Oh, who should not ascend high mountains to behold such growths?

At thy tree, O Zarathustra, the gloomy and ill-constituted also refresh themselves; at thy look even the wavering become steady and heal their hearts.

And verily, towards thy mountain and thy tree do many eyes turn today; a great longing hath arisen, and many have learned to ask: 'Who is Zarathustra?'

And those into whose ears thou hast at any time dripped thy song and thy honey – all the hidden ones, the lone-dwellers and the twain-dwellers, have simultaneously said to their hearts:

'Doth Zarathustra still live? It is no longer worth while to live, everything is indifferent, everything is useless; or else – we must live with Zarathustra!'

'Why doth he not come who hath so long announced himself?' Thus do many people ask; 'hath solitude swallowed him up? Or should we perhaps go to him?'

Now doth it come to pass that solitude itself becometh fragile and breaketh open, like a grave that breaketh open and can no longer hold its dead. Everywhere one seeth resurrected ones.

Now do the waves rise and rise around thy mountain, O Zarathustra. And however high be thy height, many of them must rise up to thee: thy boat shall not rest much longer on dry ground.

And that we despairing ones have now come into thy cave, and already no longer despair: it is but a prognostic and a presage that better ones are on the way to thee –

For they themselves are on the way to thee, the last remnant of God among men: that is to say, all the men of great longing, of great loathing, of great satiety –

All who do not want to live unless they learn again to *hope* – unless they learn from thee, O Zarathustra, the *great* hope!

Thus spake the king on the right, and seized the hand of Zarathustra in order to kiss it; but Zarathustra checked his veneration, and stepped back frightened, fleeing as it were, silently and suddenly into the far distance. After a little while however, he was again at home with his guests, looked at them with clear scrutinising eyes, and said:

My guests, ye higher men. I will speak plain language and plainly with you. It is not for *you* that I have waited here in these mountains.

('Plain language and plainly?' Good God! said here the king on the left to himself. One seeth he doth not know the good Occidentals, this sage out of the Orient!

But he meaneth 'blunt language and bluntly' – well, that is not the worst taste in these days!)

Ye may, verily, all of you be higher men, continued Zarathustra; but for me – ye are neither high enough, nor strong enough.

For me, that is to say, for the inexorable which is now silent in me, but will not always be silent. And if ye appertain to me, still it is not as my right arm.

For he who himself standeth, like you, on sickly and tender legs, wisheth above all to be *treated indulgently*, whether he be conscious of it or hide it from himself.

My arms and my legs, however, I do not treat indulgently, *I do not treat my warriors indulgently*; how then could ye be fit for *my* warfare?

With you I should spoil all my victories. And many of you would tumble over if ye but heard the loud beating of my drums.

Moreover, ye are not sufficiently beautiful and well-born for me. I require pure, smooth mirrors for my doctrines; on your surface even mine own likeness is distorted.

On your shoulders presseth many a burden, many a recollection; many a mischievous dwarf squatteth in your corners. There is concealed populace also in you.

And though ye be high and of a higher type, much in you is crooked and misshapen. There is no smith in the world that could hammer you right and straight for me.

Ye are only bridges; may higher ones pass over upon you! Ye signify steps; so do not upbraid him who ascendeth beyond you into *his* height!

Out of your seed there may one day arise for me a genuine son and perfect heir; but that time is distant. Ye yourselves are not those unto whom my heritage and name belong.

Not for you do I wait here in these mountains, not with you may I descend for the last time. Ye have come unto me only as a presage that higher ones are on the way to me –

Not the men of great longing, of great loathing, of great satiety, and that which ye call the remnant of God –

Nay! Nay! Three times Nay! For *others* do I wait here in these mountains, and will not lift my foot from thence without them –

For higher ones, stronger ones, triumphanter ones, merrier ones, for such as are built squarely in body and soul: *laughing lions* must come!

O my guests, ye strange ones – have ye yet heard nothing of my children? And that they are on the way to me?

Do speak unto me of my gardens, of my Happy Isles, of my new beautiful race – why do ye not speak unto me thereof?

This guests'-present do I solicit of your love, that ye speak unto me of my children. For them am I rich, for them I became poor: what have I not surrendered!

What would I not surrender that I might have one thing: *these* children, *this* living plantation, *these* life-trees of my will and of my highest hope!

Thus spake Zarathustra, and stopped suddenly in his discourse; for his longing came over him, and he closed his eyes and his mouth because of the agitation of his heart. And all his guests also were silent, and stood still and confounded; except only that the old soothsayer made signs with his hands and his gestures.

72 The Supper

For at this point the soothsayer interrupted the greeting of Zarathustra and his guests; he pressed forward as one who had no time to lose, seized Zarathustra's hand and exclaimed: But Zarathustra!

One thing is more necessary than the other, so sayest thou thyself; well, one thing is now more necessary *unto me* than all others.

A word at the right time: didst thou not invite me to *table?* And here are many who have made long journeys. Thou dost not mean to feed us merely with discourses?

Besides, all of you have thought too much about freezing, drowning, suffocating, and other bodily dangers: none of you, however, have thought of my danger, namely, perishing of hunger –

(Thus spake the soothsayer. When Zarathustra's animals, however, heard these words, they ran away in terror. For they saw that all they had brought home during the day would not be enough to fill the one soothsayer.)

Likewise perishing of thirst, continued the soothsayer And although I hear water splashing here like words of wisdom, that is to say plenteously and unweariedly, I – want *wine*!

Not every one is a born water-drinker like Zarathustra. Neither doth water suit weary and withered ones; we do serve wine – it alone giveth immediate vigour and improvised health!

On this occasion, when the soothsayer was longing for wine, it happened that the king on the left, the silent one, also found expression for once. *We* took care, said he, about wine. I, along with my brother the king on the right, we have enough of wine – a whole ass-load of it. So there is nothing lacking but bread.

Bread, replied Zarathustra, laughing when he spake. It is precisely bread that anchorites have not. But man doth not live by bread alone, but also by the flesh of good lambs, of which I have two –

These shall we slaughter quickly, and cook spicily with sage: it is so that I like them. And there is also no lack of roots and fruits, good enough even for the fastidious and dainty – nor of nuts and other riddles for cracking.

Thus will we have a good repast in a little while. But whoever wish to eat with us must also give a hand to the work, even the kings. For with Zarathustra even a king may be a cook.

This proposal appealed to the hearts of all of them, save that the voluntary beggar objected to the flesh and wine and spices.

Just hear this glutton Zarathustra! said he jokingly. Doth one go into caves and high mountains to make such repasts?

Now indeed do I understand what he once taught us: 'Blessed be moderate poverty.' And why he wisheth to do away with beggars.

Be of good cheer, replied Zarathustra, as I am. Abide by thy customs, thou excellent one; grind thy corn, drink thy water, praise thy cooking – if only it make thee glad!

I am a law only for mine own; I am not a law for all. He, however, who belongeth unto me must be strong of bone and light of foot –

Joyous in fight and feast, no sulker, no John o' Dreams; ready for the hardest task as for the feast, healthy and hale.

The best belongeth unto mine and me; and if it be not given us, then do we take it: the best food, the purest sky, the strongest thoughts, the fairest women!

Thus spake Zarathustra; the king on the right however answered and said: Strange! Did one ever hear such sensible things out of the mouth of a wise man?

And verily, it is the strangest thing in a wise man if over and above he be still sensible, and not an ass.

Thus spake the king on the right and wondered; the ass however, with ill-will, said YE-A to his remark. This however was the beginning of that long repast which is called 'The Supper' in the history-books. At this there was nothing else spoken of but *the higher man.*

73 *The Higher Man*

1

When I came unto men for the first time, then did I commit the anchorite folly, the great folly: I appeared on the market-place.

And when I spake unto all, I spake unto none. In the evening, however, rope-dancers were my companions, and corpses; and I myself almost a corpse.

With the new morning, however, there came unto me a new truth; then did I learn to say: 'Of what account to me are market-place and populace and populace-noise and long populace-cars!'

Ye higher men, learn *this* from me: on the market-place no one believeth in higher men. But if ye will speak there, very well! The populace, however, blinketh: 'We are all equal.'

'Ye higher men' – so blinketh the populace – 'there are no higher men, we are all equal; man is man, before God – we are all equal!'

Before God! Now, however, this God hath died. Before the populace, however, we will not be equal. Ye higher men, away from the market-place!

2

Before God! Now however this God hath died! Ye higher men, this God was your greatest danger.

Only since he lay in the grave have ye again arisen. Now only cometh the great noontide, now only doth the higher man become – master!

Have ye understood this word, O my brethren? Ye are frightened: do your hearts turn giddy? Doth the abyss here yawn for you? Doth the hell-hound here yelp at you?

Well! Take heart, ye higher men! Now only travaileth the mountain of the human future. God hath died: now do *we* desire – the Superman to live.

3

The most careful ask today: 'How is man to be maintained?' Zarathustra however asketh, as the first and only one: 'How is man to be *surpassed*?'

The Superman, I have at heart; *that is* the first and only thing to me – and *not* man; not the neighbour, not the poorest, not the sorriest, not the best –

O my brethren, what I can love in man is that he is an over-going and a down-going. And also in you there is much that maketh me love and hope.

In that ye have despised, ye higher men, that maketh me hope. For the great despisers are the great reverers.

In that ye have despaired, there is much to honour, for ye have not learned to submit yourselves, ye have not learned petty policy.

For today have the petty people become master; they all preach submission and humility and policy and diligence and consideration and the long *et cetera* of petty virtues.

Whatever is of the effeminate type, whatever originateth from the servile type, and especially the populace-mishmash – *that* wisheth now to be master of all human destiny. O disgust! Disgust! Disgust!

That asketh and asketh and never tireth: 'How is man to maintain himself best, longest, most pleasantly?' Thereby – are they the masters of today.

These masters of today – surpass them, O my brethren. These petty people: *they* are the Superman's greatest danger!

Surpass, ye higher men, the petty virtues, the petty policy, the sand-grain considerateness, the ant-hill trumpery, the pitiable comfortableness, the 'happiness of the greatest number'!

And rather despair than submit yourselves. And verily, I love you, because ye know not today how to live, ye higher men. For thus do *ye* live – best!

4

Have ye courage, O my brethren? Are ye stout-hearted? *Not* the courage before witnesses, but anchorite and eagle courage, which not even a God any longer beholdeth?

Cold souls, mules, the blind and the drunken I do not call stout-hearted. He hath heart who knoweth fear, but *vanquisheth* it; who seeth the abyss, but with *pride*.

He who seeth the abyss, but with eagle's eyes – he who with eagle's talons *graspeth* the abyss – he hath courage.

5

'Man is evil' – so said to me for consolation all the wisest ones. Ah, if only it be still true today! For the evil is man's best force.

Man must become better and eviler – so do I teach. The evilest is necessary for the Superman's best.

It may have been well for the preacher of the petty people to suffer and be burdened by men's sin. I, however, rejoice in great sin as my great *consolation* –

Such things, however, are not said for long ears. Every word, also, is not suited for every mouth. These are fine far-away things: at them sheep's claws shall not grasp!

6

Ye higher men, think ye that I am here to put right what ye have put wrong?

Or that I wished henceforth to make snugger couches for you sufferers? Or show you restless, miswandering, misclimbing ones new and easier footpaths?

Nay! Nay! Three times Nay! Always more, always better ones of your type shall succumb – for ye shall always have it worse and harder. Thus only –

Thus only groweth man aloft to the height where the lightning striketh and shattereth him: high enough for the lightning!

Towards the few, the long, the remote go forth my soul and my seeking; of what account to me are your many little, short miseries!

Ye do not yet suffer enough for me! For ye suffer from yourselves, ye have not yet suffered *from man*. Ye would lie if ye spake otherwise! None of you suffereth from what I have suffered.

7

It is not enough for me that the lightning no longer doeth harm. I do not wish to conduct it away; it shall learn – to work for me.

My wisdom hath accumulated long like a cloud; it becometh stiller and darker. So doeth all wisdom which shall one day bear *lightnings* –

Unto these men of today will I not be *light*, nor be called light. *Them* – will I blind: lightning of my wisdom, put out their eyes!

8

Do not will anything beyond your power, there is a bad falseness in those who will beyond their power.

Especially when they will great things! For they awaken distrust in great things, these subtle false-coiners and stage-players –

Until at last they are false towards themselves; squint-eyed, whited cankers, glossed over with strong words, parade virtues and brilliant false deeds.

Take good care there, ye higher men! For nothing is more precious to me, and rarer, than honesty.

Is this today not that of the populace? The populace however knoweth not what is great and what is small, what is straight and what is honest; it is innocently crooked, it ever lieth.

9

Have a good distrust today, ye higher men, ye enheartened ones! Ye open-hearted ones! And keep your reasons secret! For this today is that of the populace.

What the populace once learned to believe without reasons, who could – refute it to them by means of reasons?

And on the market-place one convinceth with gestures. But reasons make the populace distrustful.

And when truth hath once triumphed there, then ask yourselves with good distrust: 'What strong error hath fought for it?'

Be on your guard also against the learned! They hate you, because they are unproductive! They have cold withered eyes before which every bird is unplumed.

Such persons vaunt about not lying: but inability to lie is still far from being love to truth. Be on your guard!

Freedom from fever is still far from being knowledge! Refrigerated spirits I do not believe in. He who cannot lie, doth not know what truth is.

10

If ye would go up high, then use your own legs! Do not get yourselves *carried* aloft; do not seat yourselves on other people's backs and heads!

Thou hast mounted, however, on horseback? Thou now ridest briskly up to thy goal? Well, my friend! But thy lame foot is also with thee on horseback!

When thou reachest thy goal, when thou alightest from thy horse – precisely on thy *height*, thou higher man, then wilt thou stumble!

11

Ye creating ones, ye higher men! One is only pregnant with one's own child.

Do not let yourselves be imposed upon or put upon! Who then is your neighbour? Even if ye act 'for your neighbour' – ye still do not create for him!

Unlearn, I pray you, this 'for', ye creating ones; your very virtue wisheth you to have naught to do with 'for' and 'on account of' and 'because'. Against these false little words shall ye stop your ears.

'For one's neighbour' is the virtue only of the petty people; there it is said 'like and like', and 'hand washeth hand' – they have neither the right nor the power for your self-seeking!

In your self-seeking, ye creating ones, there is the foresight and foreseeing of the pregnant! What no one's eye hath yet seen – namely, the fruit – this sheltereth and saveth and nourisheth your entire love.

Where your entire love is – namely, with your child – there is also your entire virtue! Your work, your will is *your* 'neighbour': let no false values impose upon you!

12

Ye creating ones, ye higher men! Whoever hath to give birth is sick; whoever hath given birth, however, is unclean.

Ask women: one giveth birth, not because it giveth pleasure. The pain maketh hens and poets cackle.

Ye creating ones, in you there is much uncleanness. That is because ye have had to be mothers.

A new child: oh, how much new filth hath also come into the world! Go apart! He who hath given birth shall wash his soul!

13

Be not virtuous beyond your powers! And seek nothing from yourselves opposed to probability!

Walk in the footsteps in which your fathers' virtue hath already walked! How would ye rise high, if your fathers' will should not rise with you?

He, however, who would be a firstling, let him take care lest he also become a lastling! And where the vices of your fathers are, there should ye not set up as saints!

He whose fathers were inclined for women, and for strong wine and flesh of wildboar swine – what would it be if he demanded chastity of himself?

A folly would it be! Much, verily, doth it seem to me for such a one, if he should be the husband of one or of two or of three women.

And if he founded monasteries, and inscribed over their portals: 'The way to holiness', I should still say: What good is it! it is a new folly!

He hath founded for himself a penance-house and refuge-house: much good may it do! But I do not believe in it.

In solitude there groweth what any one bringeth into it – also the brute in one's nature. Thus is solitude inadvisable unto many.

Hath there ever been anything filthier on earth than the saints of the wilderness? *Around them* was not only the devil loose – but also the swine.

14

Shy, ashamed, awkward, like the tiger whose spring hath failed – thus, ye higher men, have I often seen you slink aside. A *cast* which ye made had failed.

But what doth it matter, ye dice-players! Ye had not learned to play and mock, as one must play and mock! Do we not ever sit at a great table of mocking and playing?

And if great things have been a failure with you, have ye yourselves therefore – been a failure? And if ye yourselves have been a failure, hath man therefore – been a failure?

If man, however, hath been a failure: well then, never mind!

15

The higher its type, always the seldomer doth a thing succeed. Ye higher men here, have ye not all – been failures?

Be of good cheer; what doth it matter? How much is still possible! Learn to laugh at yourselves, as ye ought to laugh!

What wonder even that ye have failed and only half-succeeded, ye half-shattered ones! Doth not – man's *future* strive and struggle in you?

Man's furthest, profoundest, star-highest issues, his prodigious powers – do not all these foam through one another in your vessel?

What wonder that many a vessel shattereth! Learn to laugh at yourselves, as ye ought to laugh! Ye higher men, oh, how much is still possible!

And verily, how much hath already succeeded! How rich is this earth in small, good, perfect things, in well-constituted things!

Set around you small, good, perfect things, ye higher men; their golden maturity healeth the heart. The perfect teacheth one to hope.

16

What hath hitherto been the greatest sin here on earth?

Was it not the word of him who said: 'Woe unto them that laugh now!'

Did he himself find no cause for laughter on the earth? Then he sought badly. A child even findeth cause for it.

He – did not love sufficiently; otherwise would he also have loved us, the laughing ones! But he hated and hooted us; wailing and teeth-gnashing did he promise us.

Must one then curse immediately, when one doth not love? That – seemeth to me bad taste. Thus did he, however, this absolute one. He sprang from the populace.

And he himself just did not love sufficiently; otherwise would he have raged less because people did not love him. All great love doth not *seek* love – it seeketh more.

Go out of the way of all such absolute ones! They are a poor sickly type, a populace-type: they look at this life with ill-will; they have an evil eye for this earth.

Go out of the way of all such absolute ones! They have heavy feet and sultry hearts – they do not know how to dance. How could the earth be light to such ones!

17

Tortuously do all good things come nigh to their goal. Like cats they curve their backs, they purr inwardly with their approaching happiness – all good things laugh.

His step betrayeth whether a person already walketh on *his own* path: just see me walk! He, however, who cometh nigh to his goal, danceth.

And verily, a statue have I not become; not yet do I stand there stiff, stupid and stony, like a pillar; I love fast racing.

And though there be on earth fens and dense afflictions, he who hath light feet runneth even across the mud, and danceth as upon well-swept ice.

Lift up your hearts, my brethren, high, higher! And do not forget your legs! Lift up also your legs, ye good dancers; and better still, if ye stand upon your heads!

18

This crown of the laughter, this rose-garland crown: I myself have put on this crown, I myself have consecrated my laughter. No one else have I found today potent enough for this.

Zarathustra the dancer, Zarathustra the light one, who beckoneth with his pinions, one ready for flight beckoning unto all birds, ready and prepared, a blissfully light-spirited one –

Zarathustra the soothsayer, Zarathustra the sooth-laugher, no impatient one, no absolute one, one who loveth leaps and side-leaps; I myself have put on this crown!

19

Lift up your hearts, my brethren, high, higher! And do not forget your legs! Lift up also your legs, ye good dancers; and better still if ye stand upon your heads!

There are also heavy animals in a state of happiness; there are club-footed ones from the beginning. Curiously do they exert themselves, like an elephant which endeavoureth to stand upon its head.

Better, however, to be foolish with happiness than foolish with misfortune; better to dance awkwardly than walk lamely. So learn, I pray you, my wisdom, ye higher men: even the worst thing hath two good reverse sides –

Even the worst thing hath good dancing-legs; so learn, I pray you, ye higher men, to put yourselves on your proper legs!

So unlearn, I pray you, the sorrow-sighing, and all the populace-sadness! Oh, how sad the buffoons of the populace seem to me today! This today, however, is that of the populace.

20

Do like unto the wind when it rusheth forth from its mountain-caves: unto its own piping will it dance; the seas tremble and leap under its footsteps.

That which giveth wings to asses, that which milketh the lionesses: praised be that good, unruly spirit, which cometh like a hurricane unto all the present and unto all the populace –

Which is hostile to thistle-heads and puzzle-heads, and to all withered leaves and weeds – praised be this wild, good, free spirit of the storm, which danceth upon fens and afflictions as upon meadows!

Which hateth the consumptive populace-dogs, and all the ill-constituted, sullen brood – praised be this spirit of all free spirits, the laughing storm which bloweth dust into the eyes of all the melanopic and melancholic!

Ye higher men, the worst thing in you is that ye have none of you learned to dance as ye ought to dance – to dance beyond yourselves! What doth it matter that ye have failed!

How many things are still possible! So *learn* to laugh beyond yourselves! Lift up your hearts, ye good dancers, high! higher! And do not forget the good laughter!

This crown of the laugher, this rose-garland crown: to you my brethren do I cast this crown! Laughing have I consecrated; ye higher men, *learn*, I pray you – to laugh!

74 *The Song of Melancholy*

1

When Zarathustra spake these sayings, he stood nigh to the entrance of his cave; with the last words, however, he slipped away from his guests, and fled for a little while into the open air.

O pure odours around me, cried he. O blessed stillness around me! But where are mine animals? Hither, hither, mine eagle and my serpent!

Tell me, mine animals: these higher men, all of them – do they perhaps not *smell* well? O pure odours around me! Now only do I know and feel how I love you, mine animals.

And Zarathustra said once more: I love you, mine animals! The eagle, however, and the serpent pressed close to him when he spake these words, and looked up to him. In this attitude were they all three silent together, and sniffed and sipped the good air with one another. For the air here outside was better than with the higher men.

2

Hardly, however, had Zarathustra left the cave when the old magician got up, looked cunningly about him, and said: He is gone!

And already, ye higher men – let me tickle you with this complimentary and flattering name, as he himself doth – already doth mine evil spirit of deceit and magic attack me, my melancholy devil –

Which is an adversary to this Zarathustra from the very heart: forgive it for this! Now doth it wish to conjure before you, it hath just its hour; in vain do I struggle with this evil spirit.

Unto all of you, whatever honours ye like to assume in your names, whether ye call yourselves 'the free spirits' or 'the conscientious', or 'the penitents of the spirit', or 'the unfettered', or 'the great longers' –

Unto all of you who like me suffer from *the great loathing*, to whom the old God hath died, and as yet no new God lieth in cradles and swaddling clothes – unto all of you is mine evil spirit and magic-devil favourable.

I know you, ye higher men, I know him – I know also this fiend whom I love in spite of me, this Zarathustra: he himself often seemeth to me like the beautiful mask of a saint –

Like a new strange mummery in which mine evil spirit, the melancholy devil, delighteth: I love Zarathustra, so doth it often seem to me, for the sake of mine evil spirit –

But already doth *it* attack me and constrain me, this spirit of melancholy, this evening-twilight devil; and verily, ye higher men, it hath a longing –

Open your eyes! It hath a longing to come *naked*, whether male or female, I do not yet know; but it cometh, it constraineth me; alas, open your wits!

The day dieth out, unto all things cometh now the evening; also unto the best things: hear now, and see, ye higher men, what devil – man or woman – this spirit of evening-melancholy is!

Thus spake the old magician, looked cunningly about him, and then seized his harp.

3

In evening's limpid air,
What time the dew's soothings
Unto the earth downpour,
Invisibly and unheard –
For tender shoe-gear wear
The soothing dews, like all that's kind-gentle –
Bethink'st thou then, bethink'st thou, burning heart,
How once thou thirstedst
For heaven's kindly teardrops and dew's down-droppings,
All singed and weary thirstedst,
What time on yellow grass-pathways
Wicked, occidental sunny glances
Through sombre trees about thee sported,
Blindingly sunny glow-glances, gladly-hurting?

Of *truth* the wooer? Thou? – so taunted they –
Nay! Merely poet!
A brute insidious, plundering, grovelling,
That aye must lie,
That wittingly, wilfully, aye must lie:
For booty lusting,
Motley masked,
Self-hidden, shrouded,
Himself his booty –
He – of truth the wooer?
Nay! Mere fool! Mere poet!
Just motley speaking,
From mask of fool confusedly shouting,
Circumambling on fabricated word-bridges,
On motley rainbow-arches,
'Twixt the spurious heavenly
And spurious earthly,
Round us roving, round us soaring –
Mere *fool*! Mere *poet*!

He – of truth the wooer?
Not still, stiff, smooth and cold,
Become an image,
A godlike statue,
Set up in front of temples,
As a God's own door-guard:
Nay! Hostile to all such truthfulness-statues,
In every desert homelier than at temples,
With cattish wantonness,
Through every window leaping
Quickly into chances,
Every wild forest a-sniffing,
Greedily-longingly, sniffing,
That thou, in wild forests,
'Mong the motley-speckled fierce creatures,
Shouldst rove, sinful-sound and fine-coloured,
With longing lips smacking,
Blessedly mocking, blessedly hellish, blessedly blood-thirsty,
Robbing, skulking, lying – roving –

Or unto eagles like which fixedly,
Long adown the precipice look,
Adown *their* precipice –
Oh, how they whirl down now,
Thereunder, therein,
To ever deeper profoundness whirling!
Then,
Sudden,
With aim aright,
With quivering flight,
On *lambkins* pouncing,
Headlong down, sore-hungry,
For lambkins longing,
Fierce 'gainst all lamb-spirits,
Furious-fierce 'gainst all that look
Sheeplike, or lamb-eyed, or crisp-woolly –
Grey, with lambsheep kindliness!

Even thus,
Eaglelike, pantherlike,
Are the poet's desires,
Are *thine own* desires 'neath a thousand guises.
Thou fool! Thou poet!
Thou who all mankind viewedst –
So God, as sheep –
The God *to rend* within mankind,
As the sheep in mankind,
And in rending *laughing* –

That, that is thine own blessedness!
Of a panther and eagle blessedness!
Of a poet and fool – the blessedness!

In evening's limpid air,
What time the moon's sickle,
Green, 'twixt the purple-glowings,
And jealous, steal'th forth –
Of day the foe,
With every step in secret,

The rosy garland-hammocks
Downsickling, till they've sunken
Down nightwards, faded, downsunken –

Thus had I sunken one day
From mine own truth-insanity,
From mine own fervid day-longings,
Of day aweary, sick of sunshine –
Sunk downwards, evenwards, shadow-wards:
By one sole trueness
All scorched and thirsty –
Bethinkst thou still, bethinkst thou, burning heart,
How then thou thirstedst?
That I should banned be
From all the trueness!
Mere fool! Mere poet!

75 Science

Thus sang the magician; and all who were present went like birds unawares into the net of his artful and melancholy voluptuousness. Only the spiritually conscientious one had not been caught: he at once snatched the harp from the magician and called out: Air! Let in good air! Let in Zarathustra! Thou makest this cave sultry and poisonous, thou bad old magician!

Thou seducest, thou false one, thou subtle one, to unknown desires and deserts. And alas, that such as thou should talk and make ado about the *truth*!

Alas, to all free spirits who are not on their guard against *such* magicians! It is all over with their freedom; thou teachest and temptest back into prisons –

Thou old melancholy devil, out of thy lament soundeth a lurement; thou resemblest those who with their praise of chastity secretly invite to voluptuousness!

Thus spake the conscientious one; the old magician, however, looked about him, enjoying his triumph, and on that account put up with the annoyance which the conscientious one caused him. Be still! said he with modest voice. Good songs want to re-echo well; after good songs one should be long silent.

Thus do all those present, the higher men. Thou, however, hast perhaps understood but little of my song? In thee there is little of the magic spirit.

Thou praisest me, replied the conscientious one, in that thou separatest me from thyself. Very well! But, ye others, what do I see? Ye still sit there, all of you, with lusting eyes –

Ye free spirits, whither hath your freedom gone! Ye almost seem to me to resemble those who have long looked at bad girls dancing naked: your souls themselves dance!

In you, ye higher men, there must be more of that which the magician calleth his evil spirit of magic and deceit – we must indeed be different.

And verily, we spake and thought long enough together ere Zarathustra came home to his cave, for me not to be unaware that we *are* different.

We *seek* different things even here aloft, ye and I. For I seek more *security;* on that account have I come to Zarathustra. For he is still the most steadfast tower and will –

Today, when everything tottereth, when all the earth quaketh. Ye, however, when I see what eyes ye make, it almost seemeth to me that ye seek *more insecurity* –

More horror, more danger, more earthquake. Ye long (it almost seemeth so to me: forgive my presumption, ye higher men) –

Ye long for the worst and most dangerous life, which frighteneth *me* most – for the life of wild beasts, for forests, caves, steep mountains and labyrinthine gorges.

And it is not those who lead *out of* danger that please you best, but those who lead you away from all paths, the misleaders. But if such longing in you be *actual*, it seemeth to me nevertheless to be *impossible*.

For fear – that is man's original and fundamental feeling; through fear everything is explained – original sin and original virtue. Through fear there grew also my virtue: that is to say, Science.

For fear of wild animals – that hath been longest fostered in man, inclusive of the animal which he concealeth and feareth in himself: Zarathustra calleth it 'the beast inside'.

Such prolonged ancient fear, at last become subtle, spiritual and intellectual – at present, methinketh, it is called *Science*.

Thus spake the conscientious one; but Zarathustra, who had just come back into his cave and had heard and divined the last discourse, threw a handful of roses to the conscientious one, and laughed on account of his 'truths'. Why! he exclaimed, what did I hear just now? Verily, it seemeth to me, thou art a fool, or else I myself am one; and quietly and quickly will I put thy 'truth' upside down.

For *fear* – is an exception with us. Courage, however, and adventure, and delight in the uncertain, in the unattempted – *courage* seemeth to me the entire primitive history of man.

The wildest and most courageous animals hath he envied and robbed of all their virtues: thus only did he become – man.

This courage, at last become subtle, spiritual and intellectual, this human courage, with eagle's pinions and serpent's wisdom: *this*, it seemeth to me, is called at present –

Zarathustra! cried all of them there assembled, as if with one voice, and burst out at the same time into a great laughter; there arose, however, from them as it were a heavy cloud. Even the magician laughed, and said wisely: Well! It is gone, mine evil spirit!

And did I not myself warn you against it when I said that it was a deceiver, a lying and deceiving spirit?

Especially when it showeth itself naked. But what can I do with regard to its tricks! Have I created it and the world?

Well! Let us be good again, and of good cheer! And although Zarathustra looketh with evil eye – just see him! He disliketh me –

Ere night cometh will he again learn to love and laud me; he cannot live long without committing such follies.

He – loveth his enemies: this art knoweth he better than any one I have seen. But he taketh revenge for it – on his friends!

Thus spake the old magician, and the higher men applauded him; so that Zarathustra went round, and mischievously and lovingly shook hands with his friends – like one who hath to make amends and apologise to every one for something. When however he had thereby come to the door of his cave, lo, then had he again a longing for the good air outside, and for his animals – and wished to steal out.

76 *Among Daughters of the Desert*

1

Go not away! said then the wanderer who called himself Zarathustra's shadow. Abide with us – otherwise the old gloomy affliction might again fall upon us.

Now hath that old magician given us of his worst for our good, and lo, the good, pious pope there hath tears in his eyes, and hath quite embarked again upon the sea of melancholy!

Those kings may well put on a good air before us still; for that have *they* learned best of us all at present! Had they however no one to see them, I wager that with them also the bad game would again commence –

The bad game of drifting clouds, of damp melancholy, of curtained heavens, of stolen suns, of howling autumn winds –

The bad game of our howling and crying for help! Abide with us, O Zarathustra! Here there is much concealed misery that wisheth to speak, much evening, much cloud, much damp air!

Thou hast nourished us with strong food for men, and powerful proverbs; do not let the weakly, womanly spirits attack us anew at dessert!

Thou alone makest the air around thee strong and clear! Did I ever find anywhere on earth such good air as with thee in thy cave?

Many lands have I seen, my nose hath learned to test and estimate many kinds of air; but with thee do my nostrils taste their greatest delight!

Unless it be – unless it be – do forgive an old recollection! Forgive me an old after-dinner song, which I once composed amongst daughters of the desert –

For with them was there equally good, clear, Oriental air; there was I furthest from cloudy, damp, melancholy Old-Europe!

Then did I love such Oriental maidens and other blue kingdoms of heaven, over which hang no clouds and no thoughts.

Ye would not believe how charmingly they sat there, when they did not dance, profound, but without thoughts, like little secrets, like beribboned riddles, like dessert-nuts –

Many-hued and foreign, forsooth, but without clouds; riddles which can be guessed: to please such maidens I then composed an after-dinner psalm.

Thus spake the wanderer who called himself Zarathustra's shadow; and before any one answered him, he had seized the harp of the old magician, crossed his legs, and looked calmly and sagely around him – with his nostrils, however, he inhaled the air slowly and questioningly, like one who in new countries tasteth new foreign air. Afterward he began to sing with a kind of roaring.

2

The deserts grow: woe him who doth them hide!

– Ha!
Solemnly!
In effect solemnly!
A worthy beginning!
Afric manner, solemnly!
Of a lion worthy,
Or perhaps of a virtuous howl-monkey –
But it's naught to you,
Ye friendly damsels dearly loved,
At whose own feet to me,
The first occasion,
To a European under palm-trees,
A seat is now granted. Selah.

Wonderful, truly!
Here do I sit now,
The desert nigh, and yet I am
So far still from the desert,
Even in naught yet deserted:
That is, I'm swallowed down
By this the smallest oasis –
It opened up just yawning,
Its loveliest mouth agape,

Most sweet-odoured of all mouthlets:
Then fell I right in,
Right down, right through – in 'mong you,
Ye friendly damsels dearly loved! Selah.

Hail, hail, to that whale, fishlike,
If it thus for its guest's convenience
Made things nice – (ye well know,
Surely, my learned allusion?)
Hail to its belly
If it had e'er
A such loveliest oasis-belly
As this is: though however I doubt about it –
With this come I out of Old-Europe,
That doubt'th more eagerly than doth any
Elderly married woman.
May the Lord improve it!
Amen!

Here do I sit now,
In this the smallest oasis,
Like a date indeed,
Brown, quite sweet, gold-suppurating,
For rounded mouth of maiden longing,
But yet still more for youthful, maidlike,
Ice-cold and snow-white and incisory
Front teeth; and for such assuredly
Pine the hearts all of ardent date-fruits. Selah.

To the there-named south-fruits now,
Similar, all-too-similar
Do I lie here; by little
Flying insects
Round-sniffled and round-played,
And also by yet littler,
Foolisher, and peccabler
Wishes and phantasies –
Environed by you,
Ye silent, presentientest
Maiden-kittens,

Dudu and Suleika –
Roundsphinxed, that into one word
I may crowd much feeling:
(Forgive me, O God
All such speech-sinning!)
Sit I here the best of air sniffling,
Paradisal air? Truly,
Bright and buoyant air, golden-mottled,
As goodly air as ever
From lunar orb downfell –
Be it by hazard,
Or supervened it by arrogancy,
As the ancient poets relate it?
But doubter, I'm now calling it
In question: with this do I come indeed
Out of Europe,
That doubt'th more eagerly than doth any
Elderly married woman.
May the Lord improve it!
Amen.

This the finest air drinking,
With nostrils out-swelled like goblets,
Lacking future, lacking remembrances,
Thus do I sit here, ye
Friendly damsels dearly loved,
And look at the palm-tree there,
How it, to a dance-girl like,
Doth bow and bend and on its haunches bob –
One doth it too, when one view'th it long –
To a dance-girl like, who as it seem'th to me,
Too long, and dangerously persistent,
Always, always, just on *single* leg hath stood –
Then forgot she thereby, as it seem'th to me,
The *other* leg?
For vainly I, at least,
Did search for the amissing
Fellow- jewel –
Namely, the other leg –

In the sanctified precincts,
Nigh her very dearest, very tenderest,
Flapping and fluttering and flickering skirting.
Yea if ye should, ye beauteous friendly ones,
Quite take my word:
She hath alas, *lost* it!
Hu! Hu! Hu! Hu! Hu!
It is away!
For ever away!
The other leg!
Oh, pity for that loveliest other leg!
Where may it now tarry, all-forsaken weeping,
The lonesomest leg?
In fear perhaps before a
Furious, yellow, blond and curled
Leonine monster? Or perhaps even
Gnawed away, nibbled badly –
Most wretched woeful! Woeful! Nibbled badly! Selah.

Oh, weep ye not,
Gentle spirits!
Weep ye not, ye
Date-fruit spirits!
Milk-bosoms!
Ye sweetwood-heart
Purselets!
Weep ye no more,
Pallid Dudu!
Be a man, Suleika! Bold! Bold!
– Or else should there perhaps
Something strengthening, heart-strengthening,
Here most proper be?
Some inspiring text?
Some solemn exhortation? –
Ha! Up now! Honour!
Moral honour! European honour!
Blow again, continue,
Bellows-box of virtue!
Ha! Once more thy roaring,

Thy moral roaring!
As a virtuous lion
Nigh the daughters of deserts roaring!
– For virtue's out-howl,
Ye very dearest maidens,
Is more than every
European fervour, European hot-hunger!
And now do I stand here,
As European,
I can't be different, God's help to me!
Amen!

The deserts grow: woe him who doth them hide!

77 *The Awakening*

1

After the song of the wanderer and shadow, the cave became all at once full of noise and laughter; and since the assembled guests all spake simultaneously, and even the ass, encouraged thereby, no longer remained silent, a little aversion and scorn for his visitors came over Zarathustra, although he rejoiced at their gladness. For it seemed to him a sign of convalescence. So he slipped out into the open air and spake to his animals.

Whither hath their distress now gone? said he, and already did he himself feel relieved of his petty disgust – with me, it seemeth that they have unlearned their cries of distress –

Though, alas! not yet their crying. And Zarathustra stopped his ears, for just then did the YE-A of the ass mix strangely with the noisy jubilation of those higher men.

They are merry, he began again, and who knoweth? Perhaps at their host's expense; and if they have learned of me to laugh, still it is not my laughter they have learned.

But what matter about that! They are old people, they recover in their own way, they laugh in their own way; mine ears have already endured worse and have not become peevish.

This day is a victory; he already yieldeth, he fleeth, *the spirit of gravity,* mine old arch-enemy! How well this day is about to end which began so badly and gloomily!

And it is *about to* end. Already cometh the evening; over the sea rideth it hither, the good rider! How it bobbeth, the blessed one, the home-returning one, in its purple saddles!

The sky gazeth brightly thereon, the world lieth deep. Oh, all ye strange ones who have come to me, it is already worth while to have lived with me!

Thus spake Zarathustra. And again came the cries and laughter of the higher men out of the cave; then began he anew:

They bite at it, my bait taketh; there departeth also from them their enemy, the spirit of gravity. Now do they learn to laugh at themselves: do I hear rightly?

My virile food taketh effect, my strong and savoury sayings; and verily, I did not nourish them with flatulent vegetables! But with warrior-food, with conqueror-food: new desires did I awaken.

New hopes are in their arms and legs, their hearts expand. They find new words, soon will their spirits breathe wantonness.

Such food may sure enough not be proper for children, nor even for longing girls old and young. One persuadeth their bowels otherwise; I am not their physician and teacher

The *disgust* departeth from these higher men; well, that is my victory. In my domain they become assured; all stupid shame fleeth away; they empty themselves.

They empty their hearts, good times return unto them; they keep holiday and ruminate – they become *thankful.*

That do I take as the best sign: they become thankful. Not long will it be ere they devise festivals, and put up memorials to their old joys.

They are *convalescents*! Thus spake Zarathustra joyfully to his heart and gazed outward; his animals, however, pressed up to him, and honoured his happiness and his silence.

2

All on a sudden however, Zarathustra's ear was frightened; for the cave which had hitherto been full of noise and laughter became all at once still as death – his nose, however, smelt a sweet-scented vapour and incense-odour, as if from burning pine-cones.

What happeneth? What are they about? he asked himself, and stole up to the entrance, that he might be able unobserved to see his guests. But wonder upon wonder! What was he then obliged to behold with his own eyes!

They have all of them become *pious* again; they pray. They are mad! said he, and was astonished beyond measure. And forsooth, all these higher men, the two kings, the pope out of service, the evil magician, the voluntary beggar, the wanderer and shadow, the old soothsayer, the spiritually conscientious one, and the ugliest man – they all lay on their knees like children and credulous old women and worshipped the ass. And just then began the ugliest man to gurgle and snort, as if something unutterable in him tried to find expression; when, however, he had actually found words, behold, it was a pious, strange litany in praise of the adored and censed ass. And the litany sounded thus:

Amen! And glory and honour and wisdom and thanks and praise and strength be to our God, from everlasting to everlasting!

– The ass, however, here brayed YE-A.

He carrieth our burdens, he hath taken upon him the form of a servant, he is patient of heart and never saith Nay; and he who loveth his God chastiseth him.

– The ass, however, here brayed YE-A.

He speaketh not, except that he ever saith Yea to the world which he created: thus doth he extol his world. It is his artfulness that speaketh not: thus is he rarely found wrong.

– The ass, however, here brayed YE-A.

Uncomely goeth he through the world. Grey is the favourite colour in which he wrappeth his virtue. Hath he spirit, then doth he conceal it; every one, however, believeth in his long ears.

– The ass, however, here brayed YE-A.

What hidden wisdom it is to wear long ears, and only to say Yea and never Nay! Hath he not created the world in his own image, namely, as stupid as possible?

– The ass, however, here brayed YE-A.

Thou goest straight and crooked ways; it concerneth thee little what seemeth straight or crooked unto us men. Beyond good and evil is thy domain. It is thine innocence not to know what innocence is.

– The ass, however, here brayed YE-A.

Lo, how thou spurnest none from thee, neither beggars nor kings. Thou sufferest little children to come unto thee, and when the bad boys decoy thee, then sayest thou simply, YE-A.

– The ass, however, here brayed YE-A.

Thou lovest she-asses and fresh figs, thou art no food-despiser. A thistle tickleth thy heart when thou chancest to be hungry. There is the wisdom of a God therein.

– The ass, however, here brayed YE-A.

78 The Ass-festival

1

At this place in the litany, however, Zarathustra could no longer control himself; he himself cried out YE-A, louder even than the ass, and sprang into the midst of his maddened guests. Whatever are you about, ye grown-up children? he exclaimed, pulling up the praying ones from the ground. Alas, if any one else, except Zarathustra, had seen you –

Every one would think you the worst blasphemers, or the very foolishest old women, with your new belief!

And thou thyself, thou old pope, how is it in accordance with thee, to adore an ass in such a manner as God?

O Zarathustra, answered the pope, forgive me, but in divine matters I am more enlightened even than thou. And it is right that it should be so.

Better to adore God so, in this form, than in no form at all! Think over this saying, mine exalted friend; thou wilt readily divine that in such a saying there is wisdom.

He who said 'God is a Spirit' – made the greatest stride and slide hitherto made on earth towards unbelief: such a dictum is not easily amended again on earth!

Mine old heart leapeth and boundeth because there is still something to adore on earth. Forgive it, O Zarathustra, to an old, pious pontiff-heart!

And thou, said Zarathustra to the wanderer and shadow, thou callest and thinkest thyself a free spirit? And thou here practisest such idolatry and hierolatry?

Worse verily doest thou here than with thy bad brown girls, thou bad, new believer!

It is sad enough, answered the wanderer and shadow. Thou art right; but how can I help it! The old God liveth again, O Zarathustra, thou mayst say what thou wilt.

The ugliest man is to blame for it all; he hath reawakened him. And if he say that he once killed him, with Gods *death is* always just a prejudice.

And thou, said Zarathustra, thou bad old magician, what didst thou do! Who ought to believe any longer in thee in this free age, when *thou* believest in such divine donkeyism?

It was a stupid thing that thou didst; how couldst thou a shrewd man do such a stupid thing!

O Zarathustra, answered the shrewd magician, thou art right, it was a stupid thing – it was also repugnant to me.

And thou even, said Zarathustra to the spiritually conscientious one, consider, and put thy finger to thy nose! Doth nothing go against thy conscience here? Is thy spirit not too cleanly for this praying and the fumes of those devotees?

There is something therein, said the spiritually conscientious one, and put his finger to his nose. There is something in this spectacle which even doeth good to my conscience.

Perhaps I dare not believe in God; certain it is however, that God seemeth to me most worthy of belief in this form.

God is said to be eternal, according to the testimony of the most pious; he who hath so much time taketh his time. As slow and as stupid as possible: *thereby* can such a one nevertheless go very far.

And he who hath too much spirit might well become infatuated with stupidity and folly. Think of thyself, O Zarathustra!

Thou thyself – verily, even thou couldst well become an ass through superabundance of wisdom.

Doth not the true sage willingly walk on the crookedest paths? The evidence teacheth it, O Zarathustra – *thine own* evidence!

And thou thyself, finally, said Zarathustra, and turned towards the ugliest man, who still lay on the ground stretching up his arm to the ass (for he gave it wine to drink). Say, thou nondescript, what hast thou been about!

Thou seemest to me transformed, thine eyes glow, the mantle of the sublime covereth thine ugliness; *what* didst thou do?

Is it then true what they say, that thou hast again awakened him? And why? Was he not for good reasons killed and made away with?

Thou thyself seemest to me awakened. What didst thou do? Why didst *thou* turn round? Why didst *thou* get converted? Speak, thou nondescript!

O Zarathustra, answered the ugliest man, thou art a rogue!

Whether *he* yet liveth, or again liveth, or is thoroughly dead – which of us both knoweth that best? I ask thee.

One thing however do I know – from thyself did I learn it once, O Zarathustra: he who wanteth to kill most thoroughly, *laugheth.*

'Not by wrath but by laughter doth one kill' – thus spakest thou once, O Zarathustra, thou hidden one, thou destroyer without wrath, thou dangerous saint, – thou art a rogue!

2

Then, however, did it come to pass that Zarathustra, astonished at such merely roguish answers, jumped back to the door of his cave, and turning towards all his guests, cried out with a strong voice:

O ye wags, all of you, ye buffoons! Why do ye dissemble and disguise yourselves before me!

How the hearts of all of you convulsed with delight and wickedness, because ye had at last become again like little children – namely, pious –

Because ye at last did again as children do – namely, prayed, folded your hands and said 'good God'!

But now leave, I pray you, *this* nursery, mine own cave, where today all childishness is carried on. Cool down, here outside, your hot child-wantonness and heart-tumult!

To be sure: except ye become as little children ye shall not enter into *that* kingdom of heaven. (And Zarathustra pointed aloft with his hands.)

But we do not at all want to enter into the kingdom of heaven; we have become men – *so we want the kingdom of earth.*

3

And once more began Zarathustra to speak: O my new friends, said he – ye strange ones, ye higher men, how well do ye now please me –

Since ye have again become joyful! Ye have, verily, all blossomed forth: it seemeth to me that for such flowers as you, *new festivals* are required –

A little valiant nonsense, some divine service and ass-festival, some old joyful Zarathustra fool, some blusterer to blow your souls bright.

Forget not this night and this ass-festival, ye higher men! *That* did ye devise when with me, that do I take as a good omen – such things only the convalescents devise!

And should ye celebrate it again, this ass-festival, do it from love to yourselves, do it also from love to me! And in remembrance of *me*!

Thus spake Zarathustra.

79 The Drunken Song

1

Meanwhile one after another had gone out into the open air, and into the cool, thoughtful night; Zarathustra himself, however, led the ugliest man by the hand, that he might show him his night-world, and the great round moon, and the silvery waterfalls near his cave. There they at last stood still beside one another; all of them old people, but with comforted, brave hearts, and astonished in themselves that it was so well with them on earth; the mystery of the night, however, came nigher and nigher to their hearts. And anew Zarathustra thought to himself: Oh, how well do they now please me, these higher men! But he did not say it aloud, for he respected their happiness and their silence –

Then, however, there happened that which in this astonishing long day was most astonishing: the ugliest man began once more and for the last time to gurgle and snort, and when he had at length found expression, behold, there sprang a question plump and plain out of his mouth, a good, deep, clear question which moved the hearts of all who listened to him.

My friends, all of you, said the ugliest man, what think ye? For the sake of this day – I am for the first time content to have lived mine entire life.

And that I testify so much is still not enough for me. It is worth while living on the earth; one day, one festival with Zarathustra, hath taught me to love the earth.

'Was *that* – life?' will I say unto death. 'Well! Once more!'

My friends, what think ye? Will ye not, like me, say unto death: 'Was *that* – life? For the sake of Zarathustra. Well! Once more!' Thus spake the ugliest man; it was not, however, far from midnight. And what took place then, think ye? As soon as the higher men heard his question, they became all at once conscious of their transformation and convalescence, and of him who was the cause thereof: then did they rush up to Zarathustra, thanking, honouring, caressing him, and kissing his hands, each in his own peculiar way; so that some laughed and some wept. The old soothsayer, however, danced with delight; and though he was then, as some narrators suppose, full of sweet wine, he was certainly still fuller of sweet life, and had renounced all weariness. There are even those who narrate that the ass then danced; for not in vain had the ugliest man previously given it wine to drink. That may be the case, or it may be otherwise; and if in truth the ass did not dance that evening, there nevertheless happened then greater and rarer wonders than the dancing of an ass would have been. In short, as the proverb of Zarathustra saith: 'What doth it matter!'

2

When, however, this took place with the ugliest man, Zarathustra stood there like one drunken: his glance dulled, his tongue faltered and his feet staggered. And who could divine what thoughts then passed through Zarathustra's soul? Apparently, however, his spirit retreated and fled in advance and was in remote distances, and as it were 'wandering on high mountain-ridges', as it standeth written, 'twixt two seas –

Wandering 'twixt the past and the future as a heavy cloud. Gradually, however, while the higher men held him in their arms, he came back to himself a little, and resisted with his hands the crowd of the honouring and caring ones; but he did not speak. All at once, however, he turned his head quickly, for he seemed to hear something; then laid he his finger on his mouth and said: *Come!*

And immediately it became still and mysterious round about; from the depth however there came up slowly the sound of a clock-bell. Zarathustra listened thereto, like the higher men; then, however, laid he his finger on his mouth the second time, and said again: *Come! Come! It is getting on to midnight!* – and his voice had changed. But still he had not moved from the spot. Then it became yet stiller and more mysterious, and everything hearkened, even the ass, and Zarathustra's noble animals, the eagle and the serpent – likewise the cave of Zarathustra and the big cool moon, and the night itself. Zarathustra, however, laid his hand upon his mouth for the third time, and said:

Come! Come! Come! Let us now wander! It is the hour: let us wander into the night!

3

Ye higher men, it is getting on to midnight; then will I say something into your ears, as that old clock-bell saith it into mine ear –

As mysteriously, as frightfully and as cordially as that midnight clock-bell speaketh it to me, which hath experienced more than one man –

Which hath already counted the smarting throbbings of your fathers' hearts – ah, ah, how it sigheth! How it laugheth in its dream, the old, deep, deep midnight!

Hush! Hush! Then is there many a thing heard which may not be heard by day; now however, in the cool air, then even all the tumult of your hearts hath become still –

Now doth it speak, now is it heard, now doth it steal into overwakeful, nocturnal souls: ah, ah, how the midnight sigheth, how it laugheth in its dream!

Hearest thou not how it mysteriously, frightfully and cordially speaketh unto *thee*, the old deep, deep midnight?

O man, take heed!

4

Woe to me! Whither hath time gone? Have I not sunk into deep wells? The world sleepeth –

Ah! Ah! The dog howleth, the moon shineth. Rather will I die, rather will I die, than say unto you what my midnight-heart now thinketh.

Already have I died. It is all over. Spider, why spinnest thou around me? Wilt thou have blood? Ah! Ah! The dew falleth, the hour cometh –

The hour in which I frost and freeze, which asketh and asketh and asketh: 'Who hath sufficient courage for it?

Who is to be master of the world? Who is going to say: *Thus* shall ye flow, ye great and small streams!'

The hour approacheth: O man, thou higher man, take heed! This talk is for fine-ears, for thine ears – *what saith deep midnight's voice indeed?*

5

It carrieth me away, my soul danceth. Day's-work! Day's-work! Who is to be master of the world?

The moon is cool, the wind is still. Ah! Ah! Have ye already flown high enough? Ye have danced; a leg, nevertheless, is not a wing.

Ye good dancers, now is all delight over; wine hath become lees, every cup hath become brittle, the sepulchres mutter.

Ye have not flown high enough; now do the sepulchres mutter: 'Free the dead! Why is it so long night? Doth not the moon make us drunken?'

Ye higher men, free the sepulchres, awaken the corpses! Ah, why doth the worm still burrow? There approacheth, there approacheth the hour –

There boometh the clock-bell, there thrilleth still the heart, there burroweth still the wood-worm, the heart-worm. Ah! Ah! *The world is deep!*

6

Sweet lyre! Sweet lyre! I love thy tone, thy drunken, ranunculine tone! How long, how far hath come unto me thy tone, from the distance, from the ponds of love!

Thou old clock-bell, thou sweet lyre! Every pain hath torn thy heart, father-pain, fathers'-pain, forefathers'-pain; thy speech hath become ripe –

Ripe like the golden autumn and the afternoon, like mine anchorite heart – now sayest thou: 'The world itself hath become ripe, the grape turneth brown –

Now doth it wish to die, to die of happiness.' Ye higher men, do ye not feel it? There welleth up mysteriously an odour –

A perfume and odour of eternity, a rosy-blessed, brown, gold-wine-odour of old happiness –

Of drunken midnight-death happiness, which singeth; the world is deep, *and deeper than the day could read*!

7

Leave me alone! Leave me alone! I am too pure for thee. Touch me not! Hath not my world just now become perfect?

My skin is too pure for thy hands. Leave me alone, thou dull, doltish, stupid day! Is not the midnight brighter?

The purest are to be masters of the world, the least known, the strongest, the midnight-souls, who are brighter and deeper than any day.

O day, thou gropest for me? Thou feelest for my happiness? For thee am I rich, lonesome, a treasure-pit, a gold chamber?

O world, thou wantest *me*? Am I worldly for thee? Am I spiritual for thee? Am I divine for thee? But day and world, ye are too coarse –

Have cleverer hands, grasp after deeper happiness, after deeper unhappiness, grasp after some God; grasp not after me –

Mine unhappiness, my happiness is deep, thou strange day, but yet am I no God, no God's-hell: *deep is its woe.*

8

God's woe is deeper, thou strange world! Grasp at God's woe, not at me! What am I! A drunken sweet lyre –

A midnight-lyre, a bell-frog, which no one understandeth, but which must speak before deaf ones, ye higher men! For ye do not understand me!

Gone! Gone! O youth! O noontide! O afternoon! Now have come evening and night and midnight; the dog howleth, the wind –

Is the wind not a dog? It whineth, it barketh, it howleth. Ah! Ah! How she sigheth! How she laugheth, how she wheezeth and panteth, the midnight!

How she just now speaketh soberly, this drunken poetess! Hath she perhaps overdrunk her drunkenness? Hath she become overawake? Doth she ruminate?

Her woe doth she ruminate over, in a dream, the old deep midnight – and still more her joy. For joy, although woe be deep, *joy is deeper still than grief can be.*

9

Thou grape-vine! Why dost thou praise me? Have I not cut thee! I am cruel, thou bleedest – what meaneth thy praise of my drunken cruelty?

'Whatever hath become perfect, everything mature – wanteth to die!' So sayest thou. Blessed, blessed be the vintner's knife! But everything immature wanteth to live; alas!

Woe saith: 'Hence! Go! Away, thou woe!' But everything that suffereth wanteth to live, that it may become mature and lively and longing –

Longing for the further, the higher, the brighter. 'I want heirs,' so saith everything that suffereth, 'I want children, I do not want *myself*' –

Joy, however, doth not want heirs, it doth not want children – joy wanteth itself, it wanteth eternity, it wanteth recurrence, it wanteth everything eternally-like-itself.

Woe saith: 'Break, bleed, thou heart! Wander, thou leg! Thou wing, fly! Onward, upward, thou pain!' Well! Cheer up, O mine old heart! *Woe saith: 'Hence! Go!'*

10

Ye higher men, what think ye? Am I a soothsayer? Or a dreamer? Or a drunkard? Or a dream-reader? Or a midnight-bell?

Or a drop of dew? Or a fume and fragrance of eternity? Hear ye it not? Smell ye it not? Just now hath my world become perfect, midnight is also midday –

Pain is also a joy, curse is also a blessing, night is also a sun – go away, or ye will learn that a sage is also a fool!

Said ye ever Yea to one joy? O my friends, then said ye Yea also unto all woe. All things are enlinked, enlaced and enamoured –

Wanted ye ever once to come twice; said ye ever: 'Thou pleasest me, happiness! Instant! Moment!' then wanted ye *all* to come back again!

All anew, all eternal, all enlinked, enlaced and enamoured. Oh, then did ye *love* the world –

Ye eternal ones, ye love it eternally and for all time and also unto woe do ye say: 'Hence! Go, but come back! *For joys all want – eternity!'*

11

All joy wanteth the eternity of all things, it wanteth honey, it wanteth lees, it wanteth drunken midnight, it wanteth graves, it wanteth grave-tears' consolation, it wanteth gilded evening-red –

What doth not joy want! It is thirstier, heartier, hungrier, more frightful, more mysterious, than all woe: it wanteth *itself*, it biteth into *itself*, the ring's will writheth in it –

It wanteth love, it wanteth hate, it is over-rich, it bestoweth, it throweth away, it beggeth for some one to take from it, it thanketh the taker, it would fain be hated –

So rich is joy that it thirsteth for woe, for hell, for hate, for shame, for the lame, for the *world* – for this world. Oh, ye know it indeed!

Ye higher men, for you doth it long, this joy, this irrepressible, blessed joy – for your woe, ye failures! For failures longeth all eternal joy.

For joys all want themselves, therefore do they also want grief! O happiness, O pain! Oh break, thou heart! Ye higher men, do learn it, that joys want eternity –

Joys want the eternity of *all* things; they *want deep, profound eternity!*

12

Have ye now learned my song? Have ye divined what it would say? Well! Cheer up! Ye higher men, sing now my roundelay!

Sing now yourselves the song, the name of which is 'Once more', the signification of which is 'Unto all eternity!' Sing, ye higher men, Zarathustra's roundelay!

O man! Take heed!
What saith deep midnight's voice indeed?
'I slept my sleep –
From deepest dream I've woke, and plead:
The world is deep,
And deeper than the day could read.
Deep is its woe –
Joy – deeper still than grief can be:
Woe saith: Hence! Go!
But joys all want eternity –
Want deep, profound eternity!'

80 The Sign

In the morning, however, after this night, Zarathustra jumped up from his couch, and having girded his loins, he came out of his cave glowing and strong, like a morning sun coming out of gloomy mountains.

Thou great star, spake he, as he had spoken once before, thou deep eye of happiness, what would be all thy happiness if thou hadst not *those* for whom thou shinest!

And if they remained in their chambers whilst thou art already awake, and comest and bestowest and distributest, how would thy proud modesty upbraid for it!

Well! They still sleep, these higher men, whilst I am awake; *they* are not my proper companions! Not for them do I wait here in my mountains.

At my work I want to be, at my day; but they understand not what are the signs of my morning. My step – is not for them the awakening-call.

They still sleep in my cave; their dream still drinketh at my drunken songs. The audient ear for *me* – the *obedient* ear – is yet lacking in their limbs.

This had Zarathustra spoken to his heart when the sun rose: then looked he inquiringly aloft, for he heard above him the sharp call of his eagle. Well! called he upwards, thus is it pleasing and proper to me. Mine animals are awake, for I am awake.

Mine eagle is awake, and like me honoureth the sun. With eagle-talons doth it grasp at the new light. Ye are my proper animals; I love you.

But still do I lack my proper men!

Thus spake Zarathustra; then, however, it happened that all on a sudden he became aware that he was flocked around and fluttered around, as if by innumerable birds – the whizzing of so many wings, however, and the crowding around his head, was so great that he shut his eyes. And verily, there came down upon him as it were a cloud, like a cloud of arrows which poureth upon a new enemy. But behold, here it was a cloud of love, and showered upon a new friend.

What happeneth unto me, thought Zarathustra in his astonished heart, and slowly seated himself on the big stone which lay close to the exit from his cave. But while he grasped about with his hands, around him, above him and below him, and repelled the tender birds, behold, there then happened to him something still stranger: for he grasped thereby unawares into a mass of thick, warm, shaggy hair; at the same time, however, there sounded before him a roar – a long, soft lion-roar.

The sign cometh, said Zarathustra, and a change came over his heart. And in truth, when it turned clear before him, there lay a yellow, powerful animal at his feet, resting its head on his knee – unwilling to leave him out of love and doing like a dog which again findeth its old master. The doves, however, were no less eager with their love than the lion; and whenever a dove whisked over its nose, the lion shook its head and wondered and laughed.

When all this went on Zarathustra spake only a word: *My children are nigh, my children* – then he became quite mute. His heart, however, was loosed, and from his eyes there dropped down tears and fell upon his hands. And he took no further notice of anything, but sat there motionless, without repelling the animals further. Then flew the doves to and fro, and perched on his shoulder, and caressed his white hair, and did not tire of their tenderness and joyousness. The strong lion, however, licked always the tears that fell on Zarathustra's hands, and roared and growled shyly. Thus did these animals do –

All this went on for a long time, or a short time; for properly speaking, there is *no* time on earth for such things. Meanwhile, however, the higher men had awakened in Zarathustra's cave, and marshalled themselves for a procession to go to meet Zarathustra, and give him their morning greeting; for they had found when they awakened that he no longer tarried with them. When, however, they reached the door of the cave and the noise of their steps had preceded them, the lion started violently; it turned away all at once from Zarathustra, and roaring wildly, sprang towards the cave. The higher men, however, when they heard the lion roaring, cried all aloud as with one voice, fled back, and vanished in an instant.

Zarathustra himself, however, stunned and strange, rose from his seat, looked around him, stood there astonished, inquired of his heart, bethought himself, and remained alone. What did I hear? said he at last, slowly. What happened unto me just now?

But soon there came to him his recollection, and he took in at a glance all that had taken place between yesterday and today. Here is indeed the stone, said he, and stroked his beard. On *it* sat I yester-morn; and here came the soothsayer unto me, and here heard I first the cry which I heard just now, the great cry of distress.

O ye higher men, your distress was it that the old soothsayer foretold to me yester-morn –

Unto your distress did he want to seduce and tempt me: O Zarathustra, said he to me, I come to seduce thee to thy last sin.

To my last sin? cried Zarathustra, and laughed angrily at his own words. *What* hath been reserved for me as my last sin?

And once more Zarathustra became absorbed in himself, and sat down again on the big stone and meditated. Suddenly he sprang up –

Fellow-suffering! Fellow-suffering with the higher men! he cried out, and his countenance changed into brass. Well! *That* – hath had its time!

My suffering and my fellow-suffering – what matter about them! Do I then strive after *happiness*? I strive after my *work*!

Well! The lion hath come, my children are nigh, Zarathustra hath grown ripe, mine hour hath come –

This is my morning, *my* day beginneth: *arise now, arise, thou great noontide*!

Thus spake Zarathustra and left his cave, glowing and strong, like a morning sun coming out of gloomy mountains.

BIBLIOGRAPHY

Part One: Thus Spake Zarathustra, the German text

Thus Spoke Zarathustra Parts I – IV was written in the years 1882-85. Zarathustra's Preface was written shortly thereafter. For an authoritative edition of the full text see Friedrich Nietzsche, *Sämtliche Werke, Kritische Studienausgabe*, ed. G. Colli and Mazzino Montinari: Munich, Deutscher Taschenbuch Verlag; Berlin, Walter de Gruyter, 1980. Volume 4.

Part Two: Thus Spake Zarathustra, English translations

Thus Spake Zarathustra, translated by Alexander Tille, *The Works of Friedrich Nietzsche*, Vol 8. Henry and Co. London 1896. Republished in 1899 in London and Leipzig by T. Fisher Unwin

Thus Spake Zarathustra: A Book For All and None, translated by Alexander Tille, Macmillan, New York and London 1896

Thus Spake Zarathustra: A Book For All and None, translated by Thomas Common with critical and bibliographical notes, William Reeves, London 1898

Thus Spake Zarathustra, A Book for All and None, Nietzsche's Works in 4 Volumes, T. F. Unwin, London 1899

Thus Spake Zarathustra, translated by Alexander Tille, Macmillan, New York and London 1906

Thus Spake Zarathustra, A Book for All and None, second revised edition, published in four parts 1906-09. Good European Library i-iv, 1906-09

Thus Spake Zarathustra, in *The Complete Works of Friedrich Nietzsche*, ed. Dr Oscar Levy, translated by Thomas Common, notes by A. M. Ludovici, T. N. Foulis, Edinburgh and London 1909-13. Vol 11.

Thus Spake Zarathustra, ed. Dr Oscar Levy, translated by Thomas Common, revised by Oscar Levy and J. L. Beevers, George Allen and Unwin, London 1932

Thus Spake Zarathustra, translated by Alexander Tille and revised by M. M. Bozman, introduction by Ernest Rhys, J. M. Dent and Sons, London; E. P. Dutton and Co., New York; 1933 and 1957

Thus Spoke Zarathustra, translated by R. J. Hollingdale, Penguin Books, Harmondsworth 1969

Thus Spoke Zarathustra, A Book for All and None, translated by and with preface by Walter Kaufmann, Penguin, New York and Harmondsworth 1978

Thus Spoke Zarathustra, A Book for Every One and No One, edited by Michael Tanner, Penguin, Harmondsworth, forthcoming (1998)

Part Three: Nietzsche, philosophical commentaries

The following is a selected bibliography of critiques and commentaries on Nietzsche. For specific recent studies of *Thus Spake Zarathustra*, see the works of Lampert, Rosen and Shapiro listed below.

H. Alderman, *Nietzsche's Gift*, Ohio University Press, Athens 1977

D. B. Allison, *The New Nietzsche: Contemporary Styles of Interpretation*, MIT Press, Cambridge, Mass. 1977

W. Kaufmann, *Nietzsche: Philosopher, Psychologist, Antichrist*, Princeton University Press 1950

S. Kofman, *Nietzsche and Metaphor*, Stanford University Press 1993

L. Lampert, *Nietzsche's Teaching: An Interpretation of Thus Spake Zarathustra*, Yale University Press, New Haven 1986

B. Magnus, *Nietzsche's Existential Imperative*, Indiana University Press, Bloomington 1978

A. Megill, *Prophets of Extremity, Nietzsche, Heidegger, Foucault, Derrida*, University of Californian Press, Berkeley

A. Nehamas, *Nietzsche, Life as Literature*, Harvard University Press, Cambridge, Mass. 1985

J. Richardson, *Nietzsche's System*, Oxford University Press 1996

S. Rosen, *The Mask of the Enlightenment, Nietzsche's Zarathustra*, Cambridge University Press 1995

O. Schutte, *Beyond Nihilism: Nietzsche Without Masks*, Chicago University Press 1984

G. Shapiro, *Nietzschean Narratives*, Indiana University Press, Bloomington 1989

G. Shapiro, *Alcyone, Nietzsche on Gifts, Noise and Women*, State University of New York, Albany 1991

G. Shapiro, 'The Rhetoric of Nietzsche's Zarathustra', in *Philosophical Style*, ed. B. Lang, Nelson-Hall, Chicago 1980

A. Shrift, *Nietzsche and the Question of Interpretation, Between Hermeneutics and Deconstruction*, Routledge, New York 1990

R. Solomon and K. Higgins, *Reading Nietzsche*, Oxford University Press, New York 1988